THE GUIDE TO THE

MYSTERIOUS LAKE DISTRICT

THE GUIDE TO THE
MYSTERIOUS
LAKE
DISTRICT

GEOFF HOLDER

The History Press

In memory of Ivor Cutler, Ken Campbell
and John Peel (not the huntsman, the other one)

First published 2009

The History Press
The Mill, Brimscombe Port
Stroud, Gloucestershire, GL5 2QG
www.thehistorypress.co.uk

British Library Cataloguing in Publication Data.
A catalogue record for this book is available from the British Library.

ISBN 978 0 7524 4987 6

Typesetting and origination by The History Press
Printed in Great Britain

CONTENTS

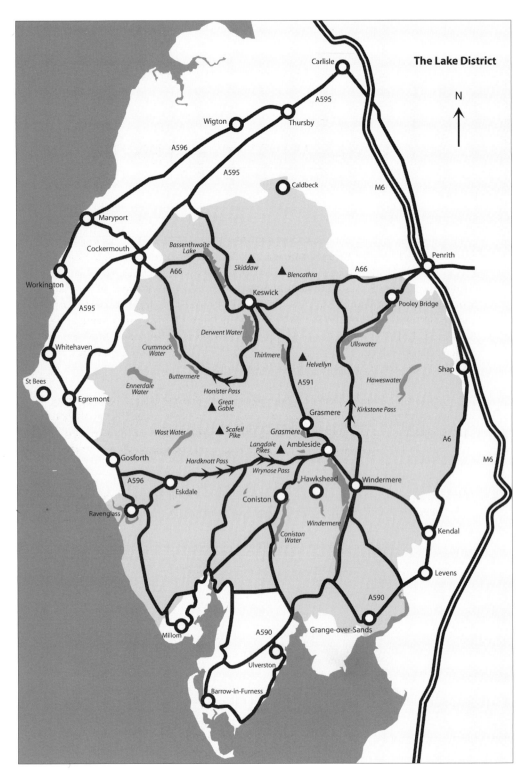

Map of the Lake District.

ACKNOWLEDGEMENTS

I would like to thank the following fine individuals and institutions: Andrew Hoyle and Curator Jamie Barnes of Keswick Museum and Art Gallery; Brian Wilkinson, Keswick historian; Peter Harding, licensee of the Twa Dogs, Keswick; the respective staff of the Armitt, Kendal and Ruskin Museums; Phil Hazlehurst, General Manager of the Rum Story, Whitehaven; Jenni Lister, Local Studies Librarian, Cumbria Record Office and Local Studies Library, Whitehaven; David Bradbury of www.pastpresented.info; Ian Caruana of the Cumberland and Westmorland Antiquarian and Archaeological Society; Margaret Reid, House Manager, Sizergh Castle; Jenni Wilson for the map; and Ségolène Dupuy, for all the usual and very best reasons.

The photographs on pages 10, 11 (right), 12 (right), 65 (left), 84 (lower left), 86, 92, 99, 102, 108 (lower three), 137, 162, 164 and 173 (lower left) are by Ségolène Dupuy. All other photographs are by the author. The photograph of the desiccated cat on page 57 is by kind permission of Keswick Museum. The photographs on pages 149 and 150 were kindly supplied by Muncaster Castle.

This book is part of an ongoing series of similar titles. If you would like to share any stories of the weird and wonderful, or wish to find more information, please visit my website: www.geoffholder.co.uk.

INTRODUCTION

Toutes les histoires anciennes, comme le disait un de nos beaux esprits, ne sont que des fables convenues.
[All ancient histories, as one of our fine spirits puts it, are nothing but convenient fictions.]

Voltaire, *Jeannot et Colin* (1764)

This is a guide to all things strange and supernatural, paranormal and peculiar, and magical and mysterious in the Lake District. It includes archaeology, history, contemporary reports, folklore, pagan beliefs, religion, bizarre behaviour, architecture and literature. There are rumours, hoaxes, customs, superstitions, miracles, folk magic and myths of the past and the present. Expect to find ghosts of executed murderers and descriptions of ancient graveyards jostling against Wordsworth's poetry, eye-witness sightings of UFOs and big cats, and tales of ape-men and giant spiders taken from recent newspaper reports.

The book is organised geographically. You can find everything mysterious and weird about one location in the same place and the descriptions flow logically, with the traveller in mind. Ordnance Survey map grid references are given, which are essential for hard-to-find sites – the 1:25000 Explorer maps OL4 to OL7 cover the area between them. Cross-references between locations are shown in SMALL CAPS. The Guide covers the whole area of the Lake District National Park and several places on its boundary such as Penrith, Kendal, Grange-over-Sands and Cockermouth. Sadly space has precluded such potentially fertile locations as Carlisle, the Eden Valley, Barrow-in-Furness, Whitehaven and the west coast, but these will be covered in a later book, *Paranormal Cumbria*.

Castlerigg Stone Circle, near Keswick.

Cup-and-ring marked stone, now in St Oswald's Church, Dean.

THINGS TO SEE AND PLACES TO VISIT

As well as including all the legends and lore relating to a specific site, there are extensive descriptions of what can be seen today. These typically include:

Stone circles, standing stones and other prehistoric monuments – all of which are mysterious and wonderful in themselves, and link to ancient rituals, ceremonies and belief systems.

Prehistoric rock art – such as cupmarks or cup-and-ring-marks. Despite extensive scholarly theorising – taking in everything from agricultural tallies to star maps, signposts and shamanic journeying – no one really knows what these enigmatic marks actually mean.

Churches – often the repository of many different kinds of sculpture, from pre-Christian images to Viking hogback tombstones, medieval graveslabs, wooden misericords, and wonderfully elaborate crosses. Stained-glass windows often feature supernatural beings such as angels or demons, or miracles associated with saints.

Graveyards – especially those with fantastically carved eighteenth- and nineteenth-century gravestones. *Memento mori* indeed.

Holy Wells – wells or springs associated with saints and/or healing.

Museums – containing objects with a ritual, funerary or bizarre association.

Caves, castles, abbeys, lakes and mountains – associated with stories of the strange or the supernatural.

Simulacra – a simulacrum is nature imitating art: a natural shape in a rock or tree that the pattern-recognition software in our foolish mammal brains misinterprets as a face, figure or, in Coleridge's case, something rather naughtier (see POOLEY BRIDGE).

Lucks – items linked to a particular family's fortunes, or 'luck.' Lucks were usually cups or bowls gifted by royalty or the fairies. The MUNCASTER Luck is still on display.

Secret Tunnels – every castle, abbey or old house must have, by an act of folk law, a secret passage. Sadly such tunnels are one thing that you will never find.

Macabre mementos – plague stones, corpse roads, coffin rests, and execution and murder sites.

Gargoyles – the demons and monsters that observe us from on high. There are two specific sub-categories:

Green Men – faces either composed of leaves (a 'foliate head') or spewing vegetation from the mouth, nose or eyes. The supposed pagan/fertility origins are much debated. They may alternatively represent Adam, Christ or resurrection, although several Cumbrian Green Men are decidedly demonic.

Sheela-na-gigs – sexually-explicit female carvings, some of the strangest medieval sculptures found in churches.

MAGIC AND THE SUPERNATURAL – KEY CONCEPTS

Apotropaic – Sheelas are often thought to be apotropaic, which means that which protects against evil. Apotropaic actions include making the sign of the cross, speaking a charm or wearing an amulet. Many of the rituals and items in this book are apotropaic in purpose, such as the dobbie stones in KENDAL MUSEUM and BLEAZE HALL.

Liminality – that which is betwixt and between, a transition, a threshold. A liminal time – such as Halloween – or place – such as a boundary between two properties, a 'no man's land' - can either make a supernatural event more likely to occur, or it can provide the right conditions to make an act of magic more powerful. Cumbria is full of liminal places such as mountain tops, caves, bogs and sands, portals between this realm and the Otherworld.

Magical Thinking – Apotropaism and liminality both depend on magical thinking. This is the state of mind you need to believe in magic, charms or witchcraft. In magical thinking, certain items – a perforated stone, or the gallows where a criminal was hanged, or water from a holy well – are thought to possess power. One of the most common objects of power was the relic of a saint.

Above left: Lichened gravestone, St Kentigern's Church, Keswick.

Above right: Gargoyle, Holy Trinity Church, Kendal.

Left: Stained glass of St Cuthbert carrying the severed head of St Oswald. St Kentigern's Church, Keswick.

Below: St Michael the Archangel, one dead dragon and two tongue-protruding bearded monks emerging out of greenery on a misericord in St Andrew's Church, Greystoke.

SAINTS

The Dark Ages were a time of holy men, Christians of power and influence who later came to be regarded as saints. In many cases the saint achieved lasting fame when his *Life* was written, often several hundred years after his death. Hagiography – the writing of the biographies of saints – was a medieval growth industry, and *Lives* were often a rich stew of documentary evidence, hearsay, legend, miracle stories and propaganda. Several saints are intimately connected with Cumbria.

St Kentigern was a Celtic holy man based in the Glasgow area in the late sixth century. His *Life* states that he was forced into exile and spent some time in Cumbria. There are churches dedicated to him at the places he allegedly preached, including KESWICK and CALDBECK, while Mungrisdale is named for his alternative moniker, St Mungo. His symbols are fourfold: a bell, bird, tree and a fish with a ring.

St Cuthbert was a seventh-century Anglo-Saxon monk from Lindisfarne, famed for his posthumous miracles. When Viking raiders attacked the monastery the monks took Cuthbert's body on a seven-year circuit of safety around southern Scotland and northern England. Many church dedications to St Cuthbert are said to date from a site where his coffin temporarily stopped. (For a miracle caused by Cuthbert's relics see DACRE.) Cuthbert is often shown holding the severed head of St Oswald, a seventh-century King of Northumbria, whose skull was interred with Cuthbert's remains when he was finally laid to rest in Durham Cathedral.

St Michael was not a man but a Biblical archangel, God's premier warrior. As such he is usually depicted despatching the Devil, often in the shape of a dragon. Michael can be distinguished from his dragon-slaying compatriot-in-arms St George – a Middle Eastern hero with no connection to England, of which he is the patron saint – by the fact that Michael, being of the heavenly host, has wings. A church dedication to St Michael often indicates the site was originally pagan.

'LET ME TELL YOU A (GHOST) STORY ...'

There is amplitude of legend ...There are stories of pigmies and giants who lived in the
wildernesses, of fairies and evil spirits who wail over shapeless mounds of rock, ruins of cities of
uncouth days.

A.H. Eaton Cooper & W.M.T. Palmer, *The English Lakes* (1908)

The Lake District is an elephants' graveyard of legends.

Melvyn Bragg, *Land of the Lakes* (1983)

'What is Truth?' said jesting Pilate; and would not stay for an answer.

Francis Bacon, *Essays* (1625)

There are many ghost stories in this book. Even if there are such things as ghosts – a notion
on which I am neither convinced nor unconvinced – not all of these stories are authentic.
Or, to put it another way, many of them are simply made up. As noted in the scabrous and
sarcastic Gavin D. Smith's *Lake District: An Alternative View of the Lakes*, 'There is a great
and honourable tradition of lying in Cumbria ... as "natives" in scenic places throughout
the world know, one of the finest pleasures ... is Telling Lies to Tourists.' Educated
tourists in the eighteenth and nineteenth centuries brought with them an expectation
of certain kinds of ghost story. The locally-available variety, with its mix of intense place-
consciousness, dialect words, pre-Christian Norse elements and deeply-lived agricultural
folklore, was not particularly palatable. And so, conscious of the tourist economy, many
people then – and since – have been quite happy to keep the ghost-hungry customer
satisfied. 'Telling Lies to Tourists' has never gone out of fashion. As demonstrated at several
points throughout this book, some of the Lake District's more famous spooks – from
the Crier of Claife to the Calgarth Skulls and the Beckside Boggle – are almost entirely
fabrications. It's often the less well-known spectres that are much more intriguing.

It was suggested that Lakelanders were, by virtue of the 'isolated' and 'rugged' land
in which they spent their 'unsophisticated' existence, particularly superstitious – and
thus those who holidayed in the Lakes were given the frisson of being close to the
primitive. Hutchinson's *History of the County of Cumberland* (1794) claims, 'this part of
the country ... abounds in all the *aniles fabellae* of fairies, ghosts and apparitions.' In 1867
Mr Whitfield MP gave a talk in Cockermouth, and his conclusions were included in
Daniel Scott's *Bygone Cumberland and Westmorland* (1899) – and have been much quoted
since – 'the superstitions in the Border country concerning fairies and brownies were
more developed, and the belief in spells and enchantments more common than in many
other parts of the country.'

In contrast to this, Dorothy Wordsworth, who noted in her *Journals* every trivial detail
her neighbours gossiped about, never mentions anything supernatural. Coleridge, restlessly
questioning every peasant and peddler he could accost on his walks, again finds nothing.
It appears that by the early decades of the nineteenth century many superstitions had passed

out of use or even living memory. And Henry Swainson Cowper, archaeologist, antiquarian and lifelong collector of local lore, wrote in his magisterial survey *Hawkshead* (1899), 'The dalesmen never were, like Celtic races, highly superstitious, and the churchyards, waterfalls, and wells, were never peopled with pixies, fairies, wraiths, or other "peculiar people", as we find in some districts.'

This is not to say that there were no tales of 'pixies, fairies, wraiths, or other "peculiar people",' just that they were no greater in number than anywhere else in England. F.J. Carruthers, in *Lore of the Lake Country* (1975), basing his ideas on earlier writers such as Cowper and Molly Lefebure, suggests a way of distinguishing between folklore and 'fakelore': if the spirit had a dialect name like 'boggle' or 'dobbie' it was intended for domestic consumption; if it rattled chains, lived in a grand house or appeared in a book by an outsider, it was probably invented.

Boggles often had their origin in the memory of a murder or suicide. Once the spot had been imprinted by the red hand of violence, it was thereafter deemed 'uncanny' – and boggles thrived in such fertile territory. For the architects of standard ghost stories – with their neat narratives and clear purposes such as revenge from beyond the grave – boggles were frustratingly protean. They were not confined to any pattern, and could manifest as human, animal, vegetable or mineral, or even as just a noise. They could change shape or speed, and frustratingly, often refused to communicate.

Many nineteenth-century books on the Lakes merely copy or elaborate on the folklore and legends of earlier works, so my approach has been to go back to the earliest available published source. Only in this way is it possible to glimpse what was going on at the time. However, those seeking what is potentially the genuinely paranormal, with names, dates and addresses, have to contend not only with this unholy brew of superstition and the wholesale invention of legends, but with a triple whammy of peculiarly local challenges. In her book *Cumberland Heritage* (1970), Molly Lefebure encountered the sheer persistence of long-term folk memory: an old couple gave her a vivid, first-hand description of a terrible mine disaster – which had actually taken place in the eighteenth century. Rain, fog, twilight, lonely moors and windswept peaks are perfect conditions for 'seeing things' – in *The English Lake District* (1964) Lefebure described how on the fells she had met what she first thought were yaks and bears (actually sheep distorted in mist) and an elephant (two lovers entwined with a loose anorak sleeve dangling in front). And in the same book she gave a fine example of the Cumbrian capacity for telling tall tales. A man had a large yellow dog which, when pitted against the farmers' hounds, easily killed them; when asked where he got the dog, he said his son had brought it back from Africa, but it was so ugly he sheared the great mane from its shoulders …

Of all the mysteries in this book, one certainly leans towards the 'reality' rather than the 'fantasy' end of the spectrum … big cats. Since the 1990s dozens upon dozens of sightings have been logged of large non-native cats in Cumbria. Most reports describe a large black creature with no markings and a long tail. As yet there is no physical specimen and no DNA evidence, but the quantity of material recorded online by the Big Cats in Britain organisation is impressive. One of the hallmarks of the phenomena reported in this book, however, is that very little is cut and dried, and sometimes the universe just seems to be toying with us. Several big black cat sightings have been in places that historically have been haunted by big black dogs. Could some of the big cats have a paranormal dimension?

THE CONTEXT – ARCHAEOLOGY AND HISTORY

The Lake District's mysteries are rooted in its history and landscape, so it is worth considering these contexts in some detail.

1. FROM PREHISTORY TO THE ROMANS – STONE CIRCLES AND STONE FORTS

Following the retreat of the glaciers that sculpted today's glorious mountain landscape, the area was visited by small bands of Mesolithic hunter-gatherer nomads. Around 3800 BC Neolithic farmers established permanent settlements and constructed burial cairns and, slightly later, henges (circular earth-banked enclosures) and stone circles. The metal-using peoples of the Bronze Age (from about 2500 BC onwards) continued erecting the circles and standing stones. The characteristic monument of the Iron Age (from about 800 BC) is the hillfort. The Iron Age is also the time of the Druids – long after the rise and decline of the stone circles with which they have been erroneously associated. By the time of the Roman conquest in the first century AD, the region was in the hands of the Carvettii, a subgroup of a loose confederation of northern clans called the Brigantes. The north-west was a military zone, and the Romans imposed a network of roads linking forts and ports. In the second and third centuries came the biggest change to the Lake District landscape, when native peoples – now called the Britons – cleared the vast upland forests to accommodate an expansion in agriculture.

2. THE DARK AGES – CUMBRIANS, ANGLO SAXONS, VIKINGS AND SCOTS

Roman procedure was to rule through favouring native client chieftains. When the legions departed Cumbria in the fifth century they left behind a cluster of British leaders with Romanised names, so that titles such as Caesarius echoed down later corridors of history and legend. The centuries known as the Dark Ages – or what archaeologists now call the Early Historic Period – are relatively poorly recorded. After some local internecine tribal warfare the British-Celtic kingdom of Rheged emerged in the sixth century, led by King Urien and then his son Owain, both celebrated in heroic ballads as Christian champions against the pagan Anglo-Saxons from the east. A very small number of crosses still survive from this period of Celtic Christianity. After Owain's death Rheged seems to have been eclipsed, being incorporated into the larger Celtic kingdom of Strathclyde, centred on the Clyde Valley in what is now Scotland. In the seventh century the Angles successfully occupied Cumbria; some, by now Christians themselves, established a number of churches. A few of their ancient crosses can still be seen.

In the late ninth and tenth centuries much of Cumbria was occupied by Norse peoples moving from Ireland and the Isle of Man. This Viking colonisation has had the longest-lasting impact on Cumbrian life, with many contemporary place names, agricultural practices and dialect words being traceable back to their Scandinavian originals. Many of the Norse were Christian and adapted pre-existing Anglian churches, although the ongoing transition from paganism can be easily seen on many carved crosses from this period, including that at GOSFORTH. A number of the older supernatural beliefs associated with Cumbria may well have their roots deep in Scandinavian soil.

During this period the island of Britain was a seething mass of competing peoples – Angles (and their various sub-groups such as the Northumbrians), Cumbrian Britons, Britons from further north, Welsh Britons, Norsemen, Picts, Scots and many others, all fighting to carve out territory. In the AD 930s a rebellion led by Constantine, king of the new nation called Scotland, broke out against Athelstan, King of Angleland or England.

Constantine forged an alliance of Scots, Britons, Vikings and Cumbrians, the last led by another Owain. Like his namesake several centuries earlier, Owain became a heroic symbol of British resistance, ending up mythologised in both Arthurian literature and in stories such as Owen Caesarius, the giant of PENRITH. Athelstan annihilated the alliance's army in 937, and Owain was killed. In 946 Athelstan's successor, Edmund, having now allied with Malcolm I, the new King of Scots, granted the whole of Cumbria to Scotland.

3. THE MIDDLE AGES – THE SCOTTISH QUESTION, CASTLES AND MONASTERIES
The interface between Cumbria and Scotland was to dominate the next few centuries. Following the Norman Conquest of England the new overlords only occupied the southern part of Cumbria, the rest being regarded as part of Scotland. The Normans pushed the border north in the late eleventh century, only for it to swing back south then back north again. By 1157 Cumbria was firmly and legally in England, but border warfare, clan raids and cattle rustling continued for centuries – Scottish chiefs, and occasionally Scottish kings, still saw Cumbria as either their property or their larder. The Normans built great defensive castles on the fringes of the mountains at Penrith, Brougham, Kendal, Millom, Egremont and Cockermouth. Brutal and devastating Scottish raids in 1138, 1216, 1316 and 1324 saw many landowners construct thick-walled stone pele towers as places of refuge – many a Cumbrian grand house, farm or even church has a pele tower at its core. The border violence remained a running sore until the Union of the Crowns in 1603, when James I of England and VI of Scotland brought the full might of unforgiving state punishment to bear on the recalcitrant border clans.

The other major influencing factor from the Middle Ages was the establishment of a number of abbeys and priories. The monks had a huge impact on the area's administration, agriculture, industries, economy and legal system – not to mention on the spread of literacy and Christian ideas. Monks turn up again and again in various Cumbrian tales of the supernatural. All the monasteries – including those at FURNESS, SHAP and CALDER – were destroyed in 1536, when Protestant religious reform coincided with Henry VIII's greed and vindictiveness.

4. MINING AND INDUSTRY
Prior to the rise of tourism, mining was probably the most important economic activity in the Lakes. The stone axe factories at LANGDALE were the workshop of Neolithic Britain. Romans and others mined and quarried for minerals and stone. The monks of FURNESS ABBEY pioneered industrial metalworking. Highly experienced German miners were imported by the government of Elizabeth I. The complex geology of the Lakes produced copper, iron-ore, slate, lead, zinc, barytes, tungsten, graphite, fluorite, granite, limestone and coal. Most, although not all, mines have now closed and abandoned mine-workings can be found on fell-sides everywhere. Heavy industry continues in Barrow-in-Furness and Workington, while the region's major industrial employer is the Sellafield nuclear plant. Both the mines and Sellafield have contributed to Cumbria's folklore (for the former see CONISTON, for the latter DRIGG).

5. THE RISE OF TOURISM AND THE INVENTION OF THE LAKE DISTRICT
In 1634 three men from the Military Co. of Norwich went on an eleven-week 800-mile (1290km) jaunt around England. Their road between Carlisle and Kendal took them on 'such ways as we hope we shall never see again, being no other but climbing and stony,

nothing but bogs and mires, or the tops of those high hills, so we were enforced to keep these narrow loose stony base ways.' Apart from the occasional antiquarian looking for ancient remains, Lt Hammond, Capt. Dehumas and their unnamed friend 'an ancient' may have been the area's first tourists. In 1698 Celia Fiennes was impressed by the 'terrible' landscape and in 1724 Daniel Defoe encountered scenery that was, 'the wildest, most barren and frightful of any that I have passed over in England.' Everyone complained about the roads and the rain. All people of taste agreed that this benighted corner of Britain was just awful.

By the later eighteenth century, however, perceptions started to change. The wars in Europe hampered continental travel and this, combined with the rise of ideas of the picturesque and the sublime in landscape, suddenly meant that the mountains were no longer vile, terrible and frightening – they were beautiful, inspiring, even spiritual. Thomas West produced the first guidebook in 1778, and the bright lights of the Romantic generation – William Wordsworth, Samuel Taylor Coleridge, Thomas de Quincey and others – venerated the area's natural beauties in prose and poetry. The county names of Cumberland and Westmorland were insufficiently felicitous for high minds, and so the area was renamed the English Lakes, or the Lake District, a place that had never until then appeared on any map or official designation.

As the Lakes increased in fame and popularity, ideas began to coalesce around what were beginning to be seen as some quintessentially English values: appreciation of wild landscape – and access to it. Hill-walking and mountain-climbing for pleasure were virtually invented in the Lakes. The National Trust, dedicated to preserving the best of the natural and historical environment and making it accessible to all, was born here, and is now the largest single owner of land within the Lake District. The National Park, England's largest, was established in 1951. Now, millions each year come to enjoy a landscape that only a few centuries ago was regarded as 'hideous'.

Much of the Lakes' popularity in the second half of the twentieth century was due to the publication of Alfred Wainwright's *Pictorial Guides to the Lakeland Fells*, a series of hand-drawn walking guides covering every peak and fell. A. Wainwright, as he styled himself, is the modern colossus of Lake District writing, and his impact cannot be overestimated. He turns up several times in this book.

6. RECENT TIMES

The National Park is entirely within the county of Cumbria, formed in 1974 from the older counties of Cumberland (roughly, the north and west of the new county), Westmorland (the south-east) and – in the locales of Furness and Cartmel to the south – part of Lancashire. Lancashire-above-the-Sands was so named because this area was separated from the great engines of the county administration at Lancaster not just by distance but by the grim barrier of the sands of Morecambe Bay, inundated twice a day by the inrushing tide. This bizarre hiccup of local government history was eliminated by the creation of the new county.

Morecambe Bay has been subject to the mythologising process. Morecambe is no ancient name – until the eighteenth century the estuary was known just as 'Kent Sands'. Then in 1771 John Whitaker's *History of Manchester* equated the sands with an unidentified estuary in north-west Britain called 'Morecambe' in Ptolemy's *Geographia*. Educated tourists liked the idea that their holiday spot may have been noticed by a Greek geographer from the second century AD, and starting using the term. And soon Kent Sands was no more, and Morecambe Bay was born.

FINDING OUT MORE

If you want to visit some of the remoter archaeological sites, a good place to start is www.themodernantiquarian.com, the user-generated site inspired by Julian Cope's book *The Modern Antiquarian*. For more excellent information on the area's ancient remains I recommend Tom Clare's *Prehistoric Monuments of the Lake District* (2007) and Robert Farrah's *A Guide to the Stone Circles of Cumbria* (2008), or any of the works by Aubrey Burl listed in the bibliography. There is much to seek out in the *Transactions of the Cumberland and Westmorland Antiquarian and Archaeological Society* (abbreviated to CWAAS in the text). For more general works on Cumbria, you cannot go wrong with anything by Molly Lefebure (see Bibliography). My guide to Lakes-related literature has been the indispensable *Literary Guide to the Lake District* by Grevel Lindop. Websites referred to in the text are listed in the bibliography.

Routes accessible for wheelchairs and buggies can be found at:
www.lake-district.gov.uk/index/enjoying/outdoors/miles_without_stiles.htm

Grinning griffin atop the Lonsdale Mausoleum, Lowther.

WINDERMERE, AMBLESIDE AND GRASMERE

WINDERMERE (THE TOWN)

At 1.35 p.m. on 8 September 1989 a mystery block of ice hit a car at what was then McCann's Garage just moments after some prospective buyers had viewed the vehicle. The *Lakeland Echo* (14 September) quoted manager David Sissons, 'Out of the corner of my eye I saw something whizzing past. I thought it was a bird but then I realised it was going too fast. The next thing we heard was a bang at the rear of the garage.' Ice was found on top of and all around the car.

St Mary Church, Windermere, at night.

Windermere has an extensive selection of water-worn stones perched on gateposts. Elsewhere (such as in ASKHAM) these stones have a guardian/apotropaic function, but here they are more likely simply a result of nineteenth-century fashion. There are Victorian gargoyles on St Mary's Church and the Old Priory (both Church Road).

THE SCREAMING SKULLS OF CALGARTH

The Sculls, though brayed and burnt, return again.
'Now, guard thee! Guard thee well, Myles Philipson,'
– So rang the curse – 'We still thy tenants stay!'
'Ours is the dearest acre thou hast won,
Its fruits misfortune, loss of friends, decay!'
A ruined hall, a name wiped out, attests
How God avenged the murderer's yeoman-guests.

H.D. Rawnsley, 'The Haunted Hall at Calgarth' (1882)

This is one of the most-told ghost stories of the Lakes. It first appeared in print in Thomas West's popular *A Guide to the Lakes* in 1778, and as this account has influenced all later ones, it is worth examining exactly what West wrote (emphases are my own):

Calgarth-park …having been a long time in the possession of farmers, who occupy but a part of it, it is much gone out of repair, and has on the whole but a melancholy appearance … many are the stories of frightful visions, and mischievous deeds, which the goblins of the place are said to have performed to terrify and distress the harmless neighbourhood. These fables are not yet entirely disbelieved. Spectres are still seen, *and there are two human skulls, which have lain in the window of a large room as long as can be remembered* …

It has been a popular tale in these parts, *of immemorial standing*, that these skulls formerly belonged to two poor old people, who were unjustly executed for a robbery; that, to perpetuate their innocence, some ghost brought them there, and that they are for that end indestructible, and, in effect, immoveable. For, it is said, to what place soever they were taken, or however used, they were still presently seen again in their old dormitory, the window. As the report goes, they have been buried, burnt, powdered, and dispersed in the wind, and upon the lake, several times to no purpose, as to their removal or destruction. So far says common fame. *Certain it is human remains still exist* …

As a more rational account of the matter (though still lame and unsatisfactory) is told by some, that there formerly lived in the house a famous doctress who had two skeletons by her, for the usual purposes of her profession; and the skulls happening to meet with better preservation than the rest of the bones, they were accidentally honoured with singular notice. But be their origin what it may, their legend is too whimsical and improbable to deserve being recorded, otherwise than as an instance of the never-failing credulity of ignorance and superstition.

Calgarth-park was purchased by Dr Watson, the late bishop of Llandaff, who built an elegant mansion thereon, which, with the other improvements in that fine situation, makes it one of the most elegant places of residence in this country.

The next report is from 1787, in James Clarke's *A Survey of the Lakes of Westmoreland, Cumberland and Lancashire*:

> Crow-garth, alias Calf-garth, alias Cold-garth, now commonly called Caw-garth, be it which it will … [there were] two human skulls, of which many strange stories are told: they were said to belong to persons whom Robin had murdered, and that they could not be removed from the place …but always returned, even though they had been thrown into the Lake; with many other ridiculous falsehoods of the same stamp: *some person, however, has lately carried one of them to London*, and as it has not yet found its way back again, I shall say nothing more on so very trivial a subject.

And William Green's *Tourist's New Guide* (1819) notes that the single skull at Calgarth had 'nearly moulded away.'

These earliest accounts suggest that the skulls were real: West, who appears to have seen the skulls on his visit in 1775, emphasises, 'Certain it is human remains still exist,' and Clarke notes that a skull had been stolen (rationalist Georgian gentlemen had a tendency to do this with 'superstitious' objects that were supposed to always return to their home – saints' bells in Scotland, for example, were frequently pilfered). West suggests that the presence of the skulls, combined with the ruinous nature of the house, created the right ambience for stories of hauntings to thrive, and that these stories were already well-known when he was writing – so we have real physical objects already interacting with folk belief. He also notes the belief that the skulls 'belonged to two poor old people, who were unjustly executed for a robbery.' Clarke fills in the details here – his 'Robin' is Robin the Devil, Col. Robin Philipson of BELLE ISLE. Clarke accuses the dashing colonel of murdering the two people who were later to haunt him.

From here the trail becomes murky. By the early nineteenth century the cast of characters had become established: the 'two poor old people' were named as Kraster and Dorothy Cook, and their persecutor as Myles Philipson (not Robin, as in Clarke's account; the supposed dates also vary from the fourteenth to the seventeenth centuries). The story went that Myles, a member of a greedy and ruthless family, coveted the Cook's land. When they refused to sell he invited them to a Christmas celebration, whereupon he falsely accused them of stealing valuables from his table. The couple were tried at Appleby and condemned to death, at which point Dorothy stood up and pronounced a dread curse which writer after writer has delighted in reproducing:

> Guard thyself, Myles Phillipson! Thou thinkest thou hast managed grandly, but that tiny lump of land is the dearest a Phillipson has ever bought or stolen, for you will never prosper, neither your breed. Whatever scheme you undertake will wither in your hand; the side you take will always lose; the time shall come when no Phillipson shall own an inch of land; and while Calgarth walls shall stand we'll haunt it night and day. Never will ye be rid of us!

Following this malison the skulls either took up permanent residence in a niche beneath the window of the staircase at Calgarth, or – depending on who is telling the story – only appeared at Christmas, at the anniversary of the Cooks' execution. Cooper and Palmer's

The English Lakes (1908) notes how 'Horrible sounds were heard, groanings and shriekings and wild lament, after any tampering with the uncanny things.' No matter what means was used to dispose of them, they kept returning, and the Philipsons' fortunes declined as prophesised, until they became landless. Eventually the skulls ceased to cause any bother, the reason being variously ascribed to: (1) they had achieved their aim in driving out the enemy, and could now rest; (2) they had been walled up somewhere in the building; (3) they had been exorcised by Bishop Watson; all of which of course contradict the testimony of earlier writers that the skulls had vanished due to ordinary reasons such as theft and decay. But here we are dealing not with historical evidence, but with a good story: the skulls are simply too juicy a tale to be allowed to succumb to a mundane fate.

It is perhaps West's mention of Bishop Watson, combined with Watson being a senior churchman conveniently on hand, that prompted the notion that he had exorcised the skulls. A typical suggestion is in John Ingram's *Haunted Homes and Family Traditions of Great Britain* (1897): 'The well-known Dr Watson, Bishop of Llandaff, was at one point an occupant of Calgarth, and, whilst residing there, in order to satisfy local fears, went through a solemn form of "laying" the two ghostly skulls.' In reality, a more unlikely candidate for exorcist would be hard to find. De Quincey recalled him in his *Literary Reminiscences*:

> Yet what an Archbishop! He talked openly at his own table as a Socinian [a sect which denied the Trinity and the divinity of Jesus]; ridiculed the miracles of the New Testament, which he professed to explain as so many chemical tricks of legerdemain, and certainly had as little devotional feeling as any man who ever lived.

Richard Watson (1737-1816) was as self-serving and materialistic an eighteenth-century fat cat as they came – he hardly ever visited his cathedral at Llandaff in Cardiff, held fifteen other ecclesiastical appointments in different parts of the country, most of which he franchised out to poor curates while he pocketed the stipend, and spent nearly thirty years at Windermere doing no work other than the farming, tree-planting and land improvement incumbent on a country gentleman. When he built himself a grand new house – which still stands (SD397996) – he demolished the decaying old Calgarth Hall (so presumably any putative walled-in skulls went into the skip as well).

The Calgarth Skulls became a Victorian Lakeland institution, a standard fixture in many a guidebook. So much so that J.P. White burlesqued the tale in 'The Armboth Banquet,' a jokey poem in *Lays and Legends of the English Lake Country* (1873):

> To Calgarth Hall in the midnight cold
> Two headless skeletons cross'd the fold,
> Undid the bars, unlatched the door,
> And over the step pass'd down the floor
> Where the jolly round porter sat sleeping.
>
> With a patter their feet on the pavement fall;
> And they traverse the stairs to that window'd wall,
> Where out of a niche, at the witch-hour dark,
> Each lifts a skull all grinning and stark,
> And fits it on with a creaking.

The newly re-skulled skeletons now head off to a spectral shindig at ARMBOTH HALL, returning at dawn:

> The skeletons two rushed through the yard,
> They pushed the door they left unbarr'd,
> Laid by their skulls in the niched wall,
> And flew like wind from Calgarth Hall
> Where still the round porter sat sleeping.
>
> As out they rattled, the wind rushed in
> And slamm'd the doors with a terrible din;
> The grey cock crew; the dogs were raised;
> And the old porter rubb'd his eyes amazed
> At the dawn so coldly breaking.

So what was the case of the screaming skulls all about? White gives us a clue: 'A burial ground was attached to the buildings of Old Calgarth; when the ground has been trenched thereabouts, quantities of human bones have frequently been turned over and re-buried.' The skulls could simply have come from one of these disinterments. But their presence, combined with a potent mix of the gloom of the decaying mansion, the actual fate of the Philipsons – whose estates declined after they supported Charles I in the Civil War – and the pleasures of a story where the rich and cruel get their comeuppance, all created an irresistible tale. White also gives us a possible alternative supernatural source – the skulls are not the Cooks, but those of disaffected Philipsons:

> There are now in the dairy of the Old Hall two flat tombstones, with the name of Philipson inscribed upon them, which not very many years ago were dug up in the garden near the house; their present use being a desecration quite in accordance with the associations which hang around the place. This circumstance may afford a clue to the re-appearance of the skulls so frequently, after every art of destruction had been tried upon them, in the mysterious chambers of Old Calgarth Hall.

Almost every source notes that the phenomena had declined by at least the 1820s, but Peter Underwood's *Guide to Ghosts & Haunted Places* (1996) suggests there may still be something skulking about, with reports of strange noises, weird atmospheres, electrical switches coming on and doors and windows moving. Calgarth Hall is private and cannot be visited.

BOWNESS-ON-WINDERMERE

St Martin's Church (Church Street) is a largely Victorian work on a thirteenth-century site. The building is virtually a book, with the surfaces and roof beams adorned with Biblical quotations, sixteenth-century instructive sayings, and a Latin inscription celebrating the failure of the Gunpowder Plot. The chancel is built over the common grave of forty-seven people who drowned on 19 October 1635 when the ferryboat overturned as they were returning from a wedding in Hawkshead, as commemorated in a book published the following year entitled *The Fatall Nupital*. Despite the folklore that has grown up since, the bride and groom were not among the victims. Seven horses were also drowned, although it is not recorded where they were buried.

The medieval bowl of the church font has two small crudely-carved heads and a pair of incised crosses, and the East Window contains rare thirteenth-century glass and St George with the dragon. In the vestry is a monument to Richard Watson, Bishop of Llandaff (see CALGARTH). The Philipson Memorial of 1631 has 'The Authors epitaph upon him selfe. Made in the tyme of his sickness.' It begins, 'A Man I was, Wormes Meate I am.'

WINDERMERE (THE LAKE)

During the Civil War, Belle Isle (private, no landing) was home to the Royalist Col. Robin Philipson, who was besieged here by the Parliamentarian army, surviving cannon fire from Cockshott Point a few hundred metres away. When the siege was raised by Philipson's brother and the Roundheads retreated, 'Robin the Devil' pursued his enemy Col. Briggs to Kendal, where he rode into the church (and local legend) on horseback (see KENDAL for the full story).

From 1781 the island belonged to the Curwen family, who brought with them the Luck of Workington, an agate cup given to their ancestors by Mary Queen of Scots in return for hosting her at Workington Hall following her retreat from the disastrous Battle of Langside in Glasgow. Like all such Lucks, it was supposed to be tied to the family's fate. According to Marjorie Rowling in *The Folklore of the Lake District*, in 1976 the Luck was still in the possession of Mr E.S.C. Curwen, and could be seen on display in the splendid Georgian Round House. The Curwens left Belle Isle in 1993 and it is not clear what has happened to the Luck.

Windermere is England's largest lake, and, as with other extensive bodies of water surrounded by high hills (such as Loch Ness), it seems to suggest something uncanny to the human imagination. In the 1890s several people wrote to the magazine *Cumbria* describing strange roaring or howling sounds heard on the lake. In 1895 the whole of the lake froze, so the noises were most likely ice shifting. One of the persistently repeated legends is that when evil is about to befall the folk around the lake, a ghostly white horse is seen walking on the water. In their round-up of these odd phenomena, Cooper and Palmer in *The English Lakes* also make mention of people seeing something like 'a faint iris on the water, rivalling in its clear tinges the very rainbow.'

The Stag's Head Hotel in Bowness is the birthplace of the local mystery animal the Tizzie-Wizzie, a shy, semi-aquatic creature with a hedgehog's body and spikes, a squirrel's tail and a pair of gossamer wings. Apparently a boatman invented the story around 1900 as an entertainment for tourists – possibly as an adjunct to the tales of Beatrix Potter's ubiquitous anthropomorphic mammals – and it continues to fulfil this role to this day.

Possibly more flesh-and-blood is 'Bownessie,' 'Windy' or the 'Bowness Monster,' the names given to a large creature spotted several times in the lake. The Lakeside Aquarium near Newby Bridge at the southern end of the lake (visitable by ferry from Bowness) displays images taken by local photographer Linden Adams in February 2007. In an interview with the *Whitehaven News* (2 March 2007) Mr Adams described the animal as around 50ft (15m) long by comparison with boats nearby, and with a head like a Labrador, only 'much, much bigger.' *Practical Photography* magazine (April 2007) had a letter from John Harker, who was looking at the lakeside from Langdale Lodge when he spotted something moving about

10mph (16kph) underwater. It was around 50ft (15m) long, with two small humps just above the surface. On 23 July 2006, standing on Watbarrow Point near Wray Castle, visitor Steve Burnip saw a fast-moving creature around 20ft (6m) long with a little head and two humps which protruded from the water. Subsequent publicity in the *Westmorland Gazette* and contact with the Centre for Fortean Zoology (CFZ) brought six further eyewitness accounts ranging from the present day to as far back as the late 1950s, including Mr and Mrs Gaskell, who in July 2006 saw something large surface and dive again, giving the impression of a dolphin without the fin. In October 2006 the CFZ team investigated the area, but did not come up with any further solid evidence. The opinion of Jon Downes and Richard Freeman of the CFZ is that the sightings are of a previously undocumented type of eel, far larger than anything previously recorded. The CFZ website has much more on the ongoing investigations into the Windermere aquatic mystery.

The Aquarium has much more of interest, including blind cave fish, poison arrow frogs, piranhas – and pike, Windermere's largest predator, which can reach 6ft (1.8m) in length. In the 1982 pulp horror novel *The Pike* ('A cold relentless killer from the murky depths,') a 12ft (3.7m) long pike goes on a slaughter spree in Windermere, creating a tourist boom as people hope to see the monster. The author, Cliff Twemlow, was an extraordinary individual, numbering theme music composition, nightclub bouncing and ultra-low-budget filmmaking among his careers. He twice attempted to film *The Pike* – once making a promo at CONISTON WATER with the star Joan Collins and a large mechanical fish – but never managed to hook the budget.

In their book *Haunted Holidays* Anne Bradford and David Taylor relate spooky happenings at an unnamed cottage on the southern end of Windermere in 1996, with three holidaymakers reporting swiftly moving shadows, sudden drops in temperature and sensations of being pushed by two hands. One morning 'Linda' was lying in bed when she heard the door open and saw and felt the bed indenting as if someone had sat down. She called out, 'There's a lot of people that love me where you are and they will be upset if they hear that you're making me frightened.' After that, there were no further phenomena.

CARTMEL FELL

The plain St Anthony's Church (SD417881) is almost unchanged from its construction in 1505. One of the pews has the game Nine Men's Morris scratched on it. The partially restored medieval stained glass from CARTMEL PRIORY has St Anthony (ignoring the pig wearing a hermit's bell trying to climb his staff) and a crucifixion where streams of blood flow from Christ's wounds to depictions of five of the seven sacraments of the church – Communion, Extreme Unction, Baptism, Ordination and Marriage.

Henry Cowper's *Hawkshead* (1899) gives an example of the role of the 'village wiseman.' A burglary had taken place at a cottage near the church. The victim bought the wiseman a few beers at the pub and received specific instructions. The next Sunday, as the congregation was leaving, he stood in the churchyard and cried out that if his property was not returned by the following Sunday, the thief would find himself sitting on the roof-beams of the chapel during the service; and this would happen because the wiseman had said so. The thief, believing in the powers of the village magus, promptly returned the stolen goods.

In 1903 H.D. Rawnsley wrote in *Lake Country Sketches* that a couple of generations earlier the approved cure for a child with whooping cough was to climb Cartmel Fell, clip 'a hair from the cross on an ass's back and then tie it round the bairn's neck as a sovereign remedy for the troublesome whoop.'

Harriet Martineau in *The English Lakes* (1855) gives the sentimental tale of a local charcoal-burner who was killed by lightning in his hut. His fiancée, Kitty Dawson, lost her mind, and did nothing but sit on the stone on which he died, and call his name. Local people made sure she was provided with food and warmth, but one winter's day a group of hunters found her dead in the hut. Inevitably it is said that there have been sightings of her seated spirit, and her voice calling a man's name has been heard.

In 1951, L.F. Newman and E.M. Wilson carried out a survey on 'Folk-Lore Survivals in the Southern "Lake Counties"' for the journal *Folklore*. One respondent described a woman who was seen spinning under Lobby Bridge over the River Winster while another informant said the spirit had a horse's head.

INGS

Reston Hall (SD457986, private) was built for Robert Bateman, a rich local marble merchant, but he died at sea before taking up residence. As a somewhat inevitable consequence, he is said to haunt not the property itself but the gates – forever looking in but never entering. A striking plaque on St Anne's Church (SD446987) records Bateman's generosity in building the church. Within is a font with four large winged souls and a lively self-portrait of woodcarver William Fell.

On 27 September 2008 the *Westmorland Gazette* reported that Windermere resident Sandra Metcalf had come forward with plaster casts of what were apparently big cat tracks found in 2003 at Hag End Farm, to the south of Ings (SD435970).

KENTMERE

Kentmere Hall (NY451042) is associated with Hugh Herd or Heard, the so-called 'Cork Lad of Kentmere,' a man of immense size and strength. He appears to have actually existed, and to have been a bit handy in a fight or when heavy lifting was required, but almost all other tales told of him are legendary. He is supposed to have lived in the fifteenth, or sixteenth, or seventeenth century, with each period casting his life in a modernised idiom. In none of the tales are we told how tall he was.

Following a flurry of reports initiated by a photograph of a strange aerial disc over Sedgwick, the *Westmorland Gazette* for 28 August 1992 reconstructed the disc's route as it crossed the area in mid-August, from Hincaster to Sedgwick, Kendal, Staveley, Windermere and Kentmere. This however, was no alien craft, but a curiously-shaped lenticular cloud, formed by wave action in layers of air with different temperatures.

TROUTBECK

In 1899 Henry Cowper recorded two examples within 'the memory of man' of brutal propitiatory sacrifices in the parish: 'in one case a bull calf being roasted alive, because the cows were all calving males; in the other, a calf was burned to death in a field because of miscarriage among the herd.'

Two drinking troughs for horses tackling the long slog up to the Kirkstone Pass still exist on the roadside, the wells being named after St John and St Margaret, although there is no record of them being holy wells. There are several ancient cairns of various sizes at Troutbeck Park (NY424076) and a double stone circle at Hird Wood (NY416059) with part of the outer circle built into a wall.

The *Westmorland Gazette* for 13 October 2000 described the sighting of a large panther-like black cat at Orrest Head on 6 October.

KIRKSTONE PASS

This mimic church … has a peculiarly fine effect in this wild situation, which leaves so far below the tumults of this world: the phantom church, by suggesting the phantom and evanescent image of a congregation, where never congregation met; of the pealing organ, where never sound was heard except of wild natural notes, or else of the wind rushing through these mighty gates of everlasting rock – in this way, the fanciful image that accompanies the traveller on his road, for half a mile or more, serves to bring out the antagonist feeling of intense and awful solitude, which is the natural and presiding sentiment – the *religio loci* – that broods for ever over the romantic pass.

Thomas de Quincey, *Recollections of the Lakes and the Lake Poets* (1862)

This is the highest road pass in the Lake District, named after a boulder resembling a kirk (church) 700yds (640m) north of the inn, although the best resemblance is seen from the car park a further 300yds (275m) north. Of course, if the rain or snow is doing its horizontal worst then such simulacrum-spotting will probably come second to getting to the inn. A travellers' rest has been here, at the junction of two precipitous roads, since medieval times. Marjorie Rowling in *The Folklore of the Lake District* notes a sixteenth-century document records the 'Rayse of Kirkstone' (Norse *hreysi*, cairn), and a burial marked by a cairn was found in 1840 when the inn was being rebuilt. So far there is no record of a Viking ghost but the Kirkstone Pass Inn seems to play host to every other type of spook. Tony Walker in *The Ghostly Guide* to the Lake District gives a rundown of the main phenomena. There's Ruth Ray, a poor woman who died in a snowstorm while keeping her child alive, and a young boy who was killed by a coach nearby. A chap in a seventeenth-century tricorn hat appeared in a family photograph in 1993 and in the 1940s a teenage workman encountered a grey woman without a face. Neville, a barman of the 1970s, died while running on the fells – his apparition was seen before his body was found, and he is said to be responsible for opening doors and moving items around. One of the tenant managers described a glass flying across the room and landing safely. One of the very few trees nearby is called the Hangman's Tree, after a woman was hanged from it for murdering a child, although this story at least, along with the name, may be apocryphal. Some guests who stay in the rooms have to leave straight away. In the middle of the night one woman went and slept in her car, and the following day she and her friends checked out two days early, despite losing their deposit. Another woman who stayed in Room 2 reported an 'ice cold thing' dragging across her feet.

The inn has now developed something of a reputation for ghosts – it was featured in the *Haunted Hotels* series on the Discovery Channel and has a prominent place in many publications and websites devoted to the supernatural. Some recent sightings could therefore be the result of expectation creating a paranormal interpretation for events which have an entirely normal cause, but the sheer number of phenomena reported at the inn remains impressive.

AMBLESIDE

> At the upper point of Winandermere lies the carcase as it were of an antient city with great ruins of walls.
>
> William Camden, *Britannia* (1586)

Camden is referring to the Roman fort of Galava, the well-interpreted excavated remains of which can be seen beside the A5075 at Waterhead (NY373035). The most striking find from the site is a double gravestone, inscribed: 'To the good gods of the underworld. Flavius Fuscinus retired from the centurionship lived 55 years. To the good gods of the underworld. Flavius Romanus Record Clerk lived 35 years. Killed in the fort by the enemy.' Flavius and Flavius may have been father and son. The stone can be viewed in the small but splendid Armitt Museum (Rydal Road, open 10-5 p.m. every day, admission charge). The museum also contains various displays mentioning folklore, several Neolithic stone axes in various states, three watercolours by Beatrix Potter of domestic Roman finds from Galava, and a number of curios including Harriet Martineau's life and hand masks, a lock of Ruskin's hair, gin traps and a nineteenth-century wooden leg. Perhaps the most unexpected item is a bust by Josephina de Vasconcellos of Richard Branson, shown with a scroll, scholar's robe and casual sweater.

Above left: The Pelican piercing her breast to feed her offspring with her own blood, a symbol of Christ. St Mary's Church, Ambleside.

Above right: The 'Turning Point' modern stone circle in Rothay Park, Ambleside.

Noah's Ark floats on a corbel on the north porch of St Mary's Church on Vicarage Road. H.A.L. Rice, in *Lake Country Towns*, notes that when the 180ft (55m) high spire was completed, and before the scaffolding was removed, a local labourer, Moses Akister, climbed up on to the weathercock and then stood on his head on the bird's back. The footpath west of the church through Rothay Park passes 'Turning Point', a modern stone circle built in 2000 around a central gravity-defying spiral sculpture.

In *Hawkshead* (1899) Cowper has a tale of fairies told to him by an old man:

> In his young days strange were the reputed doings of the little folk in Ambleside fair and market. Dressed as common folk, they would mingle with the marketing folk, and then by blowing at the women at the market stalls they became invisible, and were enabled to steal things from the stalls.

CLAPPERSGATE

Bradford and Taylor's *Haunted Holidays* relates a haunting at Grey Friar Lodge Country House Hotel. A guest, Valerie, twice saw a thin, grey-haired, bearded man aged about sixty in the dining room. He was wearing a long purple coat and looked as if he was made of organza, 'there and yet not there.' The building is a former vicarage, and owner David Veen identified the apparition as a man of the cloth who liked to warm himself by the fireside.

RYDAL

Rydal Mount (open daily from March–October 9.30 a.m.–5 p.m., thereafter Wednesday–Sunday 11 a.m.–4 p.m., admission charge) was Wordsworth's last home. In 1911 the house was rented by novelist Mrs Humphry Ward and her daughter Janet Penrose Trevelyan. In her mother's *A Writer's Recollections* Janet left an account of a curious experience on the night of 14 September. She woke up suddenly and saw 'the figure of an old man sitting in the arm-chair by the window. I said to myself, "That's Wordsworth!"' Neither Janet nor her mother – to whom she related the experience in the morning – believed she had seen a ghost, instead regarding it as 'an interesting example of the influence of mind and association on the visualizing power of the brain.'

Overlooking the lake is Nab Cottage, once home to Thomas de Quincey and Hartley Coleridge, the wayward and short-lived son of Samuel Taylor Coleridge. I assume this is the house Harriet Martineau refers to when she writes of Hartley's landlady being haunted by his ghost, 'Long after his death, she used to hear him at night laughing in his room, as he used to do when he lived there' (*Lights of the English Lake District*, 1861).

Before St Mary's Church was built at Rydal, the dead were carried to Grasmere for burial. These days, because of the Wordsworth associations, this route is the most famous and walked of the coffin roads in the Lakes, running from behind Rydal Mount under Nab Scar and past Dove Cottage in Grasmere (NY339053 to 334063). A large flat-topped boulder by the road, 200yds (183m) south of Dove Cottage, is the Coffin Stone, where the funeral party rested.

Rydal Hall, opposite Rydal Mount, is not itself open to the public but the grounds are freely accessible, and are noted for Shawn Williamson's monumental sculptures of angels, as well as other works such as an owl and a stark cross. Rydal Hall was another grand house with a Luck. Rowling's *The Folklore of the Lake District* notes it was mentioned in the will of Sir William Fleming in 1736:

Shawn Williamson's 'The Angel of Rydal Hall'.

… a pretty large gilt silver bowl with the Fleming coat of arms upon it, given by my great great grandmother … to the heirs male of the family, to be kept by them as an heirloom and a lucky piece of plate, as I have reason to believe it hath been to all those who have had the keeping of it since her death.

Rydal Old Hall was a fortified tower on a knoll about ⅔ mile (1km) south. By 1681 it was completely ruinous, and is now a barely-discernable set of foundations west of the Ambleside road (NY368055). The abandoned site soon developed the inevitable tales of buried treasure and an underground passage to the new Hall, as well as a supernatural reputation. Mary Armitt's *Rydal* (1916) gives the flavour:

> Strange sounds, strange sights, pervaded it by night. Wailing voices, as of spirits in distress; headless ghosts (three in number), that danced upon its summit; and later, a white dog that followed the terrified passenger across the Old Orchard, even, it is believed, to the middle of last century. No one now living owns to having seen the white dog, but old men and women confess to having often in childhood, laid their ear to the road-wall that leans against the How, and to thinking that they heard, while they listened in breathless expectation, strange muffled sounds issuing from its depths.

Wordsworth's *Guide to the Lakes* records a strange meteorological event on Rydal Water on 30 March 1822. The wind 'scooped the waters out of the basin, and forced them upwards in the very shape of an Icelandic Geyser, or boiling fountain, to the height of several hundred feet' with the spray driven over the mountain tops. Apparently such 'commotions' were not uncommon.

Angel and two eagles; sculpture, Rydal Hall gardens.

Above: Rydal Caves. The strange carvings are in the right-hand cave.

Left: A pagan place? Possible altar, Rydal Caves.

Below: 'Go to Bass Rock', the cryptic message in Rydal Caves.

Prehistoric cupmarks on a mound beside Broadgate Meadow carpark, Grasmere.

The upper path south of the lake passes the atmospheric Rydal Caves, an abandoned slate quarry. The larger, deeper cave, to the left, is an echoing drip-fest, but the common belief that it was used as a location in Ken Russell's adaptation of Bram Stoker's horror novel *The Lair of the White Worm* is mistaken: the movie's cave scenes were filmed at Thaw's Cavern in Derbyshire. However, there is something even better here. On the floor of the shallower cave on the right can be found what can only be a modern pagan altar: a low rhomboidal stone with a small central square hole – presumably for holding something – and recent carvings of a spiral, a concentric circle and a circle around a cupmark. Sculptor Shawn Williamson alerted me to the notion that contemporary witches met in the cave. The wall of the cave also bears the enigmatic message 'GO TO BASS ROCK.' The only Bass Rock I know of is in the Firth of Forth; quite what the connection is, occult or otherwise, between a Lake District cave and a small Scottish island, I am unable to answer.

GRASMERE

Francis Orpen Morris' *A History of British Birds* (1852) quotes the *Kendal Mercury* of 1837, in which someone claimed to have observed several swallows emerging at springtime from Grasmere lake within 'bell-shaped bubbles … from each of which a Swallow burst forth.' The newspaper's editor added, 'We give the fact, well authenticated by the parties from whom we received it, in the hope that it may prove an acceptable addition to the data on which naturalists frame their hypotheses.' This had been a folk-belief for centuries – even Dr Johnson (as recorded by Boswell) claimed, 'Swallows certainly do sleep all the winter. A number of them conglobulate together, by flying round and round, and then all in a heap throwing themselves under water, and lie in the bed of a river.' Swallows, however, actually overwinter in Africa, not in a submarine lair.

A short distance down the 'no through road' south of Dove Cottage is the Wishing Gate, subject of an eponymous poem by Wordsworth. His notes to the poem claim that the gate, 'from time out of mind, has been called the Wishing-Gate, from a belief that wishes formed or indulged there have a favorable issue.' In the village centre a sign decorated with fairies announces the Storytellers Centre and Garden, where Taffy Thomas entertains young and old with traditional tales and folklore. The garden has a tree bearing dozens of sculpted hands. At the north end of the village is Grasmere's best-kept secret – a panel of prehistoric rock art. Dozens of cupmarks adorn the outcrop on the edge of the Broadgate Meadow car park (NY338078).

The splendid Ambleside Oral History website has an interview from 1999 with 'HT,' a seventy-six-year-old local man, who told a tale handed down from his grandfather. Road widening near the churchyard turned up several unmarked graves, the bones of which were temporarily housed in the sexton's hut pending a collective re-interment. At the time Church Stile – now the National Trust shop opposite the church – was a pub, and the regulars decided to have some fun with a chap called Bob Park, a strapping, self-confident fellow who was afraid of nothing. Bob accepted a bet to go across the road in the dark, retrieve one of the skulls and bring it back to the bar. What he didn't know was that one of the pub-goers was hidden in the sexton's hut. When Bob put his hand in to pick up a skull the japester shouted out 'Leave that alone, that's mine!' Bob retreated in fear, but he couldn't return empty-handed and so ventured in once more and acquired his prize. The man again called out 'Leave that alone, that's mine!' to which Bob replied, 'Nay, thee bugger, thee can't tell thee had two heads.'

Gerald Findler, in *Ghosts of the Lake Counties*, has what sounds like another well-worn pub tale. Sometime in the 1950s or '60s a group of men had been discussing ghosts in a Grasmere pub. At the end of the night one of the group walked home over the fells, where he found himself in company with a stranger. Following a chat about the local sports, the young farmer said, 'We've been talking about ghosts but I don't believe in 'em.'

'Don't you?' said the stranger – and then promptly vanished into thin air.

Mark Fraser's *Big Cats in Britain Yearbook* 2007 records a big black cat sighting in the rear garden of Forestside Hotel on 22 January 2006. And the *Westmorland Gazette* (27 September 2008) reported a similar creature close to the A591 between Rydal and Grasmere. Another exotic animal was spotted by Peter Whittaker, who contacted the *Gazette* on 28 November 2007 with a photograph he had taken near Loughrigg Terrace. It was a coati, a raccoon-like mammal native to South and Central America. David Harpley, the conservation manager at Cumbria Wildlife Trust said there had been numerous coati sightings over the years, and indeed a post on the newspaper's website by Michelle Cresswell reported a coati at Cathedral Quarry near LITTLE LANGDALE on 17 January 2008 (for another coati sighting see SIZERGH).

2

THE LANGDALES, CONISTON AND HAWKSHEAD

Much of this chapter is indebted to a book published in 1899, *Hawkshead: (The Northernmost Parish of Lancashire) Its History, Archaeology, Industries, Folklore, Dialect, etc* by Henry Swainson Cowper. Cowper was a local archaeologist who clearly packed a lifetime's worth of folkloric gathering into his magnum opus; it's a brilliant volume.

SKELWITH BRIDGE

When Cowper was lent some papers dated 1736-51 connected with the property of Bull Close, near Skelwith Fold, he found two written charms. They had been kept in the farmer's deed box, as valuable possessions, and make for a fascinating insight into eighteenth-century rural magic. The first was to prevent bleeding:

To stop Bleeding in Man or Beast at any Distance, first you must have some Drops of ye Blood upon a Linen Ragg and wrap a Little Roman Vitrioll upon this Ragg put it under your oxter [armpit] and say these words thrice into yrself:

There was a Man Born in Bethlem of Judea

Whose name was Called Christ.

Baptized in the River Jordan

In the Watter of the flood and the Child also was meak and good and as the water stood

So I desire thee the Blood of 'Such a person or Beast' to stand in their Bodie, in the name of the father son and Holy Ghost Amen.

Then Look into the Ragg and at that moment the Blood stopth the Blew powder is Turned into Blood by sympathy.

While this charm is ostensibly Christian in content – or at least uses exclusively Christian names of power in its invocations and sympathetic magic – the second charm has a more pagan feel:

To cure Burns or Scalds by Blowing thrice and Saying these words after each Blowing:

Coutha Cold under the Clay trembleing

is there any here that would

Learn of the Dead to Cure the sores of Burning

in the Name of God And in the name of God

be it Amen

First say then Blow then say then Blow and it is done.

Cowper thought that Coutha, who was 'Cold under the Clay trembleing' might have been the name of a spirit. Or, it was a dialect word for 'cold,' giving the familiar double repetition at the start of chants, 'Cold, Cold, under the Clay trembleing ...' Here the law of opposites is being invoked – the dead, cold in their graves, being used to counter the heat of the burn. My own suggestion is that Coutha may have been a local name for one of the dead. An alternative interpretation came in an article for *Folklore* in 1996 by Owen Davies, which described an Irish version of the charm containing the sentence, 'Old clod beneath the clay,' so perhaps the Cumbrian 'cold' is simply a misspelling of 'clod.'

ELTERWATER

The *Cumberland & Westmorland Herald* (17 August 2002) reported that in the 1970s some students at what was then Langdale Outdoor Education Centre claimed they had seen an apparition of a shabby, bearded man with a pock-marked face, wearing an old-fashioned collarless shirt and leather flat cap. A sketch drawn of the visitor was said to strongly resemble John Foxcroft, who had apparently died in an explosion at the former gunpowder mill in 1916. There had also been several previous accidents at the works – the *English Lakes Visitor and Keswick Guardian* records a 'Terrific Explosion at Elterwater Gunpowder Works' which killed three men in December 1878, for example. The site is now the Langdale Estates holiday complex (NY327045). Their website claims that the Gateway building at the estate entrance is haunted by a former foreman, whose carousing one night with local wool merchant Nathaniel Hobson meant that he was still tipsy the following morning, and so caused another explosion. The gunpowder works closed in 1930. Their remains can still be seen, and a self-guided trail leaflet is available locally.

An entry on the Heritage Action website for 23 August 2005 identified a possible robbed prehistoric cairn (NY331049) on Elterwater Common. Suzanne Forster and Brian Kerr spoke to Douglas Warrell, a local historian, who told them of the Neddy Bogle or Boggle, a spirit which in the distant past emerged from the cairn to scare a local horseman.

CHAPEL STILE/GREAT LANGDALE

In 1999 prehistoric rock art was discovered on the huge Langdale Boulders, just north-west of Chapel Stile at Copt Howe (NY31400583). The westernmost boulder has the most extensive work, with numerous cupmarks, linear grooves, chevrons and multiple concentric circles, some having up to eleven rings. The eastern boulder has two partial rings. The boulders are next to a dry-stone wall just west of the road south of Harry Place Farm. They are popular with climbers and there are fears that this activity may damage the fragile rock carvings. Another cupmarked stone is beside the path through the woods by the campsite at the head of the valley (NY286056).

Great Langdale was one of Britain's first major industrial sites. During the Neolithic period, with production peaking from around 3350 BC, thousands of stone axes originated from this 'factory.' It could be argued that this was the omphalos or central focal point of prehistoric society in Britain – certainly its economic engine. Ten quarries – caves, adits, open-cast mines and even vertical faces – are known around the Langdale Pikes and Pike o' Stickle. The industry lasted for around a thousand years and may have involved specialized, skilled labour. It would have taken a month of work to convert the original quarried lump of stone to a finely polished axe head. Langdale axes have been found all over Britain and Ireland, suggesting extensive and sophisticated trade networks – the ceremonial sites at CASTLERIGG and MAYBURGH may have been the first stops on the trade routes. Finished axes would have had prestige value, suitable for gifts between high-status individuals from different tribes. If Langdale was recognised as the source of the best axes, then a Langdale axe would have been a guarantee not just of quality but also of desirability – possibly the first must-have 'designer label'.

Gabriel Blamires's 2005 book *Guidestones to the Great Langdale Axe Factories* suggests that the routes to and from the quarries were marked in ancient times by 'guidestones,' typically triangular, rhomboidal or pentagonal boulders. He gives numerous examples following routes through Great Langdale to Mickleden and up to the factories at Harrison Stickle and Pike o' Stickle. I'm not convinced by the argument – it seems to me too much depends on the eye of faith in deciding which random boulder is a guidestone – but if he's right, this is a major archaeological insight.

LITTLE LANGDALE

Cowper recorded that Busk House (NY305034) was regularly visited by brownies or house-goblins, who churned butter while the family were abed, and dropped dods of it in the nearby woods (this would be the plant Fairy Butter, *Tremella Albida*). At Fell Foot (NY300032) is an odd terraced rectangular mound which, it has been suggested, was a Viking Thing or parliament mound, making this the political centre of the Icelandic colony. Archaeologists are unconvinced, but they're not convinced it's not, either.

Alexander Craig Gibson's *The Folk-Speech of Cumberland* (1869) gives us the tale of the Oxenfell Cross dobby, which manifested itself not visually but by the sound of a furious argument between two men. Gibson's alleged informant encountered the noises on what is now the public access road between Oxen Fell High Cross on the A593 (NY328017) and Hodge Close (NY317018). The back-story has two rivals for a maiden's affections quarrelling here and one murdering the other. Writing thirty years later, Cowper could find no one who knew the story, and was convinced Gibson had made it up.

Two local people interviewed for the Ambleside Oral History Group in the 1980s gave details of old-time death and funeral customs in Little Langdale. 'AP', who was born in 1901, described how when someone died the clocks were stopped in the house, and only restarted when the body was taken to the funeral. It was also the custom that everybody entering the house had to touch the body; this was presumably an echo of the ancient belief that if a murderer's hand touched his victim's corpse, the body would bleed. 'BZ', born in 1916, recalled that a plate of salt was placed on the corpse's chest whilst it was lying in the house; this was thought to keep evil away before the funeral.

Jessica Lofthouse in *North Country Folklore* (1976) relates how her friends followed footprints in the snow from Wrynose Bottoms to Red Tarn (NY278037) where the prints simply ended, with no sign of anyone having walked back or further on.

CONISTON WATER

Donald Campbell broke the water speed record here in 1955. He went on to set land speed records and a further six world water speed records, his 1964 record coming in at 276mph (444kph). When another team looked as if they would beat this, Campbell attempted to break his own record. On 4 January 1967 his boat *Bluebird K7* disintegrated on Coniston Water while doing more than 300mph (483kph).

Veteran ghosthunter Peter Underwood recorded interviews with Donald Campbell and his wife Tonia in *Guide to Ghosts & Haunted Places*. Sir Malcolm Campbell, Donald's father, another multiple speed record holder, who had died some years earlier, had believed it was possible for the dead to communicate intelligibly with the living. Donald was completely convinced he had seen his dead father many times – whenever he was fearful about one of his speed attempts, Malcolm would appear to encourage him. During the actual attempts Donald sometimes saw his father's face in the windshield, and often he felt his presence guiding the vehicle. We will never know if he saw his father before the fatal crash. Ten years after Donald's death Tonia told Underwood, 'Donald is still guiding me from the other world … I have awakened in the middle of the night to find him standing there, but he is always helpful and never scary. I often see him in front of me yet I'm not psychic in any way.' She never felt that Donald was a ghost or that he was trying to return – he was simply helping her with problems in her life.

Campbell's body and *Bluebird* were not found and recovered until 2001, and Coniston is clearly a lake that guards its secrets well. Carol Park went missing on 17 July 1976. In 1997 her weighted body was found on a projecting ledge at a depth of 75ft (23m). At the subsequent 'Lady in the Lake' trial in 2005 Carol's husband Gordon was convicted of her murder, although the case has become a cause célèbre, with many convinced that he is innocent. As yet there have been no claims of sightings of the ghost of Carol Park on the lake, although it can surely only be a matter of time. Cumbrian lakes are popular with those seeking to dispose of female corpses (see also CRUMMOCK WATER and WAST WATER).

Several newspapers (*Metro, News & Star, Sun*) in February 2005 reported that divers had created a bathroom, complete with toilet and bathtub, at the bottom of the lake. The National Trust Steam Yacht *Gondola* plies the lake, a steam-powered Victorian-era luxury vessel with opulent décor, its prow sporting a pair of stags and a great silver coiled serpent.

CONISTON

One morning in 1980 a Mrs Hudson was drinking tea in bed in a holiday cottage when she saw on the landing a large, big-bellied man with the weather-beaten appearance of a local workman. He grinned benignly at her with blackened teeth, before vanishing. The encounter is in Bradford and Taylor's *Haunted Holidays*.

The Ruskin Museum on Yewdale Road (typically open March-November 10 a.m.-5.30 p.m. daily, and 10.30 a.m.-3.30 p.m. Wednesday-Sunday between November-February, admission charge) is another of the area's bijou but excellent museums. There are Neolithic axes from GREAT LANGDALE, Bronze-Age weapons and tools, finds from the stone circle at BANNISIDE, a lithophone (a stone xylophone), and splendid displays on Donald Campbell and *Bluebird*, and local coppermines and slate quarries. Perhaps the best part is that devoted to the great John Ruskin himself, Victorian polymath, environmentalist and social critic, noted for statements such as: 'THERE IS NO WEALTH BUT LIFE. Life, including all its powers of love, of joy, and of admiration. That country is richest which nourishes the greatest number of noble and happy human beings' (from *Unto this Last*).

Ruskin is buried in the churchyard of St Andrew's in the centre of the village (SD303975). His memorial cross, one of the finest works of its kind, was designed by his biographer and secretary W.G. Collingwood, who also painted the moving portrait of Ruskin in old age that hangs in the museum. The memorial is in the shape of a Dark-Age cross and its complex content is filled with visual references, both obvious and obscure, to Ruskin's work and achievements. Collingwood described it as 'a kind of short pictorial biography.' A display inside the church explains the key elements of the symbolism:

An artist sketching the landscape (for *Modern Painters*, Ruskin's first major book).

A boy with a lyre (representing Ruskin's love of poetry and music).

St George and the dragon (his craft organisation the Guild of St George).

The Lion of St Mark (his book *The Stones of Venice* – the winged lion is the symbol of the city).

A seven-branched candlestick (the book *The Seven Lamps of Architecture*).

The Parable of the labourers in the vineyard (the social criticism work *Unto This Last*).

Lilies and sesame cakes (*Sesame and Lilies*, essays on the duties of men and women).

The Angel of Destiny holding a club, key and nail (representing *Fors Clavigera*, 'The Nails of Fortune,' letters addressed to 'The Workmen and Labourers of Great Britain').

A crown of olives (*The Crown of Wild Olive*, lectures on the moral aspects of work and trade).

Animals, birds and wild flowers (symbolising Ruskin's love of nature).

This level of detail is important because in recent times the symbolism has, by some, been given entirely twisted interpretations. The starting point has been the swastika that sits between the two parts of Ruskin's name. It is another of Collingwood's learned references, this time to ancient Norse crosses where it was the emblem of Thor. Its meaning in the Mediterranean ancient world – as a symbol of good fortune – was re-interpreted by the early Church as referring to the Resurrection. It can be found on Christian gravestones right up to the early twentieth century. Its more recent usage as a Nazi symbol, however, has obscured all these earlier innocent meanings and given them an unwonted sinister bent. (For the record, the pacifistic, liberal, socially-concerned Ruskin died in 1900, when a certain Adolf Hitler was still in short trousers.) With the swastika as their springboard some conspiracy-minded individuals have pored over the monument and found alleged references to Zionism, Freemasonry, the Knights Templar, Communism, Fascism, the Illuminati, and anti-Christian paganism and occultism. To which there is only one appropriate response: piffle.

Until 1538 there was no burial ground in Coniston and the dead had to be taken from the church for burial in Ulverston, 25 miles (40km) distant along the corpse way. In *The Old Man; or, Ravings and Ramblings round Conistone* (1846) Alexander Craig Gibson gives the tale of how the ditch called Jenkin Syke got its name. The funeral party was taking Jenkin to his last rest, pulling him on a sled. When they arrived at Torver they noticed the coffin was missing. 'Deeming it unseemly to proceed without it,' they returned to find that it had fallen into the syke at the southern edge of Coniston village.

Gibson also gives the tale of the Devil's footprint, although here his tone clearly tells us he is having a bit of a laugh. An unnamed witch lived at the point of land where Yewdale Beck decants into Coniston Water, near where the Water Head Pier now stands (SD311971). Realising that the deal she had made with the Big Bad Man was perhaps not in her ultimate interest, she sought advice from a Fr Brian, a monk based at Bank Ground on the opposite side of the lake. He prescribed a severe penance, and told her to call upon the aid of himself and St Herbert if Satan became a problem: the Devil, learning of his disciple's apostasy, very quickly turned up at the door of the witch's hovel, so she exited through the window and ran up Yewdale Beck screaming the holy names as prescribed. His Evilness was just about to nab her at Bannock Stone Bridge, when his foot, 'not the cloven one – for neither dead Saint nor living Priest can

Above: The Lion of St Mark, representing The Stones of Venice. The Ruskin Cross, St Andrew's Church, Coniston.

Left: St George taking on a very Norse dragon. The Ruskin Cross.

Below: Candelabra symbolising the Seven Lamps of Architecture, the Ruskin Cross.

be supposed to have power over that, – but his other foot,' was trapped by the melting rock. Before the Devil was released Fr Brian, 'being well versed in this particular line of business' negotiated the woman's release from her contract. Gibson insisted the footprint was still there under the bridge, but Cowper, writing fifty years later, could find no trace of it – nor any such tradition – and concluded that Gibson had invented the story. The current Bannock Stone Bridge is over Church Beck on Lake Road; Gibson gives precise directions and places it over Yewdale Beck, about 220yds (200m) to the north, just south of the B5285 road bridge. Has the name shifted from one bridge to another, or did Gibson get his geography wrong?

Another one of Gibson's tall tales concerns a giant from TROUTBECK who settled north of Coniston. At 9ft 6in (2.9m) tall and powerfully built, 'Girt Will o' t' Tarns' was a local asset agriculturally and militarily, but he became obsessed with Barbara, the beautiful maid of Lady Eva Fleming, and one night he abducted the girl from the lakeside. Lady Eva gave the alarm and a posse of Flemings chased Will north along Yewdale Beck to a pool called Cauldron Dub where the giant killed the girl before being despatched himself. A long narrow mound near the stream was thereafter pointed out as Girt Will's grave.

Copper has been extracted in Coppermines Valley from Roman times or even earlier, although it only became systematic when the German miners invited by Elizabeth I opened nine mines. The industry declined around 1900. Many of the workings were opened up by blasting with gunpowder. Some of the shafts go down 1,100ft (335m), and many sheep and dogs were lost in them before they were covered over. The Simon Nick chasm is the centre of the area's legends. Simon apparently found a great seam of copper ore in a secret place and consequently made it rich. One night in the pub he boasted that the Devil was his partner – or, depending on whom you read, the fairies had guided him to the seam – and from then on his luck turned. He found no more copper and while setting up a blast he blew himself up. Molly Lefebure, in *The English Lake District*, says that one of the old huts is inhabited by the spirit of a miner.

THE OLD MAN OF CONISTON

On 18 December 1958 George King climbed the Old Man and performed a ritual to make the mountain holy and create a New-Age power centre. King had been requested by the Cosmic Masters to ascend a number of mountains in Britain, the USA, Australia, New Zealand, Switzerland and France. On the summits he became a conduit for extraterrestrial spiritual energy which then 'charged' the mountain so it could become a reservoir for use by later adepts. King completed his mission, known as Operation Starlight, between 1958 and 1961, creating eighteen gigantic spiritual energy batteries whose powers could be harnessed for good (the nineteenth, Mount Kilimanjaro, was personally charged by St Goo-Ling, one of the Ascended Masters of Earth; Kilimanjaro is now apparently a Spiritual Retreat of the Great White Brotherhood). On 23 August 2008, to celebrate the golden jubilee of Operation Starlight, members of King's group, the Aetherius Society, made a return pilgrimage to the Holy Mountain of the Old Man of Coniston.

King and his acolytes had a religious interpretation of the flying saucer phenomenon that swept Britain in the 1950s: the aliens were benign, spiritual, and counted among their number Ascended Masters such as Jesus, who was the original 'Charger' of a mountain in Devon. It's probably no coincidence that, of all the mountains in the Lakes, the Aetherians chose the Old Man, because it was here, on 15 February 1954, that Torver schoolboy Stephen Darbishire took one of the most famous photographs in Ufology. According to an account he gave that year, a 'strange silvery cloud' descended, looking like a 'solid, metal-like thing, with a dome.' He took two photographs which quickly became a worldwide sensation. They were similar to images of a 'Venusian scoutship' taken two years earlier by American George Adamski, who claimed he had actually met the aliens and been on board their spaceship. To true believers, it seemed confirmation of their faith. The photographs were repeatedly used to 'prove' the literal reality of alien visitors. The teenager found himself speaking to packed halls and even being invited to Buckingham Palace, where he was interviewed on behalf of Prince Philip (one of several royal and aristocratic individuals interested in 'the flying saucer question' at the time). Eventually Darbishire faded from the public eye, and became a teacher and artist.

The photographs were taken on Little Arrow Moor, above the valley of Torver Beck (around SD273969), not far from legend-rich Goat's Water (see below). On 9 October 2004, on the same site, artist Julian Claxton, as part of the FRED art project, attempted to recreate what he regarded as Darbishire's photographic hoax. He erected a sign reading 'Notice: Site of a Psychic Research Foundation experiment' and gave details of the original sighting. In the *Westmorland Gazette* the previous day he had explained his purpose, 'What I'm trying to do is adapt various methods that have been suggested to me by people ranging from UFO experts to local people as to how Stephen Darbishire might have made these photographs in the first place.' Several photographs were taken using techniques and cameras available in 1954, and although none replicated the originals, one – created by smearing Windolene on glass – came close to their style.

In response to Claxton's experiment, the now sixty-three-year-old Darbishire was still exhibiting his trickster spirit. To the *Westmorland Gazette* (8 October 2004), he was adamant the photographs were not faked:

We just went up the fell and took the photograph of it. I was with my cousin at the time. This thing, whatever it was, appeared, we took a photograph of it. I fell over the camera at one point. When we took it down, everybody laughed at us. I've no idea what it was … For two years, every weekend was taken up with people coming and sitting on the lawn. Most of the people who came were sort of on some religious trip, that's the best way to put it. To a fourteen-year-old, it was a bit of a joke.

Apparently the unwelcome attention caused him to change his story: 'I said it was a hoax to get people away but they said "you've been got at". They wanted to believe. I should have dropped it like a stone.' The following day in the *North West Evening Mail* he gave a completely different account:

It was all just a hoax. We were just a couple of lads fooling around … I drew this shape on a piece of silver paper and photographed it … when my father met me off the bus next morning he said all the national newspapers were waiting for me … I thought I would get into trouble, so I shut my mouth. I just let them believe I'd taken a picture of a UFO. I was too terrified to do anything else … I've told everybody that it was a hoax but they don't believe me. They just say I've been got at.

Gibson, in *The Old Man*, tells us that Low Water (SD275983), just below the summit, was home to enormous trout, one of which was so large and so resistant to being hooked that it was thought immortal. Sadly for this notion it was found one morning dead upon the shore. However the corpse was able to furnish a second legend – the fish's 'great age and its high stormy location,' had caused it to grow a covering of hair. Stories of hairy fish go back at least to the sixteenth century, with Ambroise Paré's *On Monsters and Marvels*, and there are several more recent legends of the fur-bearing trout in Canada, the USA and northern Europe – along with a number of faked sideshow specimens – but no genuine hair- or fur-bearing fish is known. That being said, the deceased Hairy Trout of Low Water could have been suffering from a fungal disease which caused a white or grey fur-like growth. Such moulds are well-known, and are often fatal, so it's possible part of Gibson's tale was actually authentic.

Janet Bord's *Traveller's Guide to Fairy Sites* notes that fairies have been seen guarding hidden treasure by the piles of stones at the side of Goat's Water (SD265977). The Banniside Stone Circle (SD28469670) to the south-east of the Old Man is a group of very low stones. Cowper mentions a peculiar tale associated with a sheep-shelter somewhere near the circle, above the farm then called Smartfield, 'a workman was nearly scared out of his wits and driven back to the farmhouse by the insane antics of a besom, which, leaning peacefully against a wall when he entered, suddenly dashed into the middle of the floor and executed a vigorous hornpipe round the terrified rustic.' An animated broomstick? Groovy.

TORVER

The seven stones of the tiny and charming Bleaberry Haws stone circle (SD26429465) sit among a cluster of archaeological remains, with cairns at SD26739448, 26789442 and 26569471, the last being on the summit. These cairns line a mysterious ancient earthwork, Torver High Common Dyke, which runs from south-east to north-west from Green Rigg Bank over Banks, down the valley and up to Bleaberry Haws summit, a distance of some 1,100yds (1km). There are similar dykes near HAWKSHEAD HILL.

BLAWITH

Cowper describes how, when the milk at Nibthwaite Grange (SD296881) had been bewitched, the farmer's wife obtained twigs of rowan and either stirred the milk with it or placed it in the milk to remove the curse.

CONISTON WATER (EAST SHORE)

A number of nineteenth-century folklorists have commented on the custom of 'the fire that was never allowed to go out' in different parts of the world, something they dubbed the 'hearth-cult.' Cowper mentions that the hearth fire at Low Parkamoor (SD306926) had been kept continuously for three generations, while the farmer at Lawson Park (SD317951) claimed he had his grandfather's fire, and when this accidentally went out one time he took a shovelful of embers from a local woodcutter whose fire had been originally lit from his.

Lawson Park is where Richard Adams places the animal research station in his novel *The Plague Dogs*.

OUTGATE

The *Westmorland Gazette* (8 November 2002) reported a sighting on 4 November of a large black cat on the minor road from the Drunken Duck pub to Outgate.

Cowper gives us a story told to him by an eighty-year-old local man, who was relating an episode told by his mother. An ill-regarded family – who in 1899 had only recently left Outgate, so Cowper declined to give their name – numbered among their brood a woman universally regarded as a witch. The local pack of hounds would often chase a certain hare, which always disappeared near Outgate, scent and all. One day the hare was chased into Outgate, and just as it leaped up to the window of the 'uncanny' family, one of the dogs, a black one, nipped it. 'At the same moment there came from within the building this wild screaming chorus:"Switch Granny Switch! Here comes t' black bitch!"' But it was too late – the hunters, running to the spot, found not the hare, but the injured witch. This shape-shifting story is widely told about witches all over the British countryside.

Another Outgate woman, Agnes Warriner, reportedly had the special power to cure jaundice by a spell, although possibly she had some medical skill, for the patient was required to take urine for examination. Cowper met an old man who had been thus cured in his youth.

KNIPE FOLD

Cowper mentions an item in the will of William Knipe, who in 1699 left some property to the Quaker Meeting House, and 'a gold ring, which is kept in Mary Satterthwaite's hands, yet any poor Friends may have it to wash sore eyes with.' This is an unusual example of superstition being associated with the Society of Friends.

HAWKSHEAD HILL

Marjorie Rowling notes that in 1895 an oak tree here was dressed with coloured rags and crockery, presumably some kind of fertility ritual. Some years earlier Cowper's father, making alterations at a farm at Hawkshead Hill, discovered a walled-up door close to, but a few steps above, the main front door. One of the workmen said these corpse doors were originally made as an exit for coffins. These doors were so positioned to prevent the spirit returning by way of the threshold, which was always open.

South of the hamlet at SD337982 is a cairn that Cowper dug out in 1883, finding a cremation burial and a flint knife. South of this, in Hawkshead Hall Park, he describes two earthworks, one about 440yds (400m) long, running north-east and south-west, and the other leaving it at right angles and running south-east for about ½ mile (800m). The dykes, which were no more than 2ft (60cm) high when Cowper saw them, ran up and down slopes and valleys, and were clearly not defensive, as they were often overlooked by higher ground. There is a similar dyke near TORVER. Cowper wondered if their proximity to burial cairns might be a clue – could they have been built to prevent the restless dead within these sepulchres from walking further? The dykes seemed to start and finish at becks – could the running water at each end have been regarded as a further barrier to the spirits? The whole idea is an intriguing one, and 'spirit walls' may provide a fruitful line of research for earth mysteries researchers. As for the Hawkshead Hall dykes, I fear they have been lost under forestry plantations.

HAWKSHEAD

> Haunted places, as we find them in our parish, are simply the result of a strange jumbling
> of actual tragedies and mysteries and very ancient folklore, early forms, indeed, of northern
> superstition; in fact a murder or a suicide takes place, and the people promptly crowd the site, so
> to speak, with bogeys, whose exact counterpart existed a thousand years ago.

Henry Swainson Cowper, Hawkshead (1899)

This is Cowper's healthily sceptical take on his parish's ghostlore, which he clearly enjoyed collecting while not taking it too seriously. He spoke to an old man who, in about 1825, was riding in a cart from Hawkshead Hall towards Gallowbarrow (the suitably-named hamlet north of Hawkshead), when he saw a tall woman in old-fashioned clothing perform a vertical take off, finally disappearing high in the air. He concluded the anecdote with, 'There nae doobt but ther's summat terrible queer about Haaksid Hall.'

The medieval manor house, once owned by the monks of FURNESS ABBEY, was indeed widely held to be haunted. Cowper's grandfather pulled down most of the old building and built a new farm – whereupon the ghosts apparently gave notice to quit, and moved ¼ mile (400m) down the road to Belmount (SD352993), a house built merely in the 1770s, and with no history of grisliness. It had, however, been empty for some time, and thus became suitable quarters for the dispossessed spectres. There were lights in the house when no one was home, the gates would fly open as a person passed, locked doors yawned wide, and there was many a strange noise, not to mention apparitions. Meanwhile a tall, white-robed woman was regularly seen strolling along the road between Belmount and Hawkshead Hall, or in Scarhouse Lane. When Belmount gained long-term tenants the spooks were seen no more.

Another legend associated with Hawkshead Hall was that it was supposed to be joined by a subterranean passage to FURNESS ABBEY, 19 miles (30.5km) away. Even by the credulity-stretching standards of tales of secret underground tunnels, that's a fair stretch. All that now remains of Hawkshead Hall is the Courthouse (SD349987). Entry is free, but the key must be obtained from the National Trust shop in Hawkshead.

Frankhousesteads, a farmhouse in the neighbourhood of Hawkshead, was reputed to be haunted by fairies; Cowper notes that the building was one of the hideouts of the Castlehow thieving gang, which was broken up in about 1785, and suggests that the criminals invented the legend in order to discourage prying eyes.

Cowper also collected examples of curious customs and superstitions, such as the belief that seventh sons had special powers. A Mr Tyson, originally from LITTLE LANGDALE, was a seventh son who was convinced he had no special powers. Despite this, a woman working at Coniston Copper Mines persistently sought him out to heal some problem on her arm, perhaps scrofula. She came early in the morning every week for seven weeks, and eventually the man agreed to tie some charm or spell round her neck – which actually worked, and the ailment was cured.

Bibliomancy, or divination by Bible and key, was clearly practiced up until the early nineteenth century, and possibly a little later. Thomas Martin of Fieldhead, who died in 1895 at an advanced age, told Cowper he remembered his father John Martin using the procedure to discover if a certain individual was acting maliciously towards him. Thomas could not recall the exact process, but the Bible and key appear to have been balanced against each other on end, and some words or a spell muttered.

Cowper notes that in Hawkshead, if a cow gave birth to more than one dead calf, the body was taken and buried at the threshold of the byre, an apotropaic sacrifice intended to remove the presumed bewitchment. In his book *Cumbriana* (1876) Alexander Dickinson gives further details. The charm was deemed to be particularly potent if the abortive calf was still showing signs of life when it was buried. And if a cow or herd was subject to persistent abortion, the first living abortive calf was burned alive at midnight, although it was 'allowable to despatch the calf with the aid of a pitchfork as soon as it was thrown into the fire.' Dickinson provides an astonishing detail on what would occur if this live immolation actually succeeded in effecting a cure:

> ... the evil spirit which caused the disease would enter the byre or field where the cattle were, and in parting revenge would set the whole herd bellowing like so many mad creatures. If in the byre, they would break loose, and a general fight would ensue during the burning. If in the field, they would break through the hedges, galloping furiously, with heads and tails erect, bellowing and surrounding the fire; and woe be to the man who under-took the sacrifice if he had not time to secure his safety by flight.

Because of the danger of releasing both the disease demon and the maddened cows, the operation was to be performed alone, and only by a man who had explicit faith in the outcome.

Another affliction affecting cattle was foot-and-mouth disease, known as murrain, which annihilated herds in the 1830s. Desperate times called for desperate remedies, and a rumour went round that 'Needfire' was en route from Yorkshire. Needfire was fire created by friction alone and carried hand-to-hand from farm to farm; it would not be allowed to go out, or to be taken inside the house, because this would negate its power. Its smoke would ensure a miraculous cure and the greater the smoke, the more powerful the magic. Against Dickinson's orders, one of his faithful servants lit the 'great smoke':

> The men crowded the cattle into it, and drove them in a continual ring. The ring driving was repeated till the poor animals began to sneeze, and then to cough – and so did the men – till cattle and men were nearly suffocated ... The cattle were driven staggering to their several places by the men, wondering at the strange incantations, some impressed with fear, others (unbelievers) scoffing at the ceremony, and railing not a little at the outrageous smoking they had undergone.

In Dickinson's case the charm was not effective, and he eventually controlled the disease in his herd through more conventional pastoral practices.

Cowper interviewed old farmers and found several cases of Needfire being lit around Hawkshead – at Keenground (SD347983, west of the village) and Finsthwaite Heights (SD361881), both perhaps around 1835-6, and about a decade later or so at Hollin Bank in Monk Coniston (SD320982) and Fieldhead (SD368918, near Graythwaite Hall). Cowper also quotes 'Mr Taylor's Commonplace Book,' an unpublished manuscript written by a local man between 1850 and 1874, for an episode around 1846-7:

A scene of the most ludicrous and gross superstition took place at Sawrey … A well-to-do old farmer … had recourse to the following remedy, recommended to him by a weird sister in the district as an effectual protection from the attacks of the foul fiend … The cattle were made to pass through the fire and smoke in the order of their dignity and age, commencing with the horses and ending with the swine. The ceremony having been duly gone through, the enlightened owners of the herds and flocks, along with their families, followed the example of the cattle.

In 2001 there were more 'great smokes' in the Lake District, although these came from the pyres where millions of animal corpses were burned in the campaign against a resurgence of foot-and-mouth disease.

Hawkshead was struck by plague several times in the sixteenth and seventeenth centuries. An entry in the parish register for November 1577 reads, 'In this monthe begane the pestelent sicknes in our pishe wich was brought in by one George Barwicke whereof is depted all those yt are thus marked [with a star].' Thirty-eight names are accordingly starred as victims, all from just eight families. The final 'visitation,' to use the old, chilling word for the plague, was in 1672.

The Queen's Head Hotel on Main Street holds the Girt (Great) Clog, a wooden shoe 20in (51cm) long and 16in (40cms) across, made in 1820 for John Waterson who had a form of elephantiasis in his left foot. The Red Lion Inn nearby has two carved and painted figures high on its front wall, one a farmer taking his pig to market, the other a man holding the whistle which was blown at market opening time. The war memorial, designed by W.G. Collingwood, is based on the Viking cross at GOSFORTH.

Priest Pot is a small tarn a very short distance south-east of Hawkshead, west of the Sawrey road (SD357978). The ground between the tarn and the road was once known as Gibbet Moss. In April 1672 Thomas Lancaster, formerly of Threlkeld, was convicted of using white arsenic to poison his wife, her father, her three sisters, her former fiancé, her aunt and a servant boy. As well as these eight deaths the mass murderer had tried to poison the neighbours to give the impression it was some kind of epidemic, but happily they survived. The motive was financial – Lancaster had been bribed to clear the way for the heir to the estate to get hold of his inheritance quickly (we are not told what happened to this heir). Following his trial in Lancaster the felon was taken to High Wray Farm (SD372999, on the west shore of Windermere), where the murders had been committed, and was hanged from his own front door; hanging people at the scene of the crime was commonplace at that time. The body was then taken to Priest Pot and, in the words of the Hawkshead church register, 'hunge up in iron chaynes on a gibbett, which was set up for that very purpose … and there continued until such tymes as he rotted every bone from the other.' The details of Lancaster's case are in *Bygone Cumberland and Westmorland* by Daniel Scott (1899).

Gibbeting or hanging in chains was a post-mortem punishment designed not only to remind passers-by of the fate reserved for certain criminals, but to also deny the criminal a Christian burial – something which many regarded as worse than actually being executed. The hanged body was coated in pitch and placed in a specially-constructed, made-to-measure iron cage, then suspended from a gallows in a prominent place. The corpse would be left until it had rotted away – which may have taken more than a year – and the iron cage and gallows also remained until they finally decayed.

In Cowper's day the gibbet had long gone, and the place name had faded from memory also, but in earlier times there had been a popular dread of approaching the site even in daylight. The rotting stump still stood until about 1860; sufferers from toothache would remove a splinter from the gibbet and insert it next to the tooth, which was said to immediately ease the pain.

ESTHWAITE WATER & NEAR SAWREY

The nine-year-old Wordsworth saw a drowned man's body pulled from out of Esthwaite Water, and recalled the experience in 'The Prelude,' noting that he was not scared of the corpse:

> At last, the dead man, 'mid that beauteous scene
> Of trees and hills and water, bolt upright
> Rose, with his ghastly face, a spectre shape
> Of terror; yet no soul-debasing fear,
> Young as I was, a child not nine years old,
> Possessed me, for my inner eye had seen
> Such sights before, among the shining streams
> Of faery land, the forest of romance.

Cowper gives us a rundown of the numerous spooks lurking on the banks of the lake. The Waterside Boggle, on the north end, was a shape-shifting spirit, appearing as a man in light blue, a white fox, a cow-donkey hybrid and a white calf, the latter being accompanied, as it vanished, by a sound resembling a cartload of stones being emptied. Cattle often panicked at the spot, and – as Cowper himself found – horses would shy badly. One moonlit winter night the vicar was walking here when he caught up with an old lady wearing an old-fashioned wide-brimmed bonnet – beneath which he saw 'a death-like face, with goggle eyes, which gleamed like the red bull's eye at the back of a carriage lamp.' The apparition then disappeared suddenly, and when the vicar looked back along the road he and the woman had walked, he saw only one pair of footprints in the snow – his own. An old woman told Cowper she had spoken with the boggle, and it had revealed to her it was the wraith of the reputedly murdered Roger Dugdale. Cowper later established for a fact that Dugdale's drowning was accidental, and thought the spot's bad reputation dated from a much earlier suicide – which could have been the event witnessed by young Wordsworth in 1779.

At the foot of the lake a headless lady walked, and on the west shore the road by How Farm was haunted by 'Old Nelly', a woman murdered here for her bag of guineas, who would jump onto carts passing at night. Cowper notes that the Devil's Gallop south of the lake (SD362946) and Bogley Crag (which I presume is Bogle Crag in Grizedale, SD338931) 'are sites of local superstitions,' but he gives no details.

FAR SAWREY

The 'Crier of Claife' is today one of the most-repeated local ghost stories, which is a shame as Cowper effectively laid it to rest as far back as 1899. The usual account is based on its first appearance in print, in Martineau's *Guide to the English Lakes* (1855). Many later guidebooks have 'improved' the details in pursuit of making the story even more supernatural than it already was, so it's useful to include this passage in full:

A party of travellers were making merry at the Ferry House, then a humble tavern, that a call for the boat was heard from the Nab. A quiet, sober boatman obeyed the call, though the night was dark and fearful. When he ought to be returning, the tavern guests stepped out upon the shore, to see whom he would bring. He returned alone, ghastly and dumb with horror. Next morning he was in a high fever: and in a few days he died, without having been prevailed upon to say what he had seen at the Nab. For weeks after, there were shouts, yells, and howlings at the Nab, on every stormy night, and no boatman would attend to any call after dark. The Reformation had not penetrated the region; and the monk from Furness, who dwelt on one of the islands of the lake, was applied to exorcise the Nab. On Christmas day, he assembled all the inhabitants of Chapel Island, and performed in their presence services which should for ever confine the ghost to the quarry in the wood behind the Ferry, now called the Crier of Claife. Some say that the priest conducted the people to the quarry, and laid the ghost, then and there. But laid though it be, nobody goes there at night. It is still told how the foxhounds in eager chase would come to a full stop at that place; and how, within the existing generation, a schoolmaster from Colthouse, who left home to pass the Crier, was never seen more.

Cowper decries the tale as a 'modern invention' and takes issue with the geography. The Ferry House is on the west shore, and the paranormal visitant is calling from the Ferry Nab on the east shore; yet the Crier of Claife quarry, supposedly 'in the wood behind the Ferry' is actually over 1½ miles (2.4km) north of the Ferry House in Heald Wood (SD384981) – on the opposite shore to the ghost's supposed home on Ferry Nab. Even Gibson, normally quite happy with invented spectres, was sceptical; in a paper given to the Historic Society of Lancashire and Cheshire in 1866 he described his own experience:

Riding down the woods a little south of the Ferry, on a wild January evening, I was strongly impressed by a sound made by the wind as … it came rushing up and across the lake with a sound startlingly suggestive of the cry of a human being in extremity, wailing for succour … [this] may account for much of the legend.

Cowper concluded that Martineau had amalgamated the tragedy of the drowned wedding party of 1635 (see BOWNESS) with some unrecorded local superstition surrounding the quarry, added the frightening 'cries' caused by the wind, and created a legend out of whole cloth. The former stables of the Sawrey Hotel are now the Claife Crier Bar, which has a suitably Gothic pub sign.

GRAYTHWAITE

Clarke's *Survey of the Lakes* (1787) records a belief in an underground passage at Low Graythwaite Hall (aka Graythwaite Old Hall, SD372908), from beneath a thick internal wall to a mound in the garden which was supposed to have been built over a cellar.

The B&B's website suggests this mound is an icehouse, and that, although a deep underground structure – presumably a large field drain – was discovered in 1962, there is actually a beck between the house and mound; no one is going to build a tunnel under a stream. Nearby Graythwaite Hall (SD371912) has several gargoyles on its tower (gardens only, open daily 1 April-30 August 10 a.m.-6 p.m., admission charge).

Cowper mentions the apparition of a murdered child between the great oak below Graythwaite and Baswicks Hill, on the minor road to Cunsey. In his survey *The Haunted: A Social History of Ghosts* (2007), Owen Davies notes child ghosts are very unusual in England, and suggests the tale might derive from a Norse influence.

GRIZEDALE FOREST

Way-marked trails radiate out from the Visitor Centre at SD336944, giving access to one of the Lake District's best and most unusual sights – something like eighty wood and stone sculptures located in the natural environment. It's worth picking up the sculpture guide from the shop, and allowing lots of time. For the longer trails a bicycle is a good idea – they can be hired on site. The Ridding Wood Trail (blue way markers) is accessible for wheelchairs and buggies, and has some of the best sculptures. Even if you don't venture very far, the Centre has the fantastic Ancient Forester sculpture, a 15ft (4.5m) tall figure of a forest guardian, complete with woodpecker, colossal axe and antlered hat. You may find yourself thinking of Herne the Hunter, or the axe-wielding good woodsman of fairy tales, the Horned God, the Green Man – the imaginative connections are manifold. And indeed, the forest sculptures tend to spark many imaginations, as they act as a call to something within us.

In 1995 two police officers, parked up for a mug of coffee near Grizedale, saw a pair of big black cats (the *Westmorland Gazette*, 23 July 2004).

Above left: The Ancient Forester, Grizedale Forest.

Above centre: Insect/alien sculpture, the Ridding Wood Trail, Grizedale Forest.

Above right: Larch Arch, the entrance to the Ridding Wood Trail, Grizedale Forest.

Above left: Metallic owl, the Ridding Wood Trail, Grizedale Forest.

Above right: Sheep, with carved rings reminiscent of cup-and-ring marked stones, the Ridding Wood Trail, Grizedale Forest.

SATTERTHWAITE

Cowper made a point of visiting the oldest inhabitants of the parish and pumping them for information on the beliefs and customs of the old days. Robert Scales told Cowper that around 1829 Satterthwaite had a 'wiseman,' who was consulted on issues such as cattle diseases and the recovery of stolen property. An elderly woman ascribed the birth of a calf with eight legs and two heads to witchcraft, and remembered a time when her mistress surrounded the butter churn with a chaplet of rowan to counter the witchery of one Betty Postlethwaite.

RUSLAND

Cowper relates a tradition that, to escape detection by the authorities, a hoard of counterfeit guineas was thrown into Rusland Pool, but he doubted its veracity. There is a standing stone opposite Whitestock Hall at SD332887.

FINSTHWAITE

In the graveyard of St Peter's Church (SD368879) is the grave of 'the Finsthwaite Princess,' Clementina Johannes Sobieski Douglas of Waterside, who was buried on 16 May 1771. The tradition is that she was a forgotten daughter of Bonnie Prince Charlie, Charles Edward Stuart. Cowper, like many before and since, tried and failed to get to the bottom of the tale. Maria Clementina Sobieski was Charles's mother, and Charles was known to have used the name Douglas as an alias. 'The Princess' was supposed to have arrived at

Waterside around 1745, and thereafter lived a secluded life; it is possible she was just a wealthy eccentric obsessed with the Stuart cause. But nothing can be found for certain, and in the end we are simply left with an absence of evidence.

COLTON

St Cuthbert's Well (SD318861) is on a path downhill from the remote Holy Trinity church, opposite the church gate. The water was used for church baptisms, and although the well was utilised by the monks of FURNESS ABBEY, I can find no record of it being regarded as a healing well. The marks on the church font are claimed to date from its use as a whetstone to sharpen tools and weapons.

Cowper's folkloric gleanings here included a use of bibliomancy by a servant at Hollow Oak (SD340842) in 1836 to divine if a particular groom had thrown a stone through a window.

The dobbie of Ealinghearth Brow (SD350860) was a woman in white who had committed suicide at the spot. She walked alongside pedestrians and took a seat in any cart, and was accompanied by what Cowper described as a 'waffling' sound. An eighteen-year-old youth, Christopher Cloudsdale, was so affected by the horror stories told of the dobbie by his workmates that, instead of walking back from Rusland smithy to Finsthwaite bobbin mill via Ealinghearth Brow – the direct route – he took to the upland wastes of Greenhows. It became dark, a snowstorm set in, and he became lost and died on the fell.

A rough fell-road near Colton was supposedly haunted by a phantom coach and four, an unlikely apparition as you certainly could not drive such a vehicle along the track in real life.

Cowper concluded his own sceptical survey of Hawkshead hauntings with an episode which genuinely puzzled him, and so he declined to name its location – possibly his neighbours or own family were involved. In a large modern house beside a lake (which could be Coniston Water, Windermere or Esthwaite Water), the apparition of a beautiful lady dressed in white had regularly been seen in the years before 1899. Not far from the modern house was a farm, with another, ruined, dwelling close by. The farmer found a woman's skull and several bones hidden in a hole within the wall of a small outbuilding of this ruin. The bones had been sawn in two and all had been embedded in mortar. The outbuilding had been re-roofed fairly recently, so it was presumed that the bones had been hidden after that. What struck Cowper was that some kind of unrecorded misdemeanour had clearly taken place, the bones were recent, and the white lady nearby was dressed in relatively modern costume.

3

KESWICK AND THE NORTH

DUNMAIL RAISE

> … And now have reached that pile of stones,
> Heaped over brave King Dunmail's bones;
> His who had once supreme command,
> Last king of rocky Cumberland;
> His bones, and those of all his Power
> Slain here in a disastrous hour!
>
> William Wordsworth, 'The Waggoner' (1819)

Dunmail's cairn (NY327117) sits between the two carriageways as the A591 breasts the summit, although you'd be forgiven for missing it as you speed past. There's nowhere to park and so inspection is best left to those who walk up the paths from Wythburn and are willing to chance crossing the busy road.

This cairn has almost as many legends as it has stones, many of them contradictory. The general story is that it marks a battle between Dunmail, King of the British kingdom of Cumbria, and a combined force of the Saxons and Scots. Depending on whom you read, the cairn was created:

(1) By the Cumbrians, who each placed a stone on the pile before going into battle; the stones held their souls, and those who survived would retrieve them from this 'soul depository' later. The number of stones left indicates the scale of the Cumbrian defeat.

(2) By the Saxons, who forced the defeated Cumbrians to pile stones over their slain king. (The problem with this version is that there are records of Dunmail surviving and making a pilgrimage to Rome in 975.)

(3) Simply to mark the site of the battle.

(4) To mark the border between Scotland and England, or between Cumberland and Westmorland. Of course the battle cairn could later have become a convenient marker for a boundary.

It appears not to have occurred to anyone that the cairn might be prehistoric; as far as I can tell it has not been properly excavated, although it's likely it was disturbed when the roads were improved. In 1692 it was a huge pile of stones with a wall climbing over the middle, by 1860 it had so reduced it was barely noticeable, and now appears to be midway between these two extremes.

Dunmail is also a 'sleeping king.' The basic story is that his last words as he lay dying at the battle (where, as we have seen, he did not die) were: 'My crown, bear it away, never let the Saxon flaunt it.' Dunmail's loyal bodyguard hacked their way through the Saxon forces and ascended the fell to Grisedale Tarn (NY348120) where they threw the crown into the water with the words, 'Till Dunmail come again to lead us.' And each year since, on the anniversary of the battle, his myrmidons retrieve the crown, march down to the cairn and knock on the stones, and each year a voice cries from within, 'Not yet; not yet – wait a while my warriors.' So Dunmail, like Arthur, awaits the day when he is most needed.

Everything described so far is pretty much the standard version (or versions). Cooper and Palmer's *The English Lakes* (1908) adds what appears to be an entirely original magical detail:

> When Dunmail came to the throne of the mountain-lands a wizard in Gilsland Forest held a master-charm to defeat the purpose of his [enchanted] crown … The magician was able to make himself invisible save at cock crow, and to destroy him the hero braved a cordon of wild wolves at night. At the first peep o' dawn he entered the cave where the wizard was lying. Leaping to his feet the magician called out, 'Where river runs north or south with the storm' ere Dunmail's sword silenced him for ever.

The English king heard of the episode, and after much consultation with those knowledgeable in magic, identified the place in the wizard's incomplete curse – 'Where river runs north or south with the storm' – as the Raise. With magic on his side the result was inevitable, and Edmund killed Dunmail – although he failed to acquire the enchanted crown.

A.H. Griffin, in *The Roof of England* (1970) mentions a phantom of a king seen on snowy nights pursuing a maiden on Seat Sandal (NY344114), above Grisedale Tarn. Apparently they were due to be married and he had given her his bracelet in exchange for her ring. The story is otherwise unfamiliar to me – could it be a distant cousin of Dunmail's crown? A woman from Ulverston told Griffin she once walked over Seat Sandal from Grisedale Tarn with a friend. Ahead of them, but always just out of sight, they could hear a dog barking and two men in conversation. But when they reached the summit and had a clear view for miles around, there was no one in sight.

HELVELLYN

The Gough Memorial near the summit commemorates Charles Gough, a Kendal Quaker who had fallen off Swirrel Edge above Red Tarn on 18 April 1805. It was not until 20 July that his body was found, guarded by his emaciated terrier bitch Foxie, who had somehow survived, even giving birth to a litter of puppies, although all had died. Both Sir Walter Scott ('Helvellyn') and William Wordsworth ('Fidelity') wrote poems about the episode, and Gough's posthumous literary fame prompted a minor scandal when some writers suggested that Foxie had eaten her master's dead flesh – a notion that was fiercely denied.

In Richard Adams's *The Plague Dogs* Snitter, one of the two dogs at the centre of the anthropomorphic tale, meets Foxie's ghost beside Red Tarn.

In Jack Richardson's ghost book *Jack in the Spirit* (1989) he relates a story told to him by Bill, the owner of a garage in Northumberland. Probably some time in the 1980s, Bill and two friends climbed Helvellyn. At the top they were admiring the view when they were suddenly joined by a fourth man. He was young and clean-shaven and dressed in a climbing outfit that appeared to date to the 1930s. After looking around and smiling at the trio he suddenly seemed to be out of breath, and immediately started to descend, but with difficulty. He had gone no more than 20yds (18m) when he just disappeared. His tracks in the snow stopped abruptly and there was nowhere for him to fall over or into. Thoroughly spooked, the men thought the experience might be a harbinger of disaster, but they all got down safely. Their hotel manager in Patterdale told them the phantom was often seen.

In 1855 Martineau mentioned 'the tradition of the tramp of armies over Helvellyn, on the eve of the Battle of Marston Moor.' Marston Moor, fought near York in 1644, was one of the key battles of the Civil War. I can find no other description of this phantom army.

One raw December day on the summit A.H. Griffin met an eighty-two-year-old man with a sort of miniature spirit lamp in a waistcoat pocket over his heart. He told Griffin that if it went out he would be dead within the hour. Griffin was relieved that both of them got down together safely. The account is in *The Roof of England*.

THIRLMERE

> Lights are seen there at night, the people say; and the bells ring; and just as the bells all set off ringing, a large dog is seen swimming across the lake. The plates and dishes clatter; and the table is spread by unseen hands. That is the preparation for the ghostly wedding feast of a murdered bride, who comes up from her watery bed in the lake to keep her terrible nuptials.

Thus Harriet Martineau introduces Armboth House in her 1855 *Guide to the English Lakes*. Not surprisingly, it has ever since been one of the Lake District's 'great haunts,' and many subsequent guidebooks mention it and embellish the tales, although no one ever tracked down the alleged events that were the source of Martineau's influential description. Hugh Caine's novel *Shadow of a Crime: A Cumbrian Romance* (1885), based on local events, has a clearly sceptical aside when describing 'John Jackson' – 'John has slept for twenty years in the room at Armboth in which the spiritual presence is said to walk, and has never yet seen anything more terrible than his own shadow.' In Caine's introduction he writes that he incorporated much local folklore and history into the novel – he also briefly mentions the lights which 'dance across Deer Garth Ghyll,' which may be another local phenomenon; I presume the Ghyll is above Deergarth How Island, which is just south of Armboth at NY310163.

Perhaps the only vague shred of evidence for any actual haunting at Armboth comes in Molly Lefebure's *Cumberland Heritage*. In the late 1960s she was told by a member of the Folder family that in the old days – presumably the nineteenth century – when Folders lived at Stonycroft in Newlands, some visitors arrived there who had hurriedly quit Armboth House after hearing bangs and thumps and witnessing items being thrown about and smashed. They swore nothing would make them return. It is therefore possible that Martineau's report might have been a highly romanticised reversioning of poltergeist phenomenon. Sadly the house itself is not available to investigators, having disappeared beneath the water when the original two smaller lakes were dammed and turned into Thirlmere reservoir. The house's sole remaining trace is the monkey-puzzle tree on the west shore at NY305172. You will, however, have no difficulty in finding websites which assert that 'haunted Armboth House' still exists.

J.A. Brooks' *Ghosts and Legends of the Lake District* (1988) describes how in the mid-nineteenth century John Richardson, a local schoolmaster and farmer, encountered the Park Boggle of Dale Head. Both his sheep and dogs were terrified by a large mound of earth and stones. Richardson knew boggles often took on bizarre forms, and were also sometimes amenable to persuasion, so he told it he was just a poor farmer on his way home on a dark night. The mound consequently disappeared and all animals moved forward without hindrance. Richardson later encountered another manifestation of the boggle, a column of light and sparks that mysteriously vanished.

The drive of the Dale Head Hall hotel (NY313175) – or the road above it – is supposedly haunted either by a man called Leathes, who was robbed, murdered and dumped in the lake, or by the man accused of the murder, who has returned to protest his innocence. *Shadow of a Crime* sets the story in the seventeenth century: Sim, the man wrongly accused of the murder of Old Wilson, takes to a cave in the fells to avoid the suspicions of his neighbours. Several residents at the hotel have reported strange noises, a sense of presence, and the apparition of a young girl in the older part of the building.

Around 1¼ miles (2km) north of the southern end of the lake there was once the rocky promontory of Clarke's Leap (NY320154), named after a man who jumped into the lake to drown himself. He had consulted his wife about the best method of committing suicide, and after discounting shooting, hanging or poison – all too painful or unreliable – she proposed drowning. In his 1789 *Survey* James Clarke (no relation) received confirmation of the bizarre event from the widow: 'I had the curiosity (for she is still alive) to ask it from her own mouth.' The promontory has since vanished. Caine's *Shadow of a Crime* mentions that the local people 'had heard the wail that came from Clark's Loup,' which perhaps suggests there was an associated boggle.

The beetling crags of Castle Rock (NY321196) have to some imaginations given the impression of a castellation. In Walter Scott's poem 'The Bridal of Triermain' (1813) it is a false 'fairy fortress' whose 'airy turrets' and 'mighty keep and tower' turn out to be merely a witch's enchantment to bamboozle King Arthur, and Otley's 1823 *Guidebook* names it as 'Green Crag, sometimes called the Enchanted Castle or Castle Rock of St John's.'

About 1815-6 Thomas de Quincey was out at night: 'Deadly cold as ever March night was made by the keenest of black frosts, and by the bitterest of north winds.' Passing High Bridge End Farm (NY315196) he saw in the garden an armchair, 'upon which armchair was sitting composedly – but I rubbed my eyes, doubting the very evidence of my own eyesight – a or the huge man in his shirt-sleeves; yes, positively not sunning but mooning himself – apricating himself in the occasional moonbeams.' De Quincey never worked out why the man was moonbathing. The episode is in his *Recollections*.

ST JOHN'S IN THE VALE

The *Gentlemen's Magazine* for January 1755 has a truly mysterious account of a double death. Three men were walking through the vale, the weather being low cloud with frequent lightning. About half way along one man 'complained suddenly of uncommon oppression on his lungs, and presently afterwards dropt down dead.' The survivors tried to help him but became frightened by the storm and the oncoming darkness and ran on. Then, 'soon after one of these made the same complaint, and almost instantly fell down dead.' The last man ran for his life, arrived at a house and blurted out the story. What was going on? An elaborate story to cover up a double homicide? Some kind of lightning-related atmospheric malignity? Poisonous fog?

KESWICK

The Keswick Museum and Art Gallery on Station Road (open March–October, Tuesday–Saturday, 10 a.m.–4 p.m., admission free) was ranked the third strangest museum in the world by www.helium.com. It may not be that weird but it still has much to offer, in particular:

The star item is a desiccated cat kept in a chest. Commonly called the '500-year-old cat' (although that was its estimated age when it was found in 1842, so it is has just passed its 666th birthday), it is also often mistakenly described as 'mummified,' although it actually dried out naturally within the roof where it was found. As a consequence its nostrils, ears, claws, tail and even whiskers are still intact. It had been deliberately placed between plaster and slates in the chancel roof of Clifton Church, near Penrith. Its purpose was clearly apotropaic, and it was probably killed and then walled up by the thirteenth-century masons either as a propitiatory sacrifice, or as an ongoing charm against evil. It may even have been intended as a supernatural defence against rats.

Left and Below: Open the box and you find … the 500-year-old (actually 666-year-old) desiccated cat. (Courtesy of Keswick Museum)

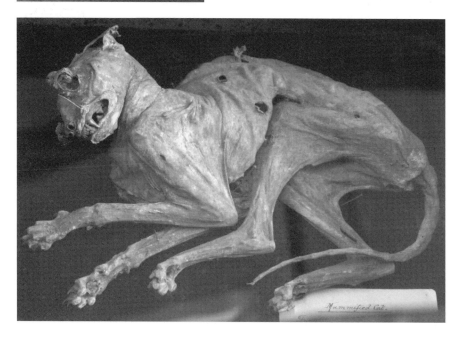

There is also a strange 'stone club' found at CASTLERIGG STONE CIRCLE. It is about 12in (30cm) long with a crude bulbous head; it is difficult to know exactly what this is, or even whether it is ancient or modern.

Several items have had their archaeological/ritual status downgraded; in each case their original and modern labels are both displayed. A 'Stone implement – hole in centre not finished' has been reassessed as 'an animal backbone' and 'two crude stone heads' found on Walla Crag in 1935, and a 'partly perforated stone implement' are now just 'interesting stones.'

A small display on superstitions, myths and legends includes anti-witchcraft rowan twigs used for stirring cream, and a fossil belemnite supposedly deposited by a lightning bolt.

There is a collection of thirty horse brasses. These evolved from holed stones which were supposed to have been made by the tongue of an adder, or a fairy; these witch-, hag- or dobbie-stones were hung above fireplaces and in stables and dairies as a charm to prevent witchcraft. Jamie Barnes, the museum's curator, passed on to me his notes about horse brasses, which had been known in England since before the twelfth century.

> They were introduced as decorations but soon became used as good luck and status symbols. By the eighteenth century and even before they were used as a talisman to ward off the Evil Eye or stay free of the Devil's hand … European gypsies seem to be credited with adding bells to the brasses to help with warding off the Evil Eye. By the mid 1800s farmers used horse brasses looking like suns and moons to help conjure up a good growing season. Other brasses had likenesses of pixies carrying lanterns in the farm fields thus coming to American folklore as 'jack-o'-lantern' of pumpkin-carving fame.

Other items in the museum's collection include:

Brasses in the forms of mandalas, wheatsheaves, spiders' webs, hearts, stylised crosses, horses, stars, shields, wheels, cameos of royalty and abstract shapes.

The head of a pike caught in Bassenthwaite Lake on 12 July 1861; it weighed 34lbs (15.4kg).

Lion teeth, a stuffed bullfrog, a death's-head hawkmoth, a sawfish saw, and Sargasso Weed collected in the Sargasso Sea in 1915.

Napoleon's cup and saucer.

Casts of an icthyosaur and dinosaur footprints, and a six-times life-size model of a trilobite.

A horseshoe enclosed in tree growth.

Three nineteenth-century mantraps for catching poachers.

Small moulds for making crucifixes and other items for sale to pilgrims heading for ST HERBERT'S ISLAND.

The painting *Ambuscade in Cumbria* by H.R. Steer. You are invited to use binoculars to spot the Celts and Romans. There are supposed to be two Romans (easy to find) and seven Celts (a tad more difficult).

A set of musical stones variously called the lithophone, stone dulcimer, rock harmonicon or geological piano. Lithophones are unique to the Lake District: the original rock music.

The museum's most intriguing possession, however, no longer exists. For decades a stuffed animal bearing the label 'The Girt Dog of Ennerdale' was on display, until a former curator decided it was just an old moth-eaten dog and threw it out. Which, to put it mildly, was something of a shame, for the 'Girt (Great) Dog' may well have been a cryptozoological marvel. In 1810 a mystery predator decimated flocks across Cumberland. Ferocious and cunning, it consistently evaded capture, caused fell dogs to cower in fear, drained its victims' blood, and, perhaps most bizarrely of all, although it was dog-shaped, its body was marked with dark, tiger-like stripes. Tales grew that it was something unnatural, even demonic. Over five months it took more than 300 sheep and lambs, often seven or eight in a night, and was observed tearing chunks out of a ram while the animal was still alive. Cumbria is hunting territory, and the monster's depredations attracted intense interest. Dickinson's *Cumbriana* gives the flavour of the year:

> He was often chased from the fells by the shepherds and their dogs, as well as by hounds … So exciting did it become, that when the cheering echoes gave notice that the game was on foot, horses were hastily unyoked from carts or ploughs, and mounted bare back, and ridden as long as they could go, and then left to take their chance whilst the riders continued the chase on foot. It was no uncommon sight to see a score or two of men running at the top of their speed after the hounds, without hats or coats.

The creature evaded these highly experienced posses for several months until it was eventually shot, escaped, shot again, and finally killed by the hounds. The remains, which weighed 8st (51kg), ended up in the museum, from whence it was thrown on the skip in the 1950s.

In a 1999 article in the Centre for Fortean Zoology's magazine *Animals & Men*, Richard Freeman was the first to suggest that the 'Girt Dog' was not, as had been thought, a vicious cross between a mastiff and a greyhound – dogs do not have stripes, for a start. Freeman opined the creature was in fact a thylacine – a marsupial wolf from Tasmania. Not only did the Girt Dog have the thylacine's stripes, it also shared what was known of its behaviour, including ferocious predation and drinking blood. Having been roundly persecuted, the thylacine is now officially extinct, although there are persistent reports that relict populations may survive in Tasmania. How did an Australian thylacine end up in Cumbria? There is no evidence for this part of the story, although Freeman speculated it may have escaped from a travelling zoo. In 2005 sculptor Shawn Williamson wrote *Mauler*, a gripping novel with the Girt Dog/thylacine rampage at its core. A young thylacine can be seen in KENDAL MUSEUM.

The burial ground of St John's Church, on St John's Street, has the grave of F.W.H. Myers (1843-1901), one of the founders of the Society for Psychical Research and author of *Phantasms of the Living* (1886), *Science and a Future Life* (1893) and the ironically posthumous *Human Personality and its Survival of Bodily Death* (1903). The *Cumberland & Westmorland Herald* (10 March 2001) reported that workmen undertaking restoration in the Moot Hall (now the Tourist Information Centre) had experienced strange phenomena over the previous weeks. One man working alone felt the clock tower chamber suddenly go very cold and saw the dark shadow of a man disappear through a wall, and a colleague felt a hand push him in the back as he was going down the stairs.

Greta Hall, a private house with self-catering apartments, was home to Robert Southey and Samuel Taylor Coleridge. Coleridge's daughter, Sara, mentioned a room on the second floor as 'a dark apple-room, which used to be supposed the abode of a bogle' (in *Memoir and Letters of Sara Coleridge*, 1874). H.A.L. Rice's *Lake Country Towns* (1974) tells us that a poet, T.E. Brown – who for twenty years spent every summer holiday at St John's Terrace – wrote that after his death one of the three places he would haunt would be Derwent Water. I have not come across any posthumous sightings of the chap.

The Cars of the Stars Museum in Standish Street (open daily Easter-December, 10 a.m.- 5 p.m., other dates vary, admission charge) displays iconic vehicles from film and television. Its star attractions include: the flying Ford Anglia from *Harry Potter and the Chamber of Secrets*; Robocop's police car; a *Back to the Future* car; the original Mad Max car; a staff car from *Raiders of the Lost Ark*; an entire fleet of James Bond vehicles; the customised Model T. Ford from *The Munsters* television series; the Lotus Super Seven driven by Patrick McGoohan at the start of the cult series *The Prisoner* (and one of the taxis that transported inmates around the sinister prison The Village); Emma Peel's Lotus Elan from the original *Avengers* series; the super-computer car KITT from *Knightrider*; a Lunar Buggy from *Space 1999*; a life-size copy of Lady Penelope's car FAB I from *Thunderbirds*; and, best of all, three Batmobiles. For anyone who is a fan of fantasy and science-fiction media, it's irresistible.

The Twa Dogs Inn on Penrith Road has the 'only known stuffed exhibit of a bogart in existence' according to its website. 'This creature, half badger and half fox is a unique animal only believed to be found in the Cumbrian Hills.' The boggart (one 'g' is optional) resides in a glass case in the bar. A sign claims, 'Killed 2 May 1946 behind Skiddaw House whilst savaging female bogart.' Peter Harding, the licensee, told me that the exhibit had been there 'for some years' and it wasn't clear when it was made or by whom. The inn also has a tree outside decorated with a face that appears to emerge from the trunk.

The *English Lakes Visitor and Keswick Guardian* for September 1882 had the following entry:

> Between three and four o'clock on Thursday morning near the bridge the policeman on duty was startled at a peculiar sound accompanied by the jangling of chains. Turning his light on he discovered one of the elephants belonging to the circus had come to the river for a drink.

Above: The boggart – half-badger, half-fox. The Twa Dogs Inn, Keswick.

Right: A real Green Man. Tree face outside the Twa Dogs Inn, Keswick.

In July 1878 the paper reported on a summer storm:

> … hailstones of what may be termed prodigious size fell in alarming quantity and with such force that all sky-light windows facing to the east suffered more or less in breakages. Some hailstones measured no less than one and a quarter inches [3.2cm] in diameter and would weigh not less than an ounce [28g].

Golfball-sized hailstones? Ouch.

The last recorded case of Needfire (see HAWKSHEAD) in the Keswick area was in 1841. Sixteen years later, in *Cumberland & Westmorland, Ancient and Modern*, Jeremiah Sullivan described what happened at one farm:

> The sacred fire was allowed to become extinct, the owner, a well-known statesman, not having sufficient faith in its virtue to take the trouble to transmit it, or even to keep it alight … he was severely rated at the time for his lack of faith. That, however, served to kill the popular belief in needfire, and even when the terrible ravages of the rinderpest, foot and mouth disease, and pleuropneumonia, were emptying the pockets and breaking the hearts of the farmers, not one of them thought of reviving the old 'cure.'

In 1564 the English government approved Daniel Hochstetter to lead a team of crack German miners in a venture to extract and smelt copper. Within a few years the Keswick Works were one of the largest copper-producing operations in Europe. It's little-known that the Germans often located metals through dowsing. Dowsing rods were a standard part of their equipment, as seen in various German documents and items: a description from 1608, silver tankards from 1652, prints of the 1720s, and a Meissen porcelain from 1750. An ivory Nativity scene from Erzebirge shows miners bringing gifts to the Infant – and a man using a divining rod. These details and images are in Christopher Bird's history of dowsing, *The Divining Hand*.

The Far Away Centre, led by Witchcraft High-Priest Marcus Katz, claims to be 'The first independent and contemporary esoteric Training Centre in the UK teaching the Esoteric and Occult Arts and Sciences for Today.' From its base in Keswick it offers a wide range of courses and workshops in, *inter alia*, Magick, Witchcraft, Kabbalah, Tarot and Alchemy, and provides rituals 'held in pagan groves, dedicated temple, caves, woods, stone circles and hilltops overlooking the lakeside.' For more see their comprehensive website.

St Kentigern's Church at Crosthwaite (NY257243, north-west of the town) is a must-see. The wonderful medieval font has numerous carvings: a Green Man spewing three strands of vegetation; trees growing out of a wolf(?) with a curled tail; a tree, vegetation and several armorial panels; the instruments of the Passion; four mutilated beast heads; Gothic 'windows'; and, on the base, four mutilated Sheela-na-gigs – to my knowledge this is a unique example of these sexually-explicit sculptures on a font. The choir stall-ends and finials have more superb carvings: the symbols of the Four Evangelists (winged bull, winged lion, eagle, man/angel); heads of a two demons, a bearded man, an African and an elf; another man's head

A gravestone with the All-Seeing Eye, St Kentigern's Church, Keswick.

Gravestone at St Kentigern's Church. Note the Devil's tail, the only part not obscured by the maiden.

Serpent threading itself through a ring: monument to the Bishop of Carlisle, St Kentigern's Church, Keswick.

emerging from foliage; a Green Man/grotesque; a boar(?) eating fruits; a bird in a tree; the Lamb of God; the symbols IHS and Alpha and Omega; and a praying female angel. The altar is inscribed with the Greek for 'In This Conquer,' the words allegedly seen below a vision of the Cross by the Emperor Constantine when he was contemplating making Christianity the official Roman religion. The beautiful mosaic floor in the sanctuary has repeated motifs of St Kentigern's symbols – the bell, bird, tree and fish with ring – and the stained glass features both Kentigern and St Cuthbert, the latter carrying his customary severed head of St Oswald. Four corbels at the east end have crowned heads. Part of a pair of damaged alabaster figures has several hollows in the lower part, as if it had been used to hold something (candles?). There is a full set of sixteenth-century consecration crosses – nine within and twelve outside the church. The south external wall has a 1602 sundial, an old Mass clock, two bewigged bearded fellows, and, high up, the names of two churchwardens and the date 1812. Another stone from 1812, marked 'A+G', is included in a buttress on the east wall, only upside down.

The extensive graveyard is equally full of diverting pleasures, with an excellent range of carved stones bearing symbols as diverse as the Ten Commandments, winged souls, a scythe and rake, skulls and crossed-bones, and an Illuminati-like all-seeing eye. A serpent threads itself through a ring on the tall Celtic cross commemorating a Bishop of Carlisle. A maiden so effectively extinguishes a dragon – or the Devil – that only a reptilian tail is visible. Old Father Time appears with his scythe and hourglass and a leafless dead tree and the legend 'Time Brings All Things To An End.' Next to him three quills and an inkpot advertise 'The Register Of Time' while an open book gives an instructive lesson:

Above: Tombstones of two sisters shown provocatively raising their skirts in defiance of Death. St Kentigern's Church, Keswick.

Right: Father Time, a dead tree and a ruined building: 'TIME BRINGS ALL THINGS TO AN END'. Gravestone, St Kentigern's Church, Keswick.

Dispose Of Time Past In Reflection; Time Present To Duty; And Time To Come To Providence.
So Make Use Of Time If Thou Lovest ETERNITY. For Yesterday Cannot Be Recalled;
Tomorrow Cannot Be Assured; Today Is Only Thine, Which If Once Lost, Is Lost For Ever.

The most amazing sight, however, is the paired end panels of the table tombs of two sisters:
on one the good ladies are holding up an hourglass, on the other a skull; and in both cases
they are raising their skirts provocatively high, revealing their thighs, an unusual graveyard
expression of sensuality in the face of King Death.

CASTLERIGG STONE CIRCLE (NY291236)

We thought this situation the most severely grand of any hitherto passed … Such sublimity
and seclusion were indeed well suited to the deep and wild mysteries of the Druids. Here, at
moon-night, every Druid, summoned by that terrible horn, never awakened but upon high
occasions, descending from his mountain or secret cave, might assemble without intrusion from
one sacrilegious footstep, and celebrate a midnight festival by a savage sacrifice.

Ann Radcliffe, *A Journey made in the Summer of* 1794 (1795)

A dismal cirque
Of Druid stones, upon a forlorn moor

John Keats, *Hyperion* (1818)

Time-honour'd pile! By simple builders rear'd,
Mysterious round, through distant times rever'd,
Ordain'd with earth's revolving orb to last,
Thou bring'st to mind the present and the past.

Dr Ogilvie, 'Fame of the Druids' Quoted in the *Saturday Magazine* No. 161, 3 January 1835

That most evocative of rings … Castlerigg.

Aubrey Burl, *Rites of the Gods* (1981)

Because Castlerigg is (a) close to Keswick (b) easy to get to and (c) wonderful, it is the
most visited stone circle in the Lakes. A *de facto* circle within a circle, its ring of forty mighty
boulders is encircled by an even grander ring of mountains. It probably dates from 3200 BC,
and as well as having a funereal function, it may have been used as a centre for ceremonies
involved in the trade and exchange of LANGDALE stone axes. In the 1998 collection
Prehistoric Ritual and Religion John Barnett describes it as one of several prehistoric 'places
of pilgrimage … where ceremonies could be performed in a majestic setting.'

The monument was first described by William Stukeley in 1725 (published in 1776 in his *Itinerarium Curiosum*), and the circle appears to have barely changed since then. In 1799 Wordsworth and Coleridge found the stones defaced with white paint, but other than this, Castlerigg has been unusually fortunate in largely avoiding the vandalism and destruction wreaked on many other major circles, probably because it was one of the first ancient monuments to be given legal protection (in 1883) and has been owned by the National Trust since 1913. However, two internal cairns recorded in 1856 have vanished, and a third, mostly ploughed out, cairn is only just visible.

Stukeley also notes: 'There seemed to be another larger circle in the next pasture toward the town,' but gives no details. There has no been no further sighting of this supposed second circle, so Stukeley may have mistaken a natural feature for an archaeological one. A modern error is giving the circle's alternative name as The Carles. A carle was a humble worker or husbandman in medieval times and this name has likely perpetuated the folkloric belief that the stones are petrified men or elders. Stukeley actually wrote, 'they call it the Carſles [not Carles], and, corruptly I suppose, Castle-rig.'

Above left: Castlerigg Stone Circle. Earthlights, druids, witches and psychometrists not shown.

Above right: An example of 'terrain echoes' at Castlerigg, with one of the stones echoing the line of the mountains behind.

Castlerigg. Another terrain echo.

The circle's most perplexing feature is the rectangle of ten stones jutting into the interior, a structure unique to Castlerigg. A perfunctory excavation in 1882 found evidence of burning but was inconclusive, and so it is not clear what its function was. In *Rites of the Gods* Aubrey Burl, the Titan of stone circles – who will no doubt one day have a megalithic monument erected in his honour – makes a strong case for the rectangle being a symbolic representation of a Neolithic sepulchral cist, 'an open-air version of a burial chamber for their rituals.'

Another pioneer of prehistory, Stan Beckensall (*British Prehistoric Rock Art*), points us to Castlerigg's very faint carvings: a lozenge and a spiral are respectively on the north and south stones on the outer part of the enigmatic rectangle, while a stone on the opposite side of the circle bears another lozenge, and the entrance to the north has a cupmark and an incomplete ring on the top of one of its stones. You will need very good lighting conditions, such as slanting sunlight, to see these carvings.

Both the circle and its setting have impressed successive generations, with interpretations couched according to the temper of the times and personal inclination. Some of these interpretations are contradictory, some may strike you as clear-sighted, some as entirely risible; Castlerigg is sufficiently enigmatic to support a panoply of opinions.

Mrs Radcliffe, quoted above, was a pioneering Gothic novelist (*The Mysteries of Udolpho* and *The Castle of Otranto*), and her trip round the Lakes was purposely designed to seek out Romantic sights that evoked sensations of the sublime and the demonic, as clearly articulated in her highly coloured descriptions. In the same account she describes the countryside around Keswick as, 'the very region, which the wild fancy of a poet, like Shakespeare, would people with witches, and shew them at their incantations, calling spirits from the clouds and spectres from the earth.' Note that Castlerigg was built several millennia before any Druids were active in the area, but antiquarians, Romantics and Gothic novelists alike find it hard to resist Druidic interpretations: there's nothing better to fire the fervid imagination than a nice bit of human sacrifice.

Reginald Smith, Keeper of British and Roman Antiquities at the British Museum and Director of the Society of Antiquaries, was a keen dowser. In the 1930s he dowsed Castlerigg and concluded it was the survivor of five concentric rings. As Tom Williamson and Liz Bellamy gently put it in their 1983 book *Ley Lines in Question*, 'This discovery has yet to be verified.'

In 1944 a mystical eccentric named John Foster Forbes – a New Ager long before the New Age – came to Castlerigg. His enthusiasm was psychometry, the practice of psychically reading the history of a place or object. His psychic friends would verbally report their impressions, which Forbes wrote down on the spot. At Castlerigg, Iris Campbell discerned that kings mourned their revered dead within the circle, with priests 'weaving different cosmic colours around the bier in order to speed the departure of the passing soul. It was done for those of higher grade in the priesthood so that they could be absolutely freed for higher work elsewhere.' The description is in Forbes' *Giants of Britain* (1945).

In 1967 Alexander Thom, a retired professor of engineering, surveyed the circle for *Megalithic Sites in Britain* and concluded there were seven alignments between the stones and celestial events (southerly extreme moon rise and set on the 18.6-year lunar cycle, midsummer sunset, midwinter sunrise, Candlemas sunrise [2 February], Equinoctial sunrise, and northerly extreme moonset). Thom's precise calculations were impenetrable to the mathematically challenged, but later writers communicated the essence, and astro-archaeology was firmly on the agenda. John Michell – who could be regarded as the archbishop of the church of intellectual-mystical hippiedom – noted in *A Little History of Astro-Archaeology* (1977) that if you extended sightlines from solar or lunar events on the horizon to the circle, they were the same lines that defined the internal geometry of

Castlerigg. In *The Traveller's Key to Sacred England* (1989) Michell describes the circle of stones within the amphitheatre of mountains as 'a gigantic work of art' and 'a passage into the ancient world' which allows a communion with the prehistoric builders: 'one has a sense – as they must have had – of being at the centre of a divinely ordered landscape.'

One of the other giants of earth mysteries research, Paul Devereux, has investigated Castlerigg several times. In 1978, as part of the Dragon Project, an attempt to scientifically record physical anomalies at stone circles, he undertook ultrasound monitoring over three dawns around the midwinter solstice. The first two mornings produced no readings, but on the third he observed 'a distinct pulsing of the meter needle when in the vicinity of one of the stones that marks the winter sunrise.' In a 1988 visit all the stones were checked with a compass; the westernmost, outward-leaning stone was the only one to deflect the compass. These observations are in *Places of Power*. In *Earth Lights Revelation* he references an experience of strange lights recorded by Mr T. Sington in *The English Mechanic and World of Science*, 17 October 1919. Here is the article:

Some years ago, during Easter, returning to Keswick from an ascent of Helvellyn with a hotel acquaintance, we saw lights, no doubt will o' the wisps. It was so dark that we had to probe for the road walls with our sticks, when we were at a point near which the track branches off to the Druidical Circle. Then, all at once we saw a rapidly moving light, as bright as the acetylene lamp of a bicycle, and we instinctively stepped to the road boundary wall to make way for it, but nothing came. As a matter of fact, the light travelled at right angles to the road, say 20 feet above our level, possibly 200 yards or so away. It was a white light, and having crossed the road it suddenly disappeared. Whether it went out or passed behind an obstruction it is impossible to say. We then saw a number of lights, possibly a third of a mile or so away, directly in the direction of the Druidical circle, but of course much fainter, due to the distance. The lights were moving backwards and forwards horizontally; we stood observing them for a long time. Whilst we were watching a remarkable incident happened – one of the lights, and only one, came straight to the spot where we were standing, at first very faint, as it approached the light increased in intensity. When it came quite near I was in doubt whether I should stoop below the boundary wall as the light would pass directly over our heads. But when it came close to the wall it slowed down, stopped, quivered and slowly went out, as if the matter producing the light had become exhausted. It was globular, white, with a nucleus, possibly six feet or so in diameter, and just high enough above the ground to pass over our heads.

This weird adventure may be describing 'earthlights,' electromagnetic anomalies created by geological stresses. There are anecdotal rumours of sightings since. It's not easy to draw any strong conclusions from these reports, but if the lights, as Devereaux suspects, were occasionally present in prehistoric times, then the site may have been regarded as the abode of the gods before the stones were erected. Devereaux contends that these naturally-occurring but little-understood lights might explain some paranormal encounters with UFOs and ghosts.

In *The Sacred Place* Devereux shows John Glover's photographs of a strikingly long shadow thrown half a mile (800m) across the valley by the tallest stone at midsummer sunset, although it is not clear what the significance of this is and what, if anything, it points to. He also demonstrates that the shape of some of the stones is an exact fit to the slopes and peaks of the mountains behind them. In 'Drawing Down the Hills: Terrain echoes at Castlerigg,' an article for *Northern Earth* magazine (No. 79, 1999) Harry Bell observed that the full set of landscape alignments, or 'terrain echoes,' could only be seen from the faint ring cairn in the north-east corner of the circle, and suggested that this was the primary structure on the site – in other words, the circle had been planned by someone standing on the pre-existing cairn. Bell, drawing on his 1984 book *Glasgow's Secret Geometry*, was a proponent of the idea that prehistoric sites were aligned on landscape features for practical, navigational purposes, and he eschewed mystical and archaeoastronomical interpretations. His work at Castlerigg can be found online at www.geocities.com/leylinequest.

Ronald Hutton's history of modern witchcraft *The Triumph of the Moon* mentions an article in the popular magazine *Illustrated* (27 Sept 1952) which states that a Cumbrian coven of eleven members held ceremonies at Castlerigg; one commented that 'you get so close to God,' an intriguing comment which may suggest these were pursuers of some form of alternative spirituality rather than 'straightforward' witches. These days several pagan groups visit the circle: the Far Away Centre (see KESWICK) regularly holds ceremonies there, as do the Cumbrian Druid Order.

Druids, dowsers, psychics, astroarchaeologists, ley line enthusiasts, terrain echoers, earthlights researchers, witches and Druids (again) – Castlerigg's stones are strong enough to support them all.

DERWENT WATER

> There have been many drownings on this lake, but invariably caused by drink … bodies are always upright, on their head or feet.

> Beatrix Potter, *Journal* (1881-1897)

The *Cumberland Chronicle or Whitehaven Intelligencer* for 27 August 1778 reports:

> John Pocklington, Esq.; who lately purchased the Vicar's isle (now called Pocklington's isle) in the lake near Keswick, has erected a fort thereon for seven cannon – in digging the foundation, the ruins of a Druid's temple was discovered, which lay hid from the eye of the traveller, for ages, but will now be preserved, with the greatest care, for the inspection of the curious.

'Lord Pocky,' a man unfamiliar with the notion of self-restraint, also enjoyed staging mock naval battles, with cannonades from his folly-fort competing with musket-fire. The 'Druid's temple' which was apparently 'discovered' was almost certainly another folly, open 'for the inspection of the curious' alongside his faux church and boathouse disguised as a Gothic chapel. All the follies have long since been swept away, and the island has reverted to a previous name, Derwent Isle (NY262224).

Lord's Island (NY265219) was formerly the home of the Earls of Derwentwater. In 1715 the Earl took part in the failed Jacobite rebellion and was executed in London. Some nights after there was a striking display of the Aurora Borealis over Keswick, and the phenomenon was thereafter known locally as 'the Derwentwater Lights.' In a paper for the CWAAS in 1903, W.G. Collingwood enumerated other fatuities associated with the island: it was formerly a peninsula, the channel between it and the mainland being artificial; the building stones for the manor house were brought from Penrith, and passed from hand to hand along a line of soldiers 18 miles (29km) long; and, inevitably, there was an underground passage to the mainland.

St Herbert's Island (NY259212) is named after an obscure Dark-Age hermit who built an oratory on the island. The legend, as recorded in Bede's *Ecclesiastical History of the English People* (AD 731) is that he had been a close friend of St Cuthbert, and as a consequence both holy men died on the same day – 20 March AD 687 – and at the same hour and minute. In the Middle Ages pilgrims visited a shrine here. A folly hermitage was built at the end of the eighteenth century, and it is the ruins of this that are now visible. Friars Crag on the east mainland shore is named for pilgrims embarking for the island. For a miracle supposedly granted by Herbert, see CONISTON.

There have supposedly been sightings of USOs (Unidentified Submerged Objects) in Derwent Water in 1994 and 2004, but I can find no solid details. One object which is definitely there is the floating island. Floating islands were something of a craze among Romantic travellers, and the Derwent Water example owes its fame to the sheer number of people who have written about it, from Jonathan Otley to William (and Dorothy) Wordsworth and John Stuart Mill, plus a gaggle of guidebook writers. It is a mat of vegetation that floats to the surface in hot summers. Scientist John Dalton collected gas from beneath the mat, an incident which inspired Ford Madox Brown's 1886 mural 'Dalton Collecting Marsh-Fire Gas' in Manchester Town Hall. The island has provided a brief raft for a brass band and a Girl Guide who planted a Union Jack on it in the 1930s and claimed it for King and Country. So far there are no reports of campers trying for a free pitch. Although many years it merely sulks at the bottom of the lake, the island is still a fairly frequent if intermittent visitor, rising in the south-eastern part of the lake, near the Lodore Boat Landings. In July 2005 Chet van Duzer, author of *Floating Islands: A Global Bibliography* (2004), found, much to his surprise, that the floating island was available for inspection, so he landed on it via canoe. In his *Addenda* to the *Bibliography* he writes: 'It was an exhilarating experience to visit and investigate this very unusual natural phenomenon.' Disappointingly, he did not plant the Stars and Stripes and claim the island for the USA.

WATENDLATH

In *The Bright Pavilions*, Sir Hugh Walpole's prequel to the *Herries Chronicles*, the hero, Nicholas Herries, is taken by his servant Gilbert to witness a moonlit witches' sabbath at Watendlath Tarn (NY274163). They watch as five women and two men dance, scream, strip naked, light a fire and sacrifice a goat. Then, in a superbly atmospheric piece of writing, the clouds shift, shadows emerge, and Nicholas seems to sense something approaching, 'did he see, or did he not see, figures flying through the air … ?' Nicholas is horrified to discover that one of the witches is the mother of Catherine Hodstetter, the girl he fancies (for more Walpolian witch-locations see GRANGE and BLENCATHRA).

GRANGE

In the most powerful and frightening sequence in Walpole's novel *Rogue Herries*, old Mrs Wilson, long suspected of being a witch, calls upon a sick woman with a similar reputation, but the beldame has already died. Mrs Wilson is ambushed by the villagers, stripped, beaten, stoned, bound, and thrown off Grange bridge into the River Derwent, where she drowns. Another character is scared of Cummacatta Wood (NY255173) because it is haunted by a suicide called Broadley, and the hill still held two stones where pagan sacrifices had taken place.

In an article in *Cumbria Life* (April/May 2007) Sue Allan relates a murder case from 1928. Dr Miao Chung-yi and his new young wife came to stay at Grange on holiday. On their second day she went missing and was later found strangled. The doctor was the only suspect. It's a story as old as the hills – he was penniless and she was an heiress. Dr Miao was hanged at Strangeways. His wife's body was discovered in a nearby wood – possibly Cummacatta.

Bull Crag, to the west (NY238183), was supposedly so-called because if a bull were kept there the echo of its own bellowings would drive it mad. I suspect a different kind of bull is at work. The *English Lakes Visitor and Keswick Guardian* for July 1881 relates the experience of James Langhorn, the Borrowdale postman, who opened the wall letterbox, near the Borrowdale Hotel, to find it occupied by a swarm of bees. He managed to gently extract the letters without being stung, but as no comb was present he was unable to take home any honey as a tip.

BORROWDALE

Dark rocks yawn at its entrance, terrific as the wildness of a maniac.
Ann Radcliffe, *A Journey made in the Summer of 1794* (1795)

Near the top of the path up Castle Crag (NY249159) is one of the strangest sights in Lakeland: the 'standing stones'. The hollows of a former quarry are dotted with dozens of piles of rocks and upright slate menhirs. All are modern, and appear to have evolved as a 'passing tradition' with walkers. Although some are toppled they appear again, and the site is dynamic, with new structures appearing each year. The effect is truly strange and eerie, especially if you happen to be alone or the mist is down.

The *Whitehaven News* for 9 September 2007 printed a sighting of a big cat by Mark Fraser of the Big Cats in Britain group. He and his girlfriend were in High Hows Wood (NY252158), close to the River Derwent, when they saw a small deer being followed by a black puma-like animal.

NEWLANDS PASS

The *Cumberland & Westmorland Herald* (9 May 2006 and 23 February 2007) reported that police had frequently been called to Rigg Beck, the purple house at the foot of Newlands Hause, because teenagers had been breaking into the boarded-up building. Apparently there had been a widespread local rumour that the house was haunted, and impromptu ghost hunts had been organised. The property has since been sold and will probably be demolished.

THORNTHWAITE

There are 'Thompson' mice (see DEAN) carved on the bishop's chair in St Mary's Church (NY226254).

BASSENTHWAITE LAKE

The miniscule Church of St Bridget and St Bega (NY226287) is only one of two churches dedicated to the semi-legendary St Bees. As John Timpson aptly puts it in *Timpson's England*, 'Churches are rich in Bridgets, but Begas are meagre.'

The lake is supposedly home to an 'Eachy,' whose standard description – slimy, gruesome, amphibious, humanoid – makes it sound like the Creature from the Black Lagoon. In 1973, a Mr Stavenglass saw a strange, fast-moving animal in the water. His inconclusive photograph shows something vague in the distance which appears to be the head and neck of an elongated creature, but it could just as easily be a duck or another lake-dwelling bird. In 2008 local cryptozoological researcher Andrew Hoyle told me that he had spent hundreds of hours fishing on Bassenthwaite, and had never seen anything the slightest bit mysterious. The *Whitehaven News* (9 July 2008) reported that angler Adam Kenyon had landed a 'monster' pike around 40in (1m) long and weighing 20-25lbs (9-11kg), twice the usual size for the lake's pike. The monster was returned to the water to lurk another day. The KESWICK MUSEUM has a Bassenthwaite pike that weighed in at 34lbs/15.4kg.

In his book *Hawkshead* Henry Cowper noted that as late as 1876 a calf was buried alive at Bassenthwaite as a charm against the miscarriages that were afflicting the herd. Bassenthwaite village regularly holds a Scarecrow Festival, which results in all sorts of delightfully surreal sights as scarecrows protrude from doorways, lean over gates and attempt to escape from vehicles.

High on the steep fell of Barf above the car park at Powterhow is a prominent white-painted stone, the Bishop of Barf. It is supposedly named after the Bishop of Derry who, in 1783, unwisely accepted an alcohol-induced bet to ride his horse up the precipitous slope. Both horse and rider were killed, and the bishop is allegedly buried near The Clerk, a smaller stone near the base of the hill. Anyone who has been to see the bishop might conclude that the only horse who could get up there is Pegasus. The whitewashing of the rock has been carried out since time immemorial, and no one really knows why.

The busy A66 flashes past the Iron-Age hillfort of Castle How at the northern end of the lake (NY201308), so the easiest approach is walking up from the road that loops past the Pheasant Inn. The levelled top and the rock-cut ditches indicate the sheer amount of labour required to construct it. Dickinson's *Cumbriana* (1876) relates the tale of fairy encounters here, although he does not give dates:

> Thomas Bell, of Thornthwaite, was born and lived at Peelwyke till grown up to a man, and gives the following proof of the superstition prevailing in his young days: A family named Watson lived near, and three or four of the young sons were accustomed to play on the Castle Hill … These boys made an excavation in the side of the hill and uncovered a neat hut roofed with slate. Dinner-time came before their exploration was completed, and they were called home. In hopes of having made a great discovery, they hurried back to the hill, but could not even find the place, for all was covered with soil and green sward as when they first found it, and no one has found the place since. Watson, the father of these boys, kept an ill-tempered cur. One evening, about sunset, he saw two tiny people dressed in green in a meadow near Peelwyke

[on the shore], and set his dog on them. The dog went fiercely to them, but immediately began to yell, and rolled over. It continued to cry out, and occasionally to tumble, till it reached Watson, and the little people were never seen after.

Which no doubt is what happens if you set your dog on fairies.

More little folk are associated with Elva Plain Stone Circle to the north-west (NY177317). In 1488 the name was recorded as Elfhow, probably derived from the Old Norse word *elfhaugr*, 'hill of malignant elves.' There are fifteen low stones here (remaining from a probable thirty originally). John Askew's *Guide to Cockermouth* (1872) noted that forty years earlier Fletcher Grave of Cockermouth described two concentric circles on the site, the inner twenty paces in circumference, the outer sixty paces. Both were of large stones, most of which were removed when the land was enclosed. In 1923 an outlying monolith was recorded to the south-west, but this too has now evaporated.

ULDALE

The website for Overwater Hall quotes an article written by a former owner, Charles de Courcy-Parry, for *Horse and Hound*. In it he described his sighting of the black woman who was reputed to haunt the hall. At 12.20 p.m. on a Friday in August she moved silently up the stairs and passed through the closed door of the best bedroom. She also exhibited her best-known characteristic – her lack of hands. The story was that she had been the mistress of Joseph Gillbanks in Jamaica. When in 1814 she followed him back to Britain he rowed her out across Overwater Tarn (NY250350) and tried to drown her; when she resisted the pitiless monster sliced off her hands with a sword. De Courcy-Parry's sighting would have been during his ownership, 1952-57, although the ghost was already well known to the servants. According to the article the maids refused to sleep in the house so cottages were built for them on the back drive. Tony Walker states the phenomena were noted again from the late 1960s, with inexplicable voices, tappings on windows, and apparitions, the latter being particularly concentrated in Room 3. Walker also mentions the ghost of a grey terrier dog seen inside the hotel.

The most intriguing episode concerned an AA hotel inspector who at breakfast animatedly told the owner about his strange experiences overnight in Room 3; when Walker spoke to the inspector only a short while later, the man had utterly forgotten all the details, except that there had been an unexplained light in the room. Despite his struggles to remember, it was as if the entire event had been erased from his mind. This is an example of a phenomenon which might be termed 'paranormal-related amnesia': there have been many cases where people have had bizarre, supernatural, once-in-a-lifetime experiences – and then forgotten all about them, only bringing them to mind when prompted. It is as if the mind says 'no, I can't accept that just happened to me' and simply suppresses the memory.

Charles de Courcy-Parry may, or may not have been, the man who shot Percy Toplis, 'the Monocled Mutineer' in 1922 (see PENRITH MUSEUM).

There are several prehistoric structures on Green How, north-east of Uldale (NY263380). They include Iron-Age enclosures and a Neolithic causewayed enclosure, the latter being an embanked arena that predates the stone circles, and was presumably used for communal gatherings. Causewayed enclosures are among the oldest and rarest prehistoric monuments in the British Isles.

CALDBECK

St Kentigern's holy well sits just outside the graveyard, north-west of the church (NY325399), a lovely spot where local brides come to have their wedding photos taken. The legend is that the well was created by Kentigern during his exiled wanderings in Cumbria, and that he baptised the area's first Christians here. There is a medieval graveslab with a sword and a foliate cross. The gravestone of the famous huntsman John Peel is in the churchyard. His son Peter predeceased him, and Peter's coffin is said to contain a fox brush placed there by his father, who had gone hunting for the tribute on the day of the funeral.

'A delicious spot … limestone rocks, hanging trees, pools, and water breaks, caves and cauldrons which have been honoured with fairy names, and no doubt continue in the fancy of the neighbourhood to resound with fairy revels.' Thus Dorothy Wordsworth, in *Recollections of a Tour Made in Scotland* (1803), introduces the riverside walk, gorge and waterfalls of The Howk, just west of the village (NY317398). Here the river passes underground for short distances and flows through large swallow holes in the limestone. When the river is in spate the apparently boiling water within the circular Fairies' Kettle justifies its name, while a 20yds (18m) long cavern nearby is named the Fairy Kirk.

In an interview in *Lake District Life* (January/February 2006) Anne Hannam described how at the full moon a lady dressed in grey supposedly walked the length of the upstairs landing of the seventeenth-century house Todcrofts, although she herself had seen nothing in almost forty years' residence. Todcrofts was where Mary Robinson, the famous 'Maid of Buttermere,' having survived a brief marriage to a charlatan and bigamist, lived happily with her second husband John Harrison.

The Branthwaite Dog, or Branthwaite Neuk Boggle, a supernatural black hound, pads it's traditional way along the road at the hamlet of Fell Side (NY305376). Perhaps even more mythical is the 'Caldbeck UFO Crash' that supposedly took place on 4 March 1954 near Roughton Gill, south of Fell Side (around NY302344). To be frank, this rumour is one of the most far-out stories in this book. As sceptically described in *Fortean Times* 197 (June 2005), it fulfils all the requirements of the by-now fully-established 'crashed saucer myth,' based on archetypes such as Roswell. There is a spectacular crash, the recovery of a strange craft with bizarre markings, the discovery of extraterrestrial corpses, covert military activity, and the buying-off of witnesses. And, of course, an official cover-up! It is more likely that the Calgarth skulls or the Crier of Claife will turn up before any evidence of alien activity does.

In his blog for 7 October 2008, Rick Gemini, clearly someone with local connections, recorded that he had quizzed an elderly life-long Caldbeck resident. Despite knowing all the local history and gossip, Gemini's contact had heard nothing about the crash. Gemini also failed to turn up anyone else in the area who had the slightest recollection of the event. You might think that a fireball hitting the fells, the discovery of a strange craft, the presence of heavy recovery vehicles and a major military and security operation might be the kind of thing people would remember. The official Freedom of Information website has a reply sent by the Ministry of Defence on 18 September 2008 to 'Ross', who had requested a FOI search on the 'Caldbeck Crash.' The official noted that, as was routine at the time, all 'UFO'-related files prior to 1967 were destroyed due to insufficient public interest, so there is nothing on the 1954 event. One of the speculations surrounding the event is that it was some kind of military aircraft that crashed, so the MOD letter concludes, 'You may also wish to know that in answer to a previous enquiry on the same subject, we were able to determine that we had no record of any RAF aircraft crashing in Cumbria on that date.' The 'UFO Files' at the National Archives can be viewed at www.nationalarchives.gov.uk/ufos.

SEBERGHAM

John Stagg's 1816 fiction *The Minstrel of the North* includes the decidedly Gothic tale of 'Lord Baldwin,' set on the banks of the River Caldew, in the forests of 'Warnell's tow'ring heights.' Warnell Fell is 1 mile (1.6km) west of Sebergham. While out hunting Baldwin, a recent widower, meets and woos a mysterious beautiful lady by the riverbank. He proposes and agrees to meet up in the churchyard at midnight, promising his body and soul to her. She repeats the phrase, 'Body and soul thou shalt be mine, for ever and for ever!' That evening Baldwin murders his mistress Emma with poison. He goes to the churchyard but at midnight Emma's ghost appears and he flees. At the castle gate he sees the mysterious beauty, who says she had impersonated Emma to try his courage. He repeats the body and soul promise and she pounces on him. It his Adelaide, his dead wife.

> Her fleshless arms his neck embrac'd,
> Her putrid lips to his were plac'd,
> Chill horror shook his soul;
> Her smell was like the scorpion's breath,
> Her icy touch as cold as death,
> And horrible the whole.

We learn that Adelaide was also poisoned. 'Body and soul thou shalt be mine, for ever and for ever!' she cries. Baldwin dies on the spot.

> Yet often, as the rustics say,
> Lord Baldwin takes his midnight way
> Along the winding stream;
> Two female forms, array'd in white,
> Pursue him thro' the live-long night,
> And hoot with hideous scream!

CARROCK FELL

A massive Iron-Age hillfort built with immense labour – and tens of thousands of boulders – encircles the exposed summit (NY342336). So spectacular and remote is the monument that its construction was ascribed to either the Devil or Michael Scot, the great medieval scholar who was reputed to command demons. The fell also hosts a large sheepfold built of the roughly-dressed stones from the fort, as well as several dozen mounds, cairns and piles of stones, at least some of which must be prehistoric.

SOUTHER FELL

Strange apparitions mocked the shepherd's sight.
The form appears of one that spurs his steed
Midway along the hill with desperate speed;
… Anon, appears a brave, a gorgeous show
Of horsemen-shadows moving to and fro;
… While silent stands the admiring crowd below,
Silent the visionary warriors go,

William Wordsworth, 'An Evening Walk' (1793)

The Phantom Army of Souther Fell is so famous it not only gets a poem by Wordsworth, it merits a mention in Book Five (The Northern Fells) of Wainwright's *Pictorial Guides*. The tale has been told and retold and through a process of paranormal Chinese Whispers, has become subtly (and not so subtly) changed from its original, so is worth going back to its first appearance in print, which was in the *Gentleman's Magazine* for 1747:

On Midsummer-eve, 1735, Wm. Lancaster's servant related that he saw the east side of Souter fell, towards the top, covered with a regular marching army for above an hour together; he said they consisted of distinct bodies of troops, which appeared to proceed from an eminence in the north end, and marched over a nitch in the top, but, as no other person in the neighbourhood had seen the like, he was discredited and laughed at. Two years after, on Midsummer-eve also, betwixt the hours of eight and nine, Wm. Lancaster himself imagined that several gentlemen were following their horses at a distance, as if they had been hunting, and, taking them for such, pay'd no regard to it till about ten minutes after; again turning his head towards the place, they appeared to be mounted, and a vast army following, five in rank, crowding over at the same place, where the servant said he saw them two years before. He then called his family, who all agreed in the same opinion, and, what was most extraordinary, he frequently observed that some one of the five would quit rank and seem to stand in a fronting posture, as if he was observing and regulating the order of their march, or taking account of the numbers, and after some time appeared to return full gallop to the station he had left, which they never failed to do as often as they quitted their lines, and the figure that did so was generally one of the middlemost men in the rank. As it grew later, they seemed more regardless of discipline, and rather had the appearance of people riding from a market than an army, though they continued crowding on and marching off as long as they had light to see them.

This phenomenon was no more seen till the Midsummer-eve which preceded the rebellion, when they were determined to call more families to be witness of this sight, and accordingly went to Wilton-hill and Souter-fell-side, till they convened about twenty-six persons, who all affirmed they then saw the same appearance, but not conducted with the usual regularity as the preceding ones, having the likeness of carriages interspersed; however, it did not appear to be less real, for some of the company were so affected with it as in the morning to climb the mountain, through an idle expectation of finding horse-shoes after so numerous an army, but they saw not the vestige or print of a foot.

Wm. Lancaster, indeed, told me that he never concluded they were real beings, because of the impracticability of a march over the precipices, where they seemed to come on; that the night was extremely serene; that horse and man, upon strict looking at, appeared to be but one being rather than two distinct ones; that they were nothing like any clouds or vapours which he had ever perceived elsewhere; that their number was incredible, for they filled lengthways near half a mile, and continued so in a swift march for above an hour, and much longer he thinks if night had kept off.

… I only give it verbatim from the original relation of a people that could have no end in imposing on their fellow-creatures, and are of good repute in the place where they live. It is my real opinion that they apprehended they saw such appearances, but how an undulating lambent meteor could affect the optics of so many people is difficult to say.

The account concludes with an earlier sighting of a phantom army in Leicestershire in 1707. Later writers added phantom armies in Ujest, Silesia (1785); Vienne, France (1848); Quigley's Point, Lough Foyle, Ireland (1848); Bannmouth, Ireland (1850); Buderich, Germany (1854); and Paderborn, Germany (1860). Clearly ghost armies were an eighteenth- and nineteenth- century craze, although they have dropped out of fashion since.

The *Gentleman's Magazine* report was anonymous. In a fine piece of detective work, F.J. Carruthers, in *Lore of the Lake Country* (1975) identifies the writer as 'GS', George Smith of Wigton, who, from an analysis of his other publications at the time, Carruthers characterises as 'not averse to creating a wrong impression among readers who were unlikely to check on his findings.' In other words, the veracity of the primary account might be open to question: the whole Souther Fell Ghost Army story could, in part, be an exaggeration; or possibly a fib.

Of course, it's never as straightforward as that. Forty years after Smith, James Clarke wrote his *Survey of the Lakes*, in which he interviewed the respectable landowning gentleman William Lancaster, who pretty much repeated what he had apparently told Smith. 'I shall give it nearly in the words of Mr Lancaster of Blakehills, from whom I had the account, and whose veracity, even if it were not supported by many concurrent testimonies, I could fully rely on.' Lancaster spoke exclusively about the 1745 sighting, and added a few additional points:

These visionary horsemen seemed to come from the lower part of Southerfell, and became visible first at a place called Knott; they then moved in regular troops along the side of the Fell, till they came opposite Blake Hills, when they went over the Mountain; thus they described a kind of curvilineal path upon the side of the Fell, till both their first and last appearance were bounded by the top of the Mountain.

Some elements of the 1737 sighting in Smith's account appear in the 1745 version:

Frequently the last, or last but one in a troop (always either the one or the other) would leave his place, gallop to the front, and then take the same pace with the rest, a regular swift walk: These would happen to every troop, (for many troops appeared) and oftener than once or twice, yet not at all times alike.

The vision was not only seen by the people at Blakehills (which is on the east side of the River Glenderamakin at NY366282, opposite Souther Fell) but 'by every person at every village within the distance of a mile.' That's a lot of witnesses (although none of them were ever interviewed or identified). Lancaster also expanded the duration of the episode, claiming it lasted two and a half hours, whereas Smith had given 'above an hour,' and noting the time of day: from 7.30 p.m. to 10 p.m., 'till the night coming on prevented the further view.' So the Ghost Army was viewed for several hours on a summer's evening, on the longest day of the year, from a location around ½ mile (800m) away.

Clarke identified William Lancaster's former servant, the first person to see the phenomenon, as Daniel Stricket, who was making a living as an auctioneer. The most extraordinary part of Clarke's report is towards the end:

> We whose names are hereunto subscribed, declare the above account to be true, and that we saw the Phenomena as above related; as witness our hands, this 21st day of July, 1785.
>
> William Lancaster, Daniel Stricket

One wonders how persuasive Clarke had to be to get them to sign this attestation.

Smith's and/or Clarke's account were then repeated in numerous later accounts, but in a sense, these are all irrelevant (other than helping to popularise the story). As the tale was recounted, however, details were changed – the number of witnesses, the number and nature of the sightings, even the dates. By the time you get to websites, the variations from the two original accounts can be legion.

The 1745 Jacobite Rebellion led by Bonnie Prince Charlie provided some writers with a spurious explanation for the phenomenon – what the witnesses had seen, they said, were 'obviously' distant mirages of the rebels exercising on the west coast of Scotland, or Government forces secretly maneuvering on the other side of the fells. Charlie, however, did not land in Scotland until late July., so the explanation falls flat There was more self-satisfied explanatory tosh about optical illusions such as the Fata Morgana or the Brocken spectre, none of which could even approach the complexity and length of the claimed phenomenon. As Charles Fort commented on his survey of the events in *New Lands*, 'there never has been an explanation that did not itself have to be explained.'

In the end the Phantom Army of Souther Fell is a genuine mystery. If the accounts written by Smith and Clarke are reliable, and if Lancaster and Strickert were telling the truth, then on Midsummer's Eve 1735, 1737 and 1745, one, several and twenty-six people respectively – not to mention apparently the entire district in the last case – watched, over an extended period each time, a non-existent army moving over a precipitous mountain where no military force could possibly operate. Why those years, and those years only? Why Midsummer's Eve? And why Souther Fell? Theories will rise and fall, but we will never really know for certain.

BLENCATHRA

The mountain is one of many under which King Arthur sleeps, ready for the crisis when he is most needed. Of the two crosses of white stones near the summit, the larger is in memory of gamekeeper John Straughan, who died in the Second World War, and the smaller has no clear provenance. The immortal pair of fish of Bowscale Tarn (NY337313) are as credible as the notion that at midday you can see the stars reflected in the water of Scales Tarn (NY329281).

In Walpole's *The Bright Pavilions* (see WATENDLATH) Frau Hodstetter, accused of shapeshifting, cattle-killing, murder and other acts of witchcraft, is burnt to death on the summit, which is a strenuous location for a spontaneous execution. The scenes of mob fury and the frenzied utterings of a fanatical Protestant clergyman are powerfully written. Hodstetter's daughter Catherine is about to be cast into the flames when Gilbert Armstrong saves her by claiming to be her fiancé – so the mob run them down the mountain to Keswick, break into Crosthwaite Church, and force them to be married.

SCALES

The White Horse Inn has a Bible which the property deeds say must never be allowed to cross the threshold.

THRELKELD

The *English Lakes Visitor and Keswick Guardian* for March 1878 announced that a cow belonging to Mr Geo Hindmoor of Setmabanning, Threlkeld, gave birth to a calf having two fully-grown and perfect heads. The animal lived but a short time.

Beard-stroking
gargoyle, Christ's
Church, Penrith.

4

ULLSWATER, PENRITH AND THE EAST

ULLSWATER

Romantic travellers came here to experience the multiple echoes, and for a fee a boat could be hired from which brass swivel-guns would be fired. The naturalist journal *Land and Water* (4 September 1869) reported an anomalous army of ladybirds over the lake, the swarm lasting thirty minutes. In Stevie Smith's slightly creepy 1962 poem 'The Frozen Lake' the narrator plunges into Ullswater in pursuit of his lady-love, a subaqueous witch who breaks through the ice from below, but he dies when stabbed by Arthur's sword Excalibur.

The ScubaSpooks website, run by Paul Renucci, gives a classic tale of an apparent 'cursed object,' in this case a coin found during a dive in Ullswater. Scrolls on it were visible to the naked eye, but under the lens of a digital camera the scrolls vanished, to be replaced by a malevolent face. Something about the coin spooked the divers. Whoever possessed the coin suffered misfortune, such as car failure, burst tyres and stomach cramps, with the problems vanishing once the coin was passed on to someone else. The 'curse' only ceased when the surface of the coin was ground down and the 'face' disappeared. The story later appeared in the *News & Star* (19 February 1997).

PATTERDALE

Supposedly the area is named after St Patrick, although the originator of the name could just as easily have been an Irish-Norse settler called Patrick. There are two Thompson mice (see DEAN) on staves within St Patrick's Church (NY393162).

Crookabeck Farm, south of Rooking (NY402155) has a rock garden complete with apparent 'standing stones' (actually old gateposts, but they look the part). In the 1999 *Transactions of the Matterdale Historical and Archaeological Society* Tim Cook relates how, clearing the garden of an old cottage he had recently bought above Patterdale, he found a large section of prehistoric cupmarks on a rock outcrop. Then his neighbours, with his encouragement, found another outcrop in their garden further down the fell, this one covered with cups both small and large, and long shallow grooves. Two more sites were uncovered further down the valley, all in an area where rock art was previously unknown.

GLENRIDDING

St Patrick's Well (NY388166) is covered by a substantial Victorian well-house by the roadside. The tradition is that Patrick was shipwrecked at Duddon Sands in AD 540, and baptised the local people here, although there is no way to confirm this. Certainly by 1348 the site was occupied by a chapel (the Capella de Patrickdale) and it was long renowned as a healing well. The spring is still flowing and is a 450yds (410m) walk south of Glenridding. For centuries Glenridding was closely associated with the Greenside Lead Mine (NY363177). When the mine closed in the early 1960s it briefly became home to Operation Orpheus, a secret Government experiment to test the nature of the seismic signals of underground atomic weapons. Two (non-nuclear) test explosions took place inside the mine.

Cottages in Glencoyne to the north rejoice in the name 'Seldom Seen'.

AIRA FORCE (NY399205)

This justifiably popular waterfall is associated with a sickeningly sentimental story of tragic love, with a knight accidentally causing the death of his sleepwalking lover. This, however, is not a traditional tale, but the story of the poem 'The Somnabulist' by Wordsworth (who writes after his name, 'Who Made The "Legend" Up').

De Quincey's *Recollections* gives a genuinely intriguing example of the 'spirit/angelic guide' genre widespread in mountains and wild places. The episode was related to him by the young witness Elizabeth Smith in winter 1800. Declining to hire the usual guide, she had climbed up alone along the side of the Force until she became lost. After a period of panic and despair she sat down to consider her position, at which point she saw a woman wearing a white muslin morning robe about 200yds (183m) away. Step by step, this lady silently indicated the correct route down, although she always kept herself at a distance. At some point Miss Smith recognized the guide as her own sister, who was supposedly studying at home. Eventually, the clear path home was reached.

> There Miss Smith paused, in order to take breath from her panic, as well as to exchange greetings and questions with her sister. But sister there was none. All trace of her had vanished; and when, in two hours after, she reached her home, Miss Smith found her sister in the same situation and employment in which she had left her; and the whole family assured her that she had never stirred from the house.

The *Westmorland Gazette* for 16 January 2008 reported a sighting of three large black cats near Aira Force.

Cockley Moor house, near Dochray, was from 1965 to 1975 the home of Sir Fred Hoyle (1915-2001), controversial astronomer and writer of science-fiction works such as *A for Andromeda*, *The Black Cloud* and *Rockets in Ursa Major*. Hoyle was a proponent of the 'Steady State' theory – in which the universe has no end or beginning, and new matter is constantly coming into existence – as opposed to the 'Big Bang' one-point-of-creation idea. The story goes that the steady state theory was inspired by the classic British horror film *Dead of Night* (1945), where the narrative loops around to end just as it began.

Hoyle, along with Chandra Wickramasinghe, then proposed that the complex molecules necessary for life originate in space, and are deposited on Earth and other planets by close encounters with comets, an evolutionary theory he termed panspermia.

POOLEY BRIDGE

It was prophesised that a princess would drown. Her father built a tower to keep her safe far from the lake, but like any spirited teenager she decided to meet up with her fella. Unfortunately as they were escaping she met an undignified end in a water butt. Moral: you can't escape fate, especially in a fairy tale. All this, taken from *The Folklore of the Lake District*, is the reason why the low circular ramparts of an Iron-Age defended settlement (NY452243, reachable by a bridleway) are known as Maiden Castle. Another Iron-Age settlement is hidden among the trees of Dunmallard Hill (NY466246).

On 18 November 1799 Coleridge looked west across from the shore near Eusemere towards Salmond's Plantation, and came over all Freudian:

> … that round fat backside of a Hill with its image in the water made together one absolutely undistinguishable Form – a kite or Paddle or keel turned to you/the road appeared a sort of suture, in many places exactly as the weiblich tetragrammaton is painted in anatomical Books! I never saw so sweet an Image!

Weiblich is 'female' in German, while *tetragrammaton* is Greek for 'four letter,' which may give you an idea of what Sam was coyly referring to. On a calm day while on the footpath running south from Pooley Bridge on the east side of the lake, you may get the sense of the particular simulacrum that got him so excited.

SANDWICK

Cumberland's last fairies were supposedly seen on Sandwick Rigg (NY424199), the grassy hill overlooking the hamlet. In 1850 Jack Wilson was returning home when he encountered many fairies 'intensely engaged in their favourite diversion' (presumably dancing, or eating and drinking). When the host spotted him they all ran up a stee (ladder) into a cloud, drawing the ladder up behind them. Jack ran forward, but fairyland was closed. He told the story many times thereafter, and the concluding words of the tale – 'yance gane, ae gane, and niver saw mair o' them' – became proverbial in the locality. (Source: Sullivan's *Cumberland and Westmorland Ancient and Modern*, 1857.) The retractable 'ladder' and hovering 'cloud' inevitably have resonances with modern descriptions of alien spacecraft.

MARTINDALE

St Martin's Church (NY434184) at the southern end of the hamlet is one of the most atmospheric churches in the Lakes. A plain sixteenth-century building with no electricity or light source other than candles, it was abandoned in favour of the new church

(St Peter's, ½ mile (800m) north) in the 1880s. The local legend is that a storm tore the roof off on the day that St Peter's was consecrated. The font is a Roman wayside altar, brought down from High Street, and was once used for sharpening tools – the grooves are still there. Estimates for the age of the yew tree in the churchyard range from 1,300 to 2,000 years – if the latter is true then this was originally a pagan site. When Tony Walker visited the yew while researching *The Ghostly Guide to the Lake District* he had a very strong, very unpleasant feeling. Some ley line enthusiasts see the church as being the terminus of a ley.

Jeremiah Sullivan gives the tale of the Henhow Boggle (Henhow is slightly further south, NY434177). In about 1834 a farm worker, out after midnight, encountered an 'uncanny' woman carrying a baby. She said she had been made pregnant by a clergyman. He attempted to procure an abortion by poison, but both the woman and her unborn child died. The tragic mother and infant were obligated to haunt the lane and house for 100 years, and had already served forty years of their manifestly unfair sentence.

DACRE

In his *magnum opus* from AD 731, *The Ecclesiastical History of the English People*, the Venerable Bede mentions a monastery at Dacre, which he calls Dacore. Excavations in the graveyard in 1929 and 1982 seem to confirm this. John Blair in *The Church in Anglo-Saxon Society* (2005) examined parish boundaries and concluded that the much larger parish of GREYSTOKE once belonged to Dacre. The assumption is that the monastery was destroyed by raiders. Bede relates a miracle from Dacre in AD 698 – Bede was always careful to give his sources, and here he was told the story by the miraculously healed monk himself, who had long suffered from an eye-threatening facial swelling. Some hairs cut from the uncorrupted body of St Cuthbert were applied to the swelling, and four hours later the monk's eye was completely cured.

The central mystery of St Andrew's Church (NY460266) is the identity of the so-called Dacre Bears. These four enigmatic sculptures stand at the corners of a notional rectangle around the church. In 1890, writing in the *Transactions* of the CWAAS, Chancellor Ferguson suggested that they told a story, the meaning of which has been lost, but the essence is: (1) north-west – the bear is asleep with his head resting on a pillar. (2) South-west – a cat or lynx has jumped on the bear's back. (3) South-east – the bear attempts to dislodge its attacker. 4) North-east – the bear has a satisfied expression and appears to have eaten the cat. The only trouble with this widely-accepted interpretation is that the main animal is clearly not ursine – it lacks a bear's snout and has a mane and a long tail, so it is probably a lion. The south-east 'bear' appears to be wearing some kind of cloak (possibly having skinned the cat?) and in the north-east sculpture my interpretation is that it is lapping milk (or blood). The 'bears' were first recorded in the churchyard in 1704, but are clearly much older. No one knows their original location – suggestions include on the church tower, or on the battlements or a gateway of Dacre Castle. Each of the four creatures also has a depression on top – too shallow for a flagpole, but just the right size for a candle or a wick floating in oil.

Elsewhere in the sheep-populated graveyard are an alms table with a broken sundial, gravestones with winged souls and hourglasses, and a monument with a skull, crossed pikes and bones. Inside the first-class church can be found a damaged but still splendid effigy of a medieval knight and a Victorian stained glass of St George in golden armour stomping on a vanquished red dragon, while a modern window features a malignant reptilian devil

Above left: The Dacre 'Bears'. The north-west creature, apparently sleeping on its pillar.

Above centre: The south-west sculpture, with the 'cat' on its back.

Above right: The south-east figure with its cloak (of catskin?). Dacre Castle is in the background.

cowering beneath saintly feet. A unique etched window has nature scenes and an image of Dalemain House. A ninth-century sculptured fragment shows a winged lion with a querulous expression, and a cross-shaft (probably Norse) is superbly carved with a beast, Abraham about to sacrifice Isaac, a hound jumping on the back of a stag – a representation of a Christian soul attacked by evil – and Adam and Eve with the tree. The serpent appears to be trying to put an apple under Eve's skirt. A small stone head of unknown age sits high up on the north wall of the nave. The pulpit is carved with the Greek symbols Alpha and Omega (the beginning and end of time), Omicron (eternity) and Delta (the Trinity), and the Chi-Rho, the abbreviation for the Greek name Christos. There is a chained Bible of 1617, the south door has a large lock dated 1671 and inscribed with the initials 'AP' for Lady Anne Clifford, Countess of Pembroke, while the floor, including the step to the vestry, re-uses several carved medieval graveslabs. Excellent guidebook available.

Dacre Castle (NY462265, private) and its impressive moat can be easily viewed from the public footpath that passes next to it. Its forbidding walls are said to be haunted by the kind of ghosts that are, frankly, the stuff of castellated legend. In the tenth century the Scottish and Cumbrian kings, having been bested militarily, paid homage to the Anglo-Saxon King Athelstan at Dacre; for no reason other than their celebrity value, the royal trio are supposed to still lurk around the castle, as allegedly does a certain Lady Dacre who, when her husband discovered her affair, was walled up with her lover's decapitated corpse.

The Horse and Ferrier pub's own website mentions they have a friendly ghost nicknamed Fred. In the village green stands a gatepost to which is attached a curious piece of ironwork that looks like a very uncomfortable three-looped set of punishment stocks, although it could be something else. Dalemain House (NY478269, open much of the year, check www.dalemain.com or telephone 017684 86450 for details) is a most enjoyable medieval, Tudor and Georgian warren, with a priest's hole off the housekeeper's room. The solar tower is claimed to be haunted by a chap in a dark brown coat.

Above left: The north-east animal, lapping up blood or milk. The candle-sized hole is clearly visible at the top.

Above right: One of the 'bears' showing a very un-bear-like mane and tail. The Dacre Lions, anyone?

Below left: Norse cross-slab, St Andrew's Church, Dacre. A long-necked beast; Abraham and Isaac; a hound attacking a stag; and Adam and Eve with the Tree and a naughty Serpent.

Below right: Crossed pikes, crossed bones, Cross, hope and anchor. Note the vegetation growing out of the skull, symbolising resurrection. St Andrew's Church, Dacre.

HUTTON JOHN

There is a St Mary's Well at NY440272 just north of the pele tower, but I can find no traditions connected with it.

TIRRIL

Neil Coates' *Best Pub Walks in the Lakeland Fringes* notes that over several decades the teetotal owner of the cottage adjoining the Queens Head pub resisted attempts to buy her out, and subsequently haunted the pub when she died in the early 1900s. A house dated 1765 has the legend 'To know thyself is a Proof of Wisdom.' Charles Gough (see HELVELLYN) was buried in the Quakers' burial ground, but there are no gravestones.

GREYSTOKE

The highlight of the wonderful, expansive St Andrew's Church (NY443308) is the medieval carving in the choir stalls. The misericords include: Green Men and Women; faces lasciviously licking their lips; three men, one with a hammer, cudgeling a donkey for its stupidity; the Christian symbols of the pelican who feeds her young with her own blood; the unicorn being speared by a hunter while surrendering to a virgin; and St Michael thrusting a spear down a dragon's throat. The stall angels have bearded heads while the finials on the stall ends are carved into irreverent chaps poking tongues out, pulling beards or grasping their head in anxiety. Another finial has two lions vertically aligned bottom-to-bottom, while tiny heads, lions and coiled serpents adorn the fronts of the stalls.

The rood beam bridging the chancel arch is a pre-Reformation survival and carries angels with shields and flowers representing the five wounds of Christ. The corbels of the north chancel wall are helmeted barons, facing a row of gentler-visaged provosts on the opposite wall.

The local story is that the medieval glass of the east window was hurriedly buried when Cromwell's iconoclasts approached, and was restored in 1848. The restorers were unable to accurately replicate the original, so some pieces have strayed – such as the red devil beneath the feet of the bishop on the left, who originally was tempting Eve in a scene set in the Garden of Eden. The 'Bestiary' window has panels depicting real and mythical creatures from the medieval bestiaries – an eagle, antelope, mongoose, ass, phoenix and caladrius, the latter a bird which can draw sickness into itself and burn the disease off in the sun. If the caladrius looks away from you, however, your fate is sealed.

There are excellent effigies of the 14th Baron Greystoke, dressed like the Black Prince at Canterbury, and his grandson the 16th Baron. For 250 years these sculptures lay outside, and farmers would break lumps of alabaster off them to sharpen their scythes and to rub on sheep scab (the latter probably magical in intent). The enormous nave contains a wooden sculpture of the Madonna and Child, carved by two German prisoners of war with just a penknife, and an evocative crucified Christ by Josefina de Vasconcellos. The base of the altar of St Andrew's Chantry is never dry and could have been built over the sanctified well that marked the site of the earliest wooden Saxon church. Several churches in Cumbria were built near pagan wells. There is a memorial brass in the floor in this chapel and three tiny brasses lurk near the west wall of the south aisle. The church has an excellent booklet, *The Story of St Andrews Greystoke*.

Above left: Cheeky chappie on the choir stall, St Andrew's Church, Greystoke.

Above right: Three men trying to shift a stubborn donkey. Probably illustrating a medieval proverb. Misericord, St Andrew's Church, Greystoke.

The path from the south porch leads to the house where the horse-drawn hearse was kept, and the graveyard has an alms table with a sundial, several Gothic monuments, and a winged soul on one gravestone. The footpath north (which may be part of a corpse road from Johnby) passes the easy-to-miss Plague Stone, where food and money were exchanged remotely. At a time when the average yearly death toll in the parish was forty-five, the plague years of 1598 and 1623 saw 182 and 163 burials respectively.

A Sanctuary Stone is protected by an iron grille by the swimming pool, a short distance west along the church access road; there are no records of it being invoked for felons seeking sanctuary within the church bounds.

A Roman road can be traced parallel to the minor road west across Greystoke Moor. Close to the east side of the B5288 road from Greystoke to Motherby lies a former sacred spring known as Icold or Eye Keld, the well of the eye (NY442306). This is probably the Tolly Keld mentioned in Marjorie Rowling's *The Folklore of the Lake District*. Before the 1850s the local children of the village used to visit the well on 'Bottle Shaking Sunday' with bottles of liquorice water. Once there they shook the bottles vigorously until the mixture frothed and then drank it quickly, giving them such a sugar rush that it was impossible to get them to Sunday School or to any of the children's services. The origins of the custom were unknown.

Greystoke Castle (NY435309) scores highly on the Castle cliché-ometer by having both ghosts and a secret tunnel. The passage in question, somewhat inevitably, was alleged to run from a bedroom to the church. The story goes that the monk who used the tunnel for extra-pastoral visits was trapped when both ends were bricked up simultaneously. He still hangs around, keeping company with a houseguest who died in the room with the former passage. The notion that Tarzan of the Apes was Lord Greystoke lies firmly in the imagination of the King of the Jungle's creator, Edgar Rice Burroughs. But you can't keep a good fiction down. In 1988 and 1997 the Edgar Rice Burroughs Society held their annual get-together at the castle; at the first event the group's entry was heralded by the theme music from the 1984 film *Greystoke* – and the Tarzan yell. The castle is not open to the public, but is now a venue for corporate hospitality, adventure sports and weddings. The B5288 Greystoke Road to Penrith passes the three farm follies associated with the castle. Charles Howard, the 11th Duke of Norfolk (1746-1815) took every opportunity to annoy his neighbour the Duke of Portland, a staunch Tory. Portland loathed the rebels of the American War of Independence, so Norfolk named two farms after British defeats. The best is Fort Putnam (NY452309), with a battlemented screen wall and turrets and a quasi-cloister within. Hatt and Sharp's *British Castles Follies and Monuments* (1967) considered this would benefit the cattle while annoying the Tories, as expressed in their mellifluous phrase, 'Perhaps we may be sure that there was enraged bellowing on one side of the wall, and contented mooing on the other.' Bunkers Hill (NY458308) has another castellated screen and tower, while Spire House (NY464313) – built to peeve a tenant who despised ostentatious church architecture – has a suitably ecclesiastical spire.

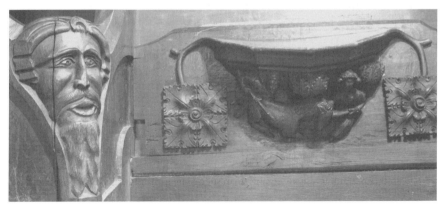

Top: Tiny leering faces carved on front of choir stalls, St Andrew's Church, Greystoke.

Above: Bearded bench-end and misericord with a virgin stroking the Unicorn's horn while the hunter spears it. The Unicorn was seen as symbolic of Christ. St Andrew's Church, Greystoke.

Right: The Fort Putnam fortified farm folly, Greystoke.

PENRITH

Penrith Museum, Middlegate (open Monday-Saturday 10 a.m.-5 p.m., free, wheelchair access to ground floor only) is modest in size but full of interest. The highlights include:

A perforated dobbie stone or hag's stone. Probably a line or net sinker, this apotropaic device protected livestock against disease and witches.

Fossils – ammonites (regarded as magical 'snakestones'), curved Gryphaea oyster shells (aka Devil's toenails) and crinoids (threaded into necklaces or rosaries and called St Cuthbert's beads).

'Elf shot' flint arrowheads, which were said to be fired by fairies to cause elf-stroke. Once found, they also acted as a charm against fairies.

A wooden griffin weathervane pattern.

Four Neolithic stone axes, regarded from the Iron Age to recent times as storm-created 'thunderstones' or 'thunderbolts' and hence built into the walls of buildings as anti-lightning devices. They were also boiled in water which was then drunk to cure diseases.

A horseshoe.

A drawing of the Luck of Edenhall, a vessel reputedly gifted by the fairies.

There is also a display exploring the Neolithic and Bronze-Age stone circles, rock art and henges in the area. The display includes finds from field-walking investigations, five cup-and-ringmarked stones, stone axes that you can handle, and a photograph sequence of the autumnal equinox at MAYBURGH showing the sun setting in the 'saddle' of BLENCATHRA.

There is also a display on Percy Toplis, the so-called Monocled Mutineer. Toplis' contemporary reputation is a fine example of modern myth-making. The 1978 book *The Monocled Mutineer* and subsequent BBC drama portrayed Toplis as a class hero fighting against injustice in the trenches of the First World War. In reality not only was he an unpleasant petty criminal who graduated to murder, he wasn't even in France when the celebrated 'mutiny' he was supposed to have led took place. He was killed by police north of Penrith (see ULDALE).

A Bellarmine jar, a pot-bellied stoneware vessel bearing the face of an ugly bearded man is also on display. These bottles are named after Cardinal Bellarmino, a fervent anti-Protestant. Bellarmines are particularly interesting because many of them are 'witch-bottles.' These were typically filled with nails, urine and hair and used as a personal counterattack against witchcraft. Of around 200 English sixteenth- and seventeenth-century witch-bottles known, 130 are Bellarmines. Unfortunately there is no record of whether this particular jar was used as a witch-bottle.

My favourite mystery item is the large elephant's tooth found in the moat of Penrith Castle in 1920. How on earth did it get there?

St Andrew's Church, off Devonshire Street, has more the air of a grand metropolitan edifice than one of Cumbria's country churches, largely due to its rebuilding in expansive Georgian style in 1720 to a design by the celebrated London architect Nicholas Hawksmoor. Only the imposing tower remains from the original thirteenth-century structure. In the graveyard are two monuments steeped in a confusion of folklore, legend

Above left: The so-called Giant's Thumb, St Andrew's Church, Penrith.

Above left: Two Anglian crosses, four Viking hogback tombstones, and a hot-potch of legends: put them together and you have the 'Giant's Grave'. St Andrew's Church, Penrith.

and speculative history. The 'Giant's Thumb' is a tenth-century Norse wheel-headed cross with part of the wheel broken off. The associated story is that it was erected in memory of his father by 'Owen Caesarius,' King of Cumbria, although there is absolutely no evidence for this beyond antiquarian guesswork. In 1900 a crucifixion scene with a sun and moon was still visible on the shaft, but this has now eroded away. George Watson's 'Notabilia of Old Penrith' (1889) recorded the tradition that the holes in the cross were at one time used to pinion the arms of malefactors; the last person so punished was a young woman who was whipped here and consequently died of shame. A decade later Daniel Scott dismissed this story, noting that Penrith had perfectly serviceable stocks and pillory.

Nearer the church is the 'Giant's Grave,' a remarkable collection of unrelated individual monuments cobbled together to create a fantasy confabulation, in this case allegedly the grave of King Owen/Owain himself. It consists of two very eroded Anglian crosses, each around 11ft (3.4m) high, at either end of an arrangement of two pairs of Viking hogback tombstones (which are supposed to represent wild boars Owen killed in nearby Inglewood Forest). The best-preserved hogback has a twisting serpent, now very difficult to see because of the positioning. The distance between the crosses, around 15ft (4.6m), is claimed to be the height of the 'giant' buried here.

The monument has a confused history, and is a classic example of the manufacture of tradition. William Camden's famous *Britannia* (first published 1586) has no mention of the giant. 'Notabilia of Old Penrith' quotes a manuscript from 1670 by Mr Sandford which is not only giant-free, it describes the two crosses as being separated merely by 'the Lenth of a man,' that is about 6ft (1.8m). In 1695 a new edition of *Britannia* came out with a chapter entitled 'Additions to Cumberland' written by Dr Todd. Here, for the first time, the giant makes an appearance, and Todd describes the crosses as being 5yds (4.6m) apart. It is hard to avoid the conclusion that between 1670 and 1695 the grave had been aggrandised, and either an existing giant legend became attached to it, or the increased size promoted a new giant tradition. The memory of a recent discovery of a man's leg bones and broadsword helped the story along, as did local reverence for the semi-legendary Owen, a popular northern hero who also appeared in Arthurian romances. When the old church was pulled down in 1720 the churchwardens ordered the Giant's Thumb, hogbacks and crosses to be broken up for rubble. The locals forcibly interrupted the destruction, and the damaged parts were riveted together. At this time the eastern cross may have been broken off from its original socket-stone, and re-set in an ill-fitting modern socket. The entire setting was tidied up and made more secure in 1889, thus finalising more than two centuries of the archaeology of fantasy.

With such an impressively-sized grave, the story of the giant gained credence with visitors, and no doubt became a favourite with local guides. In the 1720s Daniel Defoe noted:

> The people told us, they were the monument of Sir Owen Caesar ... This Sir Owen, they tell us, was a champion of mighty strength, and of gygantick stature, and so he was, to be sure, if, as they say, he was as tall as one of the columns, and could touch both pillars with his hand at the same time. They relate nothing but good of him, and that he exerted his mighty strength to kill robbers, such as infested the borders much in those days, others related wild boars; but the former is most probable.

Many later visitors related similar stories. Grevel Lindop's *Literary Guide to the Lake District* relates how in 1926 James Joyce's patron, Harriet Weaver, sent him a photograph of the Giant's Grave and commissioned him to write something about it. Joyce put it into the first chapter of *Finnegan's Wake*, suitably mutated into a form only barely related to its original. Given the monument's heritage of transformation, this seems only appropriate.

Above left: Medieval gravestone in St Andrew's Church, Penrith, with the cross itself sprouting leaves from its 'trunk'.

Above right: Ex gravi Peste ... those killed by the 'pest' in the plague year 1598. St Andrew's Church, Penrith.

Daniel Scott's *Bygone Cumberland and Westmorland* records an unusual case of post-mortem punishment. Three men had insulted a bishop on his visit to Penrith, but by the time ecclesiastical justice caught up with them one had died. The bishop ordered the body to be dug up, and to lie unburied until a ceremony of absolution had been completed. Scott also tells us of the fate of two men who in 1623 had been excommunicated, and thus deprived of the right of burial in a churchyard, 'August 29th, Lanc. Wood, being excommunicate, buried on the Fell. September 5th, Richd. Gibbon, being excommunicate, buried on the Fell.'

Within the tower are two graveslabs – one where the shaft of the foliated cross itself bears leaves like a tree, the other featuring an elaborate cross and a chalice marking the grave of a priest – and full-length effigies of Anthony and Elizabeth Hutton of Hutton Hall. Both figures were commissioned when Anthony died in 1637, but Elizabeth lasted another thirty-six years, while her statue grew no older. A worn sandstone inscription and a brass copy records the death of 2,260 local people in the plague year of 1597. (The figures given for Kendal, Richmond and Carlisle are 2,500, 2,200 and 1,196 respectively.) As the population of Penrith at the time was only 2,000, with 583 deaths recorded in the parish register for that year, the number must refer to the whole of the Penrith area. A plague stone sits in the churchyard, along with gravestones with very worn winged souls and hourglasses. The splendidly ornate Gothic memorial to engineer Robert Virtue sports four heads among the tracery.

> I led my horse, and, stumbling on, at length
> Came to a bottom, where in former times
> A murderer had been hung in iron chains.
> The gibbet-mast had mouldered down, the bones
> And iron case were gone; but on the turf,
> Hard by, soon after that fell deed was wrought,
> Some unknown hand had carved the murderer's name.
> The monumental letters were inscribed
> In times long past; but still, from year to year
> By superstition of the neighbourhood,
> The grass is cleared away, and to this hour
> The characters are fresh and visible:
> A casual glance had shown them, and I fled,
> Faltering and faint, and ignorant of the road.

> William Wordsworth, 'The Prelude'

In 1775 the five-year-old Wordsworth came across the spot on Beacon Hill where in 1766 the murderer Thomas Nicholson had been hanged and his body hung in chains. The turf-cut letters that had so terrified the child were, according to Walker's *History of Penrith* (1858), visible before the execution, and read TPM, standing for 'Thomas Parker Murdered,' thus commemorating the victim. Gerald Findler, in *Legends of the Lake Counties*, suggests this was a misreading, the original being perhaps T.N. (for 'Thomas Nicholson') with the intervening 'P' actually being the sign of the gallows. The site has long been associated with Nicholson's skeletal ghost, but it is hard to tell whether this originated with Wordsworth's immortalisation

Far left: Mouthy demon, Christ's Church, Penrith.

Left: Well you'd be grumpy too if you had a drainpipe in your mouth. Gargoyle, Christ's Church, Penrith.

Below: Dragon-lion hybrid, Christ's Church, Penrith.

of the spot and his feelings of fear. The actual location of the gibbet was on Red Hill, on the east shoulder of Beacon Hill, now difficult to reach in the tree plantations. A popular walk leads up to the summit, where a monument of 1719 gives excellent views (NY 522314).

Christ Church on Stricklandgate, built in 1850, has a superb collection of gargoyles, happy, grumpy, bored, and malign, the best being a horned demon pulling his mouth open. There are more heads and angels within. Pevsner was never more wrong than when he described this church as 'dull'.

Ann Radcliffe described a supposed passage between the ruined Penrith Castle (open all hours, free) and the Gloucester Arms Inn. Being a Gothic novelist, secret tunnels were her stock-in-trade; not surprisingly, it has never been found. Castle Park has an imposing winged

Victory on its war memorial. A substantial Plague Stone stands in a small plaza outside an old people's home just north of the fire station on the A6 (NY519295). On my visit the hollowed-out depression, where money passing between town and country folk was disinfected, was filled with another kind of plague – beer cans and fast-food containers.

On 20 December 2002 the *Westmorland Gazette* reported a sighting of a big black cat in The Crescent, on the southern fringe of Penrith.

The Carleton Inn (formerly the Cross Keys Inn) at the junction of the A686 at Carleton Road is where Thomas Parker had his last drink before being murdered by Thomas Nicholson. The wooden beam over the blocked coach entrance to the barn behind the inn is claimed to be part of Nicholson's gallows.

Carletonhill, off Carleton Hill Road, was the home of novelist Frances Trollope, mother of the better-known Anthony. In his autobiography *What I Remember* (1887) her other son Thomas Adolphus recalled how, in building the drive, it was necessary 'to cause a tiny little spring that rose in the bank by the roadside to change its course in some small degree. The affair seemed to us a matter of infinitesimal importance.' Their neighbour Sir George Musgrave was of a different mind, 'We had moved, he said, a holy well, and the consequence would surely be that we should never succeed in establishing ourselves in that spot. And surely enough we never did so succeed.' Having built the house, the family lived there for less than a year before deciding to move on. Sir George 'said that he knew perfectly well that it must be so, from the time that we so recklessly meddled with the holy well.'

Above left: The Plague Stone, Penrith, where money was disinfected in vinegar.

Above right: One of a pair of guardian gargoyles on Southend Road, Penrith.

An impressive 6ft (1.8m) high standing stone lurks in the foliage beside the workshop of the Lilliput Lane Pottery at Skirsgill, just west of M6 junction 40 (NY511287). In *The Folklore of the Lake District* Marjorie Rowling described the Luck of Skirsgill Hall, an armorial goblet engraved with a tulip and vine and 'September 1st, Anno 1732.' It was probably made to mark the betrothal of William Whelpdale and Mary, daughter of John Brougham, and there is no record of it being regarded as a charm or Luck in the traditional sense. It was sold at Sothebys in 1968 and bought by Lloyds Antiques of London. Skirsgill once had a well around which an annual fair was held, and where a 'well waking' ceremony was held on the first Sunday in May. It had steps leading down and a water jug carved on the lintel. All this appears to have vanished.

The Rheged Discovery Centre (open all year 10 a.m.-6 p.m.) just west of Penrith scores with its free Discovering Cumbria Exhibition, which gives an exciting introduction to Celts, Romans, King Arthur, the Dark Ages and the Vikings. The giant IMAX-style movies are also hugely enjoyable, especially *Dinosaurs: Giants of Patagonia*, *Mysteries of Egypt*, *Vikings: Journey to New Worlds* and *Rheged: The Lost Kingdom*, the last of which brings together local history and legends (which one could argue are interchangeable for Dark-Age Cumbria).

In the *Fortean Times* of July 2004 Dennis Rowlandson of Penrith described how his dog Judy always went through the same affectionate ritual whenever his mother arrived from a shopping trip (waggy-tailed greeting in the lounge, biscuit in the kitchen, leaning against legs in the lounge). When Dennis' mother died Judy was distraught for weeks. One day, she stood up, tail wagging, as if greeting a visitor at the lounge door. The dog then trotted into the kitchen, came back into the lounge and sat down by his mother's old chair, leaning against nothing. After about thirty minutes the contented dog returned to the rug, and thereafter regained her *joie de vivre*.

On the night of 22 September 2008 a man contacted Cumbrian police to report a sighting of a slow-moving aerial object with a white front and orange mid-section, emitting what looked like a trail of sparks. According to the report in the *News & Star* (2 October) the police investigation, which involved contacting an RAF base and Edinburgh's Seismic Research Centre, drew a blank, and they told the witness it must have been a natural phenomenon. During my researches several people told me informally that the M6 corridor was a UFO hotspot, although there were no specific sightings apart from one witness who described 'strange aurora-like lights' near Brougham. A few hours later I saw the phenomenon myself – the nightly lightshow from the CenterParcs holiday village south-east of Brougham, reflecting off the low clouds.

The *News of the World* (1 June 1986) described how John Lennon's ex-wife Cynthia had found a desiccated jackdaw perfectly preserved in 1956 newspapers behind an old fireplace at her then home in Penrith. Inevitably a link had to be found with the dead Beatle: apparently John had told his and Cynthia's son Julian that if there was life after death, he would send him a feather, so Julian supposedly believed it to be a message from his father. This celebrity-centric journalistic stretching aside, there is a genuine mystery here: why would someone hide a jackdaw behind a fireplace in 1956? Was it an apotropaic act? A ritual deposition of a tame or injured bird? Was it placed by a child or teenager acting out some personal drama? We'll never know.

EAMONT BRIDGE

> He passed Red Penrith's Table Round
> For feats of chivalry renowned;
> Left Mayborough's mound and stones of power
> By Druids raised in magic hour

> Sir Walter Scott, *The Bridal of Triermain* (1813)

Here cuddled in close proximity are two of Cumbria's most impressive and enigmatic prehistoric structures, Mayburgh Henge and the henge known as King Arthur's Round Table. Henges are spaces enclosed by a bank constructed for ritual or ceremonial purposes rather than for defence, and may pre-date the earliest stone circles. There was once a third, smaller henge to the south of the Round Table, but this has been almost entirely annihilated. In *Prehistoric Henges* Aubrey Burl suggests the cluster of three different types of earthworks means 'they may have been the separate sanctuaries of strangers from different parts where they could meet, perhaps trade, in safety' and speculates that all three were the nearest market to the stone axe factories of the LANGDALE mountains. The practical elements of trade and exchange may have combined with the reverence attached to the axes to create spaces that were both secular and sacred.

Above: King Arthur's Round Table.

Right: The bank, single remaining standing stone and vast amphitheatre of Mayburgh Henge.

The Millennium Stone
near Mayburgh Henge.

King Arthur's Round Table (NY 522284) consists of a circular bank within which is a
ditch crossed by a causeway to a central platform. There were once two entrances, but
only the south-east one survives, its partner opposite having been obliterated by the
B5320. Two large stones once stood outside this entrance and appear on a drawing made
in the sixteenth century by Sir William Dugdale. Excavation found a cremation burial.
Irrespective of the damage done by the two roads, the current state of the monument is
misleading. The causeway and central flat 'disc', which may be on the site of a prehistoric
mound, were in fact created in 1820 when William Bushby, the owner of the pub opposite,
cut away the inner bank of the henge, deepened the ditch, and used the resulting spoil to
produce a circular platform suitable for tea parties. There is an uncertain claim that one of
the entrance megaliths now sees service as a planter in the pub car park.

In the Middle Ages Arthur's name was commonly invoked to explain many mysterious
monuments. If the giants or the fairies hadn't built it, then Arthur was the name on the
docket. Certainly the name was well established in the early 1540s when John Leland – the
only person ever to be named the King's Antiquarian – wrote 'the ruin is of sum caulled
the Round Table, and of summe Arture's Castel.' (Leland's work was eventually published
in 1769 as *The Itinerary of John Leland Antiquary*.) There may have also a local connection
to the name. In the early fourteenth century English nobles were all members of Arthur's
fan-club, and they behaved accordingly, giving their children, dogs and castles Arthurian
names. Robert de Clifford renamed Mallerstang as Pendragon Castle after Arthur's father
Uther. When the Cliffords became the owners of nearby BROUGHAM CASTLE they may have
been delighted to find a ready-made 'Round Table' on their doorstep. Seventeenth- and
eighteenth-century visitors were consistently told that the henge was used for sports such
as wrestling, and that in the distant past it had been a jousting site. In *Itinerarium Curiosum*

(1724) Stukeley wrote 'The site is used to this day for a country rendezvous, either for sports or for military exercises, shooting with bows, etc.' Although there is no evidence for it, it is possible that the Cliffords, with their Arthurian enthusiasms, arranged feasting and jousting entertainments here, with participants masquerading under the names of Arthur's knights. Such social events are well attested to in Plantagenet castles elsewhere.

As with other sites around Penrith, the Round Table is associated with the giant Tarquin. Celia Fiennes' *Travel Book* of 1698 notes 'It was the table a great Giant 6yds tall used to dine at and there entertained another of 9yds tall which he afterwards killed.' Tarquin, however, is not a local figure – he too has been added to the landscape because of his Arthurian connection. When Thomas Malory compiled *Morte d'Arthur* in 1469 he included a number of already familiar tales of Arthur's knights, one of which told of the single combat between Lancelot du Lac and Tarquin, resulting in the victorious Lancelot releasing sixty-four knights of Arthur's court. The story was also told in a ballad, *Sir Lancelot du Lac*, which was published by Thomas Deloney sometime before 1600, and was so well known that Shakespeare has Falstaff sing an extract from it in *Henry IV Part II*.

West, across the road, is Mayburgh Henge (NY 519284), a colossal amphitheatre-like structure that dwarfs the Round Table. The denuded bank, still standing proud up to 21ft (6.5m) high, is composed of hundreds of thousands of waterworn cobbles, indicating the immense labour required to build this imposing site. Within the enclosed area is a single standing stone 9ft (2.8m high), the last remnant of a group of four, with another two formerly at the entrance, all long lost to gunpowder and greed. Stone circle researcher Robert Farrah has shown that Mayburgh is aligned on the mountain of BLENCATHRA, and that at the autumn equinox the sun rises between the portals of the henge entrance and sets in the saddle of Blencathra. Sightlines from the centre of the Round Table, and just over the road, where its now-destroyed entrance once stood, give views of Blencathra's saddle framed within Mayburgh's entrance, views which vary dramatically as you move towards Mayburgh – a direct alignment suggesting the two monuments were linked, and that there was a processional way from the smaller henge to the larger.

A stone axe was found ritually buried at Mayburgh's entrance; perhaps Blencathra represented the mountain source of the axes, which were presumably exchanged and traded at this site. Mayburgh therefore brings together the sacred and the mundane, a solar belief system that combines practical appreciation of the value of stone tools with veneration of the sacred mountain source, the construction of entrances and sightlines to emphasise the interplay between the landscape and the sun at significant dates, and the ritual burial/sacrifice of symbolic axes.

Mayburgh was active in the Neolithic and Bronze Age. In 1944 Iris Campbell (see CASTLERIGG) gave her psychometric reading of the site: according to her it was built about 15000 BC (when Britain was actually still in the grip of the Ice Age) and was 'an experimental area for the trying out of the sun's rays at certain angles and conditions.' In later years it declined because of black magic:

> There were two kinds of magic in force, one evil and one good; it was a truly concentric area where the magnetism was induced from the four points of the compass … an excess of magic of various kinds caused eventually its break-up and downfall; it subsequently received too much power and was broken up from within.

This somewhat eccentric view is in John Foster Forbes' *Giants of Britain*.

A 50-tonne block of granite was placed by the roadside close to Mayburgh to mark the Millennium. Carved with a cross, the number 2,000, and the symbols for Alpha and Omega, some saw the siting of this explicitly Christian monument as an attempt to counter the pagan sacred site.

BROUGHAM HALL (NY527284)

For my money, the Hall – really a castle wall with an extensive courtyard – is one of the best sites in the Lakes. The main door has a fantastic bronze beast head, a copy of the famous Durham Cathedral doorknocker. A stone head lurks on the exterior, while within are two fierce boars' heads and a modern squinting face. A weathervane is in the form of Old Father Time, carrying his scythe and supported by a stick. The underground icehouse is a vast dark chamber. A large figure of Christ lashed to the cross lies fallen in the former chapel. Because there are a number of craft shops, entry is free, with a donation suggested.

Brougham Hall is another site with a home-loving skull that resisted relocation. All attempts to bury it or dispose of it at sea precipitated poltergeist-like phenomena, and the skull always turned up again. Eventually it was bricked up and peace was restored. If this had been the full extent of our knowledge of the skull, we could just dismiss it as another legend. But in 1989, as part of the renovations to the castle which are still ongoing, Christopher Terry found the skull. It was in a niche in the lower part of a wall, and bore the marks of blunt force trauma. Based on the state of the teeth, Mr Terry's dentist estimated the man had been around thirty-five when he died, although the actual age of the skull was not determined. The tradition was that Brougham would suffer if the skull was removed, so Mr Terry placed the skull in a ceramic pot with some other bones and several modern coins, glued the lid with strong adhesive, and sealed it up in a secret location. In 2007 the castle played host to the television programme *Most Haunted*, and it regularly holds paranormal events and ghostwatches.

St Wilfrid's Chapel, next to the castle, is nineteenth century, but contains a collection of carved medieval woodwork, possibly purloined from France. The figures include Green Men and a woman emerging from the mouth of a dragon. Unfortunately on my visit it was closed for repairs.

BROUGHAM CASTLE

This attractively ruined medieval fortress was built on the site of Brocavum Roman fort (English Heritage. Open 1 March-30 September, 10 a.m.-5 p.m. daily. Admission charge. Wheelchair access to exhibition and a circuit of the site.), the faint outline of which can still be traced to the south. The exhibition features inscribed tombstones from the fort. In 1794 Ann Radcliffe visited, and found it satisfyingly gloomy and grisly:

Dungeons, secret passages and heavy iron rings remain to hint of unhappy wretches, who were, perhaps, rescued only by death from these horrible engines of a tyrant's will. We were tempted to enter a ruinous passage below, formed in the great thickness of the walls; but it was soon lost in darkness, and we were told that no person had ventured to explore the end of this, or of many similar passages among the ruins, now the dens of serpents and other venomous reptiles.

Above: Door knocker, Brougham Hall.

Right: Brougham Hall. 'Brougham' is pronounced 'broom'.

Below: Christ figure. The old chapel, Brougham Hall.

Decoration on the
Countess Pillar, near
Brougham Castle.

In 1789 James Clarke added a new element: 'what is called the Sweating Pillar, from its being continually covered with moisture or dew.' None of these Gothic horrors are now in evidence, if they ever existed at all.

An easy walk east from the castle leads to the Countess Pillar (NY547289), a monument erected by Lady Anne Clifford in memory of her mother. Among its decorations are a skull and crossbones. Next to it is the Dolestone, where alms were distributed to the poor. Note that there is no access from the A66.

CLIFTON

Carvings on the choir stalls of St Cuthbert's Church (NY532271) are virtual duplicates of those in GREYSTOKE. In the graveyard are buried some of the Government troops killed in the Battle of Clifton on 18 December 1745, the last battle fought in England. A number of Jacobites were hanged from the Rebels' Tree close to the George and Dragon Inn. The pub sign has a fine fire-breathing dragon and its walls display prints of the Lowther Estate including LOWTHER CASTLE. A footpath past the Clifton Hall pele tower crosses the M6 to reach the fine pair of standing stones at NY532259.

LOWTHER

St Michael's Church (NY519245) is a seventeenth-century structure built round the previous church's medieval columns. Carvings include an owl, a pig, a rabbit, a foliaceous lion and monster, and a particularly fiendish Green Man. One of the columns has four faces on its base. A Viking hogback stone has a naval and land-based force of shield-bearing Vikings above a fish and what might be a coiled sea serpent. On the reverse is a row of female figures with snakes, possibly a representation of the hideous hag Hel. In the churchyard is the gloomy mausoleum of William, 2nd Earl of Lonsdale, topped with a quartet of splendid griffins.

Sir James Lowther inherited the Lowther estate in 1784. De Quincey's *Recollections* describe 'wicked Jemmy' as 'a true feudal chieftain' who had an alarming impact on the citizens of Penrith: 'such was the impression diffused about him by his gloomy temper and his habits of oppression, that the streets were silent as he traversed them, and an awe sate upon many faces.' Amongst his many misdemeanours was not paying a debt owed to Wordsworth's father. A 1792 satirical portrait by James Gillray, now in the National Portrait Gallery, is titled 'Satan in all His Glory' and shows Lowther as a winged, horned, crowned and rather stout Satan at the centre of an infernal network of malefic financial influence and political corruption. When his second wife died at their Hampshire house he became stricken with a grief-induced psychosis, first dressing her corpse to join him at the dinner table – a practice apparently abandoned when the servants could no longer stand the smell – then placing her in a glass-lidded coffin, and finally having her buried at Paddington Cemetery with a company of Cumberland militia ordered to stand guard over the tomb for several weeks.

Perhaps inevitably, his death in 1802 could not be ordinary. Jeremiah Sullivan's *Cumberland and Westmorland, Ancient and Modern* of 1867 has an astonishing account:

> This notorious character … became a still greater terror to the country after death, than he had even been during his life. He was with difficulty buried; and whilst the clergyman was praying over him, he very nearly knocked the reverend gentleman from his desk. When placed in the grave, the power of creating alarm was not interred with his bones. There were disturbances in the Hall, noises in the stables; neither men nor animals were suffered to rest … The Hall became almost uninhabitable, and out of doors there was constant danger of meeting the miscreant ghost.

Jemmy's boggle manifested in the sound, if not the shape, of a coach-and-six horses, and an exorcism was arranged.

The Lonsdale Mausoleum and St Michael's Church, Lowther.

Jemmy, however – obstinate old boggle! – stood a long siege; and when at length he offered terms of capitulation, was only willing to go to the Red Sea for a year and a day. But it was decided that these terms should not be accepted; the priest read on until he fully overpowered the tyrant, and laid him under a large rock called Wallow Crag [HAWESWATER], and laid him for ever.

I have my suspicions about Sullivan's account, partly because Lowther – clearly an acquisitive villain on a grand scale – seems, in death, to have absorbed some earlier boggle traditions from the area.

Visible from the church, and accessible by a walk across the parkland, is the faded fairytale Lowther Castle (NY523239), built in 1806 as an apogee of extravagant Romantic fantasy and now a vast roofless ruin. There is no access – it's dangerous and being repaired – but splendid views can be had through the locked gates and from elsewhere in the park.

Left: Detail of the sculptures on the Mausoleum.

Below left: Human-headed lion exhaling vegetation, St Michael's Church.

Below right: Green Man exhaling vegetation (or breath?), St Michael's Church.

The Green Goblin! St Michael's Church.

The gatehouse of the fairytale Lowther Castle.

Lowther Castle: Romantic. Rich. Ruined.

ASKHAM/HELTON

A superb walk over Moor Divock takes in a cluster of prehistoric monuments. Starting from the cul-de-sac moorland road from Helton, you first encounter the Cop Stone (NY496217). Although this single standing stone is only 5ft (1.5m) high, so cleverly is it placed, it can be seen on the horizon from many of the other monuments – and it appears larger from a distance. A route to the north-north-west – not the wellworn track – passes through two boulders, which may be a ruined monument, to a cairn circle (NY494220) with a deep central depression. Carrying on in the same direction brings you to another cairn. There is supposed to be an avenue of low stones stretching for about 125yds (115m) between the ring cairn and White Raise cairn, (NY489225) close to the main track, but this largely eluded me. The moor is so scattered with stones that discerning the artificial from the natural can be challenging. White Raise is the best preserved of all the cairns, with its stone-lined cist or grave still visible. At the junction of paths, the route to the west brings you past another cairn to the seventy-odd boulders of the wonderful Cockpit stone circle (NY483222). About 330yds (300m) to the south-south-west is a standing stone, near which are several more cairns. If you carry on south-west from here you're on High Street, the high-level road used by the Romans to traverse the fells above the marshy valleys; it follows the route of a prehistoric trackway.

BAMPTON

When a tenant moved on from a farm he left a pinch of salt on a plate. This would keep away evil and bring luck to the incoming tenant. The custom is recorded in Marjorie Rowling's *The Folklore of the Lake District*.

Above left: Apotropaic waterworn stone on gatepost, Askham.

Above right: The Cop Stone, Moor Divock.

The Cockpit Stone Circle, Moor Divock.

HAWESWATER

This is actually a reservoir, occupying the drowned valley of Mardale. When drought lowers the water level the scant remains of the village can be seen at the valley head. A path, marked on the OS map as the Old Corpse Road, leads from the lakeside (NY485119) to Shap via Swindale. Up until 1730 when Mardale Church was built, coffins would be carried on horseback along this route. The local legend is that during a storm a horse panicked and fled with the coffin. By the time it was finally found three months later it had been discovered that the deceased was a murderer, and hence the deferred burial was seen as divine punishment. Wallow Crag (NY495151) is where Jemmy Lowther, 'the bad Lord Lonsdale' is supposedly buried under the only stone heavy enough to hold him (see LOWTHER), although alternative tradition asserts that he is imprisoned under the stones of the cairn on Hugh's Laithes Pike (NY502151). Two standing stones remain on Four Stones Hill (NY491163).

SWINDALE

In *Shappe in Bygone Days* (1904) the Revd Joseph Whiteside related an episode told to him by his old friend Dick Rawes. A house at Truss Gap (NY515132) acquired the name 'Starvation Cottage' because two old people, Dick and Betty, died there from hunger and cold. It was commonly believed that they had returned from the other side, and Rawes had seen a white figure dart by him on the road near the house.

SHAP

The evocative remains of Shap Abbey (NY548153, open daily, free) sit in a slight valley. Daniel Scott's *Bygone Cumberland and Westmorland* (1899) makes the following claim:

> About the middle of the fourteenth century the abbot and canons of Shap had licence from Bishop Kirkby to remove the body of Isabella, wife of William Langley, their parishioner, famed for having miracles done by it, to some proper place within the church or churchyard of Shap, that the reliques might be reverenced by the people with freer and greater devotion.

Only an arc of six stones remains of the Kemp Howe stone circle (NY567133) south of Shap, the remainder having been obliterated by the railway line. The smoking stacks of the cement factory make for a surreal backdrop. Kemp Howe seems to have been the southern terminus of what by all accounts was one of the grandest prehistoric monuments in the north of England, a great avenue of stones that extended to the north-west. At the start of the seventeenth century William Camden recorded in his *Britannia*, 'huge stones in forme of Pyramides, some 9 foote high and fourteene foot thicke, ranged directly as it were in a rowe for a mile in length,' but even by the time of this, the first published record of the monument, many of the stones were being blown up with gunpowder and cannibalised for walls and buildings. Every antiquarian report ever since has recorded fewer and fewer stones, making reconstructing this 'mini-Avebury' challenging for modern archaeologists. Finding the stones

The remaining stones of Kemp Howe stone circle, Shap, bisected by the railway and backed by a cement factory.

Above left: The Thunder Stone, one of the boulders of the former Shap Avenue.

Above right: Gunnerkeld Stone Circle, next to the M6.

on the ground can be perplexing too – the most obvious are the Giant's Foot behind the houses in Shap (NY563148), the huge wedge of the Goggleby Stone (NY559151), the Aspers Field stone next door (NY558152) and the largest stone, the Thunder Stone (NY552157). All but the last can be reached by, or at least viewed from, footpaths. For more detailed searching I recommend the books by Tom Clare and Robert Farrah, or the pioneering work done on the Shap Community website.

Just the other side of the M6 is Gunnerkeld stone circle (NY56821774), two concentric circles of large stones with a central cairn. The atmosphere of this lovely circle is somewhat affected by the constant traffic thundering past just metres away. Ask permission at Gunnerwell Farm. Access is not easy – you'll probably get at least your feet wet crossing Gunnerkeld Sike. Just opposite, on the grassy bank between the two carriageways, is a group of four boulders in a square, very probably contemporary with the motorway.

The M6 corridor around Shap summit has been the location for several sightings of big black cats, including several reports in the *Westmorland Gazette*: 5 August 2001, reported 10 August 2001; 8 November 2002 near Orton; 7 March 2004, near Tebay, reported 13 March; and 5 March 2005, reported 9 March. *The Big Cats in Britain Yearbook* 2007 also has a report from 29 January 2006. In a wonderfully appropriate coincidence, in 1904 Whiteside recorded that this area was haunted by a phantom black dog. There were several more reports of this dog in the 1930s.

5

KENDAL AND THE SOUTH-EAST

KENDAL

> Kendal has its many ghosts. They are weird demonstrations, some human, some of animal shape, spirits which rage and moan in wild voids, from innocents to murderers.

> William Palmer, *The Verge of Lakeland* (1938)

Kendal is as well-stocked with goodies of the mysterious and marvellous as it is with mintcake.

HOLY TRINITY CHURCH, KIRKLAND

This amazing building, a mere parish church, is only a few feet narrower than the mighty York Minster. The instantly striking feature is the sheer number of gurning and grinning gargoyles hanging from its stonework. The exterior also has a sundial dated 1602, a clock with a winged soul at each corner, twelve consecration crosses, and a medieval mass clock on a buttress in the south-west corner.

Many burials recorded in the church registers for 1597-8 were marked 'P', for those who had died of plague. Most were probably buried in a common grave. The register at the end of 1598 recorded 'six hundred, three score and eight' deaths 'since the nativitie of the plague.'

The huge church with its several chapels and aisles houses a treasure trove, including stained glass rescued from FURNESS ABBEY and a Victorian window brought from All Hallows' Church in Fellside featuring a strikingly solar Christ. *A Walk Around Kendal Parish Church*, available in the church, is recommended if you wish to discover more. Here are just the highlights:

THE PARR CHAPEL

This was erected by the Parr family of Kendal Castle, progenitors of Lady Katherine Parr, the sixth wife of Henry VIII. High above are four brightly painted angels carrying the symbols of the Passion – Cross, Crown of Thorns, Ladder, and Hammer and Nails. Between them are tiny painted busts of female figures with long hair – these are presumably representations of the Maiden, Katherine's badge. Another small long-haired head is carved on a nearby column. A fragment of a ninth-century Anglian cross sits on the windowsill.

THE BELLINGHAM CHAPEL

This has several sixteenth-century brasses. Overhead looms the massive modern Crown of Thorns sculpture, which is very 1968, and there is a Chinese standard embroidered with an imperial dragon. It was captured at the Battle of Ting Hai, Chunan, as a result of which Britain acquired Hong Kong (and the opium trade).

THE CENTRE AISLE

The second column from the altar, on the north side, has a block of stone where natural aging has produced a simulacrum of what appears to be a Lakeland scene of river, fell and cloud, as rendered perhaps by a disciple of J.M.W. Turner.

THE NORTH AISLE

The North Aisle is home to an entire squadron of painted angels flying across the roof, and has the church's most legend-encrusted artefact. High on the wall hang a helmet and sword that supposedly belonged to Sir Robert Philipson, 'Robin the Devil.' In 1645, during the Civil War, the Royalist Philipson had been besieged on BELLE ISLE on Windermere. When the siege was lifted he rode to Kendal in pursuit of his Parliamentarian enemy Col. Briggs, bursting into the church on his horse. Briggs was not there and, the legend goes, in the ensuing fracas Philipson lost both his helmet and sword, which have been displayed in Holy Trinity since.

The real story is slightly different. Sir Robert had indeed sacrilegiously ridden into the church on his charger. The first account was written down within fifty years of the events, in the journal of Revd Thomas Machel in 1691-2 (Machel's journal was published in 1963 as *Antiquary on Horseback*). Machel's two informants were Robert's uncle, Sir Christopher Philipson, and the Rector of Windermere – the son of a man who had probably witnessed the original affray. Machel wrote that Robert rode to Kendal with three or four companions. They rode past the watch and Robert entered the church, riding up one aisle and down another – remember, it's a huge church. He failed to find Briggs but his actions had caused consternation and he was forced to leave through the north door, at which point he was dehorsed by one of the guards, who broke his saddle girths. His companions charged and scattered the pursuers, and Robert, in a bravura display of athletic horsemanship, clapped his saddle on his horse, vaulted on without aid of stirrup or girth and galloped away. The group killed a sentinel who tried to block their flight, and they returned to Belle Isle by 2 p.m. In this, the primary account on which all others are based, there is no mention of the helmet or sword.

By and large eighteenth-century writers such as William Gilpin and Thomas West followed Machel's description. But the episode proved irresistible to storytellers of all classes. In 1813 Walter Scott changed the personnel and places and reversioned the story for Rokeby, his epic poem of the Civil War:

> All eyes upon the gate-way hung,
> When through the Gothic arch there sprung
> A Horseman armed, at headlong speed –
> Sable his cloak, his plume, his steed.

In his notes to the poem, Scott claimed that at Kendal Philipson had 'discharged a pistol at his enemy's head. In turning his horse it fell upon the pavement, notwithstanding which

Above: Holy Trinity Church, Kendal: wide, weird and wonderful.

Right and below: Three of the dozens of gargoyles on Holy Trinity Church, Kendal.

Left: The supposed Civil War helmet and sword of 'Robin the Devil' – actually nineteenth century additions, Holy Trinity Church.

Below: One of the several angels with the symbols of the Passion on the roof of the Parr Chapel, Holy Trinity Church.

he was able to raise the animal with the rein and spur, and rode out of the church as safely as he had entered.' All of which is Scott's invention. There was also a popular ballad, Dickon and the Devil, recorded in 1850 by 'YAC' who remembered being told it in childhood by his nurse. Here, the story by now was that Philipson had lost his helmet:

BALLAD OF DICK AND THE DEVIL

> The door was wide, and in does he ride,
> In his clanking gear so gay;
> A long keen brand he held in his hand,
> Our Dickon for to slay.
>
> But Dickon goodhap he was not there,
> And Robin he rode in vain,
> And the men got up that were kneeling in prayer,
> To take him by might and main.

Rob swung his sword, his steed he spurred,
He plunged right through the thrang.
But the stout smith Jock, with his old mother's crutch,
He gave him a woundy bang.

So hard he smote the iron pot,
It came down plume and all;
Then with bare head away Robin sped,
And himself was fit to fall.

This ballad was in *Notes & Queries* No. 29, Saturday 18 May 1850.

There was certainly a helmet in the church by the early nineteenth century, although no one could say for certain from whence it came. It may have been found elsewhere and brought into the church as 'proof' of the story. So by now the helmet existed in both physical and folkloric form. In 1861 Cornelius Nicholson wrote in *Annals of Kendal* that it was known as 'the Rebel's Cap' and that it had been knocked off when the mounted Cavalier's head hit the doorway. But where had the sword come from? In 1900 John Curwen's *Kirkbie Kendall* gave the answer. At the time the helmet hung above the Bellingham tomb – and for a time it was thought to have belonged to Sir Roger Bellingham. In 1863 John Broadbent, a descendant of the Bellinghams, was upgrading the tomb; he had brought a sword from London, and thought it would be fitting to place it above his noble ancestor's remains.

So the helmet probably appeared in the early nineteenth century, and the sword is definitely a Victorian addition, several hundred years after the original incident.

Right: Enigmatic stone head on an internal column, Holy Trinity Church.

Below: Simulacrum of an Impressionist painting of a Lakeland scene. The river on the right, the fell to the left, the clouds above. On column in centre aisle, Holy Trinity Church.

LOWTHER STREET, KENDAL

A statue of a Turk marks the entrance to Gawith Snuff Works.

STRICKLANDGATE, KENDAL

A plaque on a building in Angel Court off Stricklandgate marks the site of the former Angel Inn, supposedly named after a protective spirit that rescued a child from the clutches of Bonnie Prince Charlie's bloodthirsty Highlanders. The pub was demolished in the mid-twentieth century.

STRAMONGATE, KENDAL

The anonymously-published *Legends of Westmorland and the Lake District* (1874) is the source of many of the ghost stories that are now told about Kendal and area. The problem with this book is that there is nothing to anchor any of the tales in other written sources, and so there is the distinct possibility that the author simply made it all up. It describes the Stramongate Barghaist as a dual ghost, being both the spirit of a woman who came from the castle to care for the poor during a time of famine and plague, and her faithful dog. She was murdered near Blackhall Yard and the hound still whines for its mistress here, before letting out a howl and returning to the castle between midnight and dawn.

Very solidly in Blackhall Yard is the 'bristling hog,' a black pig with bristles on its back, the sign of an old brush factory (now Halifax Property Services).

The church of Holy Trinity and St George at 33 Blackhall Road has a statue of St George dispatching a diminutive dragon on the main gable, and another St George (with Crusader's shield but *sans* dragon) within.

WILDMAN STREET, KENDAL

The Castle Dairy at No. 26, now an upmarket restaurant, is Kendal's oldest inhabited building. It was probably originally a fourteenth-century dowery or dowerhouse – a dwelling granted to widows associated with the castle – and was remodelled and extended for merchant Anthony Garnett in the sixteenth century. It is full of intriguing details. Near the main door is a panel incised with the initials 'AG' and the date 1564 with what looks like a cord of knots. The windows to the left have carved faces. Another window has the very weathered inscription *Qui Vadit Plane Vadit Sane* – 'he who walks plainly, walks sanely.' The south-west wing has a cobbled floor, probably medieval, but which is claimed to be a Roman road. The first-floor bedroom in the north-east wing contains Anthony Garnett's four-poster bed with a headboard carved with three lion heads and two male heads, one of which has rat-like ears while the other sports a set of horns. Adjacent is a large ambry or cupboard with a lion's head and the inscription *Oia Vanitas Honor* [missing] *Divicie Potestas* ('All is Vanity: Honour, Wealth [and] Power'), an intriguingly reflective 'thought for the day' for a rich influential merchant. The ambry seems designed for a washing bowl – was this reminder of the transience of success the first thing he saw when he got up in the morning? The wooden supports of the vaulted ceiling have two bosses with coats of arms, and one corbel has a pair of griffons. Of the four tiny stained-glass windows, two have an eagle or vulture sitting on the circular canopy of a tree, with one claw on an infant in swaddling clothes and a papoose, and another has a miniscule grinning skull below the initials 'AG' interlaced with a knotted cord, and the phrases *Omnia Vanitas* ('all is vanity') and *Viendra le jour* ('comes the day'), both standard meditations on death and mortality.

In 'Five Specters on a Roman Road,' an article in *Fate* magazine (April 1998), Kenneth Nickel interviewed the owner Elaine Wright. She told him that on two occasions, several years apart, a group of five men had been seen sitting around a fireplace that doesn't exist anymore. Both times they were spotted by two people, but the others in their parties – another four and two respectively – saw nothing. One of those who did witness something asked if the five men were going to a fancy-dress party. There were also tales of marching Roman soldiers seen cut off under the knees, as if the ground level had changed since their vitae. In 1999 Tony Walker stated that apparitions of Romans had been seen several times, and other spectral visitors included a scullery maid and a respectable Victorian gent. As is compulsory with old buildings, there has been a long-term (and totally fatuous) rumour of a subterranean passage to the castle.

In 1981 the *Westmorland Gazette* reported on poltergeist activity in the Copper Kettle, a now-vanished café in Wildman Street. On one occasion one of the staff was pushed down-stairs by unseen hands, the lights having just gone out. She said she could feel the imprint of the hand for two hours thereafter.

KENDAL MUSEUM, STATION ROAD, KENDAL

Open Thursday-Saturday 12 p.m.-5 p.m. Admission charge. Wheelchair access to ground floor (Wainwright and World Wildlife Galleries) only.

THE WAINWRIGHT GALLERY
Named after A. Wainwright, who was the museum's Curator, this gallery gives a good overview of the archaeology of the area, as well as providing a home for the museum's 'curiosities'. There is also a recreation of Wainwright's office – you feel as if the fell-walking curmudgeon has just popped out for a moment. Highlights of the collection include:

The Neiros Cup of Fortune – an Edwardian cup and saucer designed for reading tealeaves, complete with its book of instructions. The saucer is decorated with zodiac signs, while the cup has the astrological emblems of the planets and a variety of symbols, some obvious, some cryptic – horseshoe, letter, glass, heart, bell, spades, snake, diamond, trefoil, eye, a circle with three unequal spokes radiating out, a piece of string(?) and the symbols + and)-(.

A dobby stone – an apotropaic charm used to ward away witches.

A wonderful tenth-century Hiberno-Norse stone carving of the Crucifixion, unique in England. Christ is shown on the cross with an angel above each arm, and three soldiers below.

A branks or scold's bridle – an orally invasive iron device used to punish gossiping women – and an iron girdle used with a ducking stool. The band was placed around the waist and the hands imprisoned in the attached metal cuffs.

A mummy's blackened and shrunken hand and toes. This is part of a modest collection of Egyptian items including a mummified hawk, shabti figures, a pair of small fertility figurines, a private wooden altar and reports from a 1901 excavation.

A very good diorama of a life-size Neolithic man working with stone tools beneath a skin shelter. This is associated with a display on Mesolithic and Neolithic technology, including Lake District stone axes, and other tools and weapons from the Neolithic to the Iron Age.

Objects from the Roman site of El Djem in Tunisia, including a lead curse tablet.

A display on Roman death and burial, featuring a portable stone domestic altar, three cremation urns, one containing bones, an altar, an inscribed memorial stone to ex-centurion P. Aelius Bassus, and a headless statue of the god Bacchus, the last three from the fort at Watercrook on the southern edge of Kendal (SD513907). Other Roman items include coins, a finger ring with an intaglio of Achilles (which may have served as both a signet and a protective charm), a slave shackle, a caltrop, catapult bolts, arrowheads, spikes and nails, as well as a 'face jar' with a crude face pinched out of the clay.

A model of the main gate at HARDKNOTT FORT.

A Viking sword and a bowl mount decorated with a tiny head.

A pre-Reformation wooden figure of Christ.

A Bellarmine jar (see PENRITH MUSEUM for a discussion of their magical use). The fact that it was found in the wall of a house (in Stramongate) may suggest it had an apotropaic function.

A Jacobite hand grenade.

A gamekeeper's mantrap, 6ft (1.8m) long, not designed with the comfort of the poacher in mind.

Two thumbscrews.

Grizzly bear, serval and white vole; crocodile and dolphin skulls; shark jaws; three sawfish saws; and a large pike.

The mongoose that was used by Wainwright as the model for his illustrations in Molly Lefebure's *Scratch & Co.* (see SCAFELL).

A model of the dinosaur Megalosaurus.

A very large Brain Coral. It is aptly named.

A nineteenth-century Pre-Raphaelite head of Christ, bizarrely found in a roadside tip at Endmoor near Kendal.

Another interesting item on display is a Sheela-na-gig found in PENNINGTON church. Crude in both senses of the term, the Sheela has pointed ears, a masculine-looking face, bared teeth and angled arms pointing to a well-marked vulva. Barbara Freitag's 1994 *Sheela-na-gigs: Unravelling an Enigma* traces its history. In 1925 workmen repairing the church found it on the hidden side of a stone used for a quoin (an angle-stone). They were so shocked at the sight of it they almost destroyed the carving, but a foreman intervened. In December 1925 Canon Kenworthy reported on the find in the *Pennington*

Parish Magazine, and an account was published in *A Furness Manor: Pennington and its Church* (1929) by A. Fell, and in the *Barrow News* for 14 September 1929, the latter also by Kenworthy. Kenworthy surmised that the stone had been reversed in 1826, when the church had been almost entirely rebuilt with much re use of the original medieval stones. Freitag dug up an account by Andy Roberts, who visited Pennington in the late 1920s and was told by an old resident that the local people had always called the sculpture Freya, a Norse goddess (in a deliciously accidental link, Freitag's surname is German for Friday, the day of the week named after Freya). The implication was that the Norse settlers in the area had been ambivalent about Christianity, and had inserted the figure of a pagan earth mother goddess into the church 'just to make sure.' This notion of Norse cultural survival is supported by an inscription in the church's tympanum, which is written in Scandinavian runes and dated to the mid-twelfth century, a period by which most religious inscriptions elsewhere were in Latin. In a 1983 article in the journal *Folklore* Richard Bailey noted that in 1979 he too was told by a resident that the local name for the carving was Freya. Bailey also discovered that despite the CWAAS having made a field-trip to Pennington, there was no mention of the Sheela in the Society's official account of the visit, or even in the comprehensive inventory of Westmorland antiquities. It was as if the respectable members of the CWAAS were embarrassed by the figure and wished to forget about it. Freitag says that the sculpture was allegedly removed from the church to the museum because the Pennington parson thought that the pagan image 'might put a curse on people.' Freya was associated with fertility, and the Sheela's vulva may show signs of rubbing; in *The Earth Goddess* (1991) Cheryl Straffon records that at some point before 1991 the sheela was taken out and exhibited at a village festival, after which several local women became pregnant, including the vicar's wife.

THE WORLD WILDLIFE GALLERY

Here you can see a Thylacine, the extinct-or-is-it? 'Tasmanian Wolf' (see KESWICK MUSEUM for much more on Thylacines). Possibly a young specimen, it looks smaller and far less ferocious than the few other stuffed specimens elsewhere. This specimen was donated by Dr W.R. Parker in 1940.

There is also a model of an alethiometer, a compass-like device known as a 'truth teller'. The alethiometer is a key element in Philip Pullman's incomparable fantasy trilogy *Dark Materials*, where it guides the adventures of the heroine, Lyra Belacqua. This model, made as part of a school project, cleverly suggests the alethiometer was discovered locally in 1883 and comes complete with a fire-damaged box and several other items mentioned in the epic. The zoological exhibits have been rearranged so that the device is guarded by two characters from the book, a polar bear and Mrs Coulter's 'Golden Monkey' daemon.

The rest of the gallery provokes both wonder and melancholy, because behind the superb display of animals and birds from every continent is the knowledge that many were slaughtered for sport by big game hunters, and a number are now extinct or severely endangered. The gallery's interpretation takes a more enlightened view and highlights conservation issues.

The highlights from the upstairs displays include an enormous giant elk skull and antlers, and 'The Helsfell mystery,' a display of the many mammal bones – including a complete wolf skeleton – found in the nineteenth century in a cavity in Helsfell Point, Kendal Fell. The bones have been dated to around 8000 BC.

CASTLE STREET, KENDAL

St George's Church dates from 1841. In September 1998 journalist Jeremy Craddock of the *Warrington Guardian* interviewed the then vicar, Canon Dr Alan Billings. At several houses in Kendal, Billings had been asked to perform a blessing in order to clear unwanted presences. A woman restoring a late eighteenth-century fireplace felt she had disturbed the spirits of the former residents, and became aware of an invisible presence when alone. Her father witnessed doors mysteriously opening and weights from weighing scales being moved. In another house a couple were forced out by scratchings in the walls, sudden drops in temperature and the sense of somebody crossing the bedroom and passing through the wall. And a distressed Hindu family felt their house was 'somehow wishing them ill.' Dr Billings explained the process of the blessing, which involved going from room to room reading a Biblical verse, saying a short prayer, sprinkling holy water and wafting incense. Dr Billings is now retired as an Anglican vicar and is the Director of the Centre for Ethics and Religion at Lancaster University.

AYNAM ROAD, KENDAL

Bearded male and crowned female heads decorate the former chapel of the Victorian Sleddal Almshouses. Building on the town's long history of weaving, William Palmer noted that old buildings sometimes hummed with the sound of spectral hand-looms. Sometime in the distant past the widow of an old weaver was told his spirit was still working away next to the river. Her response? 'Johnty never liked work so much that he would do it after he was dead. It would be more natural for him to come in grumbling that his dinner or his drink wasn't ready.' There speaks a voice from the heart. Palmer noticed that there were no ghostly tanners or dyers, probably because their jobs were too smelly to appeal to the high-falutin' denizens of the spirit world.

LOUND ROAD, KENDAL

'Empty cars collide in Kendal.' Such was the headline in the *Westmorland Gazette* on 8 April 2008. Two unoccupied cars, an Audi and a Rover, had collided in the lane at the back of Lound Road.

KIRKBARROW LANE (OFF KIRKLAND)

Near the top of this narrow lane is the Anchorite Well, a possible holy well also known as St Mary's Well, which may be near the site of the first Saxon church built in Kendal. Certainly records show an 'anchorite's house' next to St Mary's Chantry in 1430. Both well and chantry probably declined after the Reformation and the church has now been swept away by housing development, although bones have been dug up several times in the Cross Lane/Chapel Lane area, site of the old cemetery.

The 'traditional' story told of the anchorite himself was recounted in *Legends of Westmorland*, although the author candidly stately he couldn't remember where he had heard the details, or even if he had 'merely dreamed of them, sleeping, or awake.' So the whole tale could be his invention, built up from the scant historical details known about the well. In the latter part of the fourteenth century a man arrived in pilgrim's garb, built a beehive hut and devoted his time to helping lepers and cripples. Eventually he dressed in the white cassock of a penitent. He was deemed a holy man, and the spring became regarded as a site of miraculous healing. After several blameless decades he confessed on his deathbed that he was Julian de Clifford, member a noble family, and that he was a murderer. Blanche of Kendal Castle had married his brother instead of him and so he killed them both and buried the bodies beside the well, where he later worked to absolve his guilt ('Lift the stone, that with the ring at the foot of my couch, and you will find the coffin in which their remains still moulder.') A mawkishly sentimental coda, possibly invented by William Palmer in *The Verge of Lakeland* (1938) says that twice a year, on the anniversaries of the murder and Julian's death, the ghosts of his brother and Blanche were supposed to return to the well and forgive the anchorite. The well has been restored in recent years.

EAST BANKS, KENDAL

No. 21 sports a finial in the form of the figure of architect Miles Thompson, erected in 1870 by his brother Robert. In 1998 the figure blew down so the Kendal Civic Society replaced it with a terracotta copy. A footpath leads to Castle Howe, Kendal's first castle, now just an earthen motte. It may date to 1092, during the first Norman occupation. The place names nearby – Battle Place and Catcastle (a 'cat' is a siege engine) – support the tradition that a battle was fought here and possibly destroyed the wooden castle. Arthur Nicholl's *Kendal Town Trail* notes that bones have been found in the area and 'young children have been known to become slightly disturbed while walking there. Perhaps they are more sensitive to the atmosphere.' In 1788, to celebrate the centenary of the Glorious Revolution of 1688, an obelisk inscribed 'sacred to liberty' was erected on the summit.

FELLSIDE, KENDAL

The area north of Beast Banks was formerly a sloping slum, built on the steep hillside between Kendal Fell and the river valley. The streets were just narrow cobbled passageways, overcrowded and filthy. The Skye beck, a common sewer, flowed down Syke Lane into Maude's Meadow. When St Thomas' Church was built nearby in 1837 it was found that part of the chosen site was just a 12ft (3.7m) deep peaty mass of compacted faeces. It was too soft to build on so the location was changed. The evocatively-named Sepulchre Lane was named after a Quaker burial ground of 1666, now gone.

In the seventeenth century there was a great fascination with what were called 'prodigies', extremes of human or animal behaviour or anatomy. One such class of prodigies were 'fasters', people who appeared to eat very little or even nothing. There is a remarkable example entitled 'the Fasting Woman of Westmoreland' in *The Diary and Correspondence of Dr John Worthington*, published in 1847. In a letter to Samuel Hartlib dated 24 June 1661 Worthington included an account sent to him by a friend who had gone to Kendal specifically to view the woman:

> The woman (who is about a mile from this town) about fifteen years since buried a child whom she dearly loved, and returning home, expressed her discontent in these words,

'That God had now done his worst to her that he could.' She continued well a good while after; but within a year she fell into a deep melancholy, which brought her into that condition wherein she now lies; and in which she hath continued fourteen years. I went about a year since to see her; and had this account of her, beside what mine own eyes informed me of her. She eats not anything, only 2 or 3 spoonfuls of milk each day before twelve a clock; (for after that hour she will eat nothing.) She hath no evacuations. Her body is much worn (except her face, which is somewhat fleshy and fresh) and as cold as clay. She moves not ordinarily, but as she is moved by others, Yet twice she leapt out of bed, and was met out of the chamber upon her hands and feet; which was occasioned the one time by an extraordinary noise of an hue and cry passing by; and the other time by a sudden breaking in of light, the curtain of the window falling down. When I was with her, one took her by the hand, and she endeavoured to bite him. She sometimes groans much. There is an unpleasing smell comes from her; yet not so bad as might be expected. They have formerly had physitians, and (lest any means should be wanting, right or wrong) popish priests and conjurers; who have told them, 'tis a mere corpse kept in its form by the power of the devil; and that it may continue so till Domes-day.

That phrase ''tis a mere corpse kept in its form by the power of the devil;' is a nice touch.

The *Sunday People* for 14 July 1974 reported the case of Derek Halliwell, who was driving his empty taxi between Kendal and Kirkby Lonsdale when he glanced in the mirror and saw a woman on the back seat. He stopped, looked around, but the seat was empty. Another mile further on he saw the woman again in his mirror – but she was not in the seat. Her image persisted in the mirror even after Derek wiped it. Then she vanished again, this time for good.

Following the *Westmorland Gazette* ('Yoga outstripping church worship') on 15 October 2004, most UK broadsheets – and BBC1's *Newsnight* – reported on the Kendal Project, a Lancaster University research project which studied the current state of religion and spirituality in the town and treated it as a microcosm of the UK. The study, and the subsequent book *The Spiritual Revolution: Why Religion is Giving Way to Spirituality*, by Paul Heelas and Linda Woodhead, claimed that traditional Christianity had lost so much ground to alternative beliefs – including yoga, tarot, Reiki, Alexander technique, herbalism, Buddhism and paganism – that if the relative decline and growth continued at the same rate, alternative spirituality would eclipse Christianity in the 2030s, an event the authors termed 'the spiritual revolution.'

On 5 October 1869 the *Carlisle Journal* reported a shower of spiders' webs over Kendal. Earlier large numbers of spiders had fallen from the sky over Carlisle. It was in the newspaper – it must be true.

Big black cats have frequently been seen around Kendal. The *Westmorland Gazette* logged sightings at the back of the Helm, near Oxenholme (10 April 2002, reported 19 April), in the Heron Hill estate towards Esthwaite Green (7 March 2003, reported 13 March), in Kendal (28 July 2006), and in the Castle Green Lane area (4 August 2006). Note that several of these locations are in built-up areas. Two correspondents in the *Big Cats in Britain Yearbook* 2007 recorded sightings at New Hutton, Old Hutton and Killington, and Low Fold farm, Kendal. In all cases the cat was described as large and black, and either puma- or panther-like.

UNDERBARROW

Legends of Westmorland has the tale of the Leyburnes of Cunswick Hall (SD485934, private). Sometime in the Middle Ages Roger de Leyburne acquired his inheritance by murdering his father, Sir Charles, claiming he had been swept away in a flood. Two of Sir Charles' friends accidentally found his body by the riverside; the corpse was perfectly preserved, in keeping with the common belief that God would not permit the decay of the body of a suicide or victim of 'unnatural' murder until such time as the person would have died naturally. The stab wound being clearly visible, Roger confessed, and, being a church-hating bad egg, killed the monk who had come to attend him, before dying himself. A prophecy was recalled, saying that one Leyburne would disgrace the family name and his bones would 'whiten the rocks of Cunswick Scar,' while his spirit would haunt the Scar and the Hall. Once again, the whole thing may be fiction. William Palmer, in *The Verge of Lakeland*, adds the detail that Roger's body, being under an interdict for the murder of the priest, was refused burial in consecrated ground. The funeral party were heading back towards Cunswick Hall when they were overtaken by a storm. The corpse was abandoned and never recovered, the bones then being scattered over Cunswick Scar (SD492937) by animals, thus fulfilling the prophecy.

North of the Hall in the field centred at SD487938, west of Cunswick Tarn, are several pillow mounds, medieval artificial rabbit warrens.

It was once common to inform the bees when a death occurred in the household. In 1916 this happened at a farm in Underbarrow, as recalled by Marjorie Rowling's husband in her *Folklore of the Lake District*. The hive was gently tapped and the bees told what had happened. Later they were given crumbs from the funeral feast. If neither of these customs had been observed, the bees would have departed. Rowling also wrote that a fire in Tullithwaite Hall (SD473909) never went out for a hundred years, but the Women's Institute records where this was noted did not give the dates.

CROSTHWAITE

The 1878 church has wooden angels on its roof supports. *Cumbria Within Living Memory*, published by the Cumbria Federations of Women's Institutes in 2005, records that around 1927 a thunderbolt landed in Crosthwaite, creating a furrow along the road and setting fire to the choir stalls in the church, so services had to be held in the Memorial Hall. The lightning knocked down a farmer and killed a cow, and a woman at Tarnside Farm 750yds (686m) away was thrown across the room by another strike, which also made cracks in the walls.

In 1841 local man William Pearson submitted a paper entitled 'A Sketch of some of the Existing and Recent Superstitions of Westmoreland' to the Kendal Natural History Society. Within living memory fire sacrifices had been practised at Fell Side in Crosthwaite (S(445900) and Hodge Hill on CARTMEL FELL (SD419882), where, to prevent the death of calves after birth, large fires were set near to the farmhouse and a living calf burnt to death. Pearson had talked with a farmer who had actually been present at one of the ceremonies. On 15 November 1840 Pearson witnessed the Needfire in Crosthwaite. It had been set in the narrow Kirk Lane, where about half a dozen cattle were hemmed in and being given a 'good smoke.' The Needfire had come from Crook and had previously been at Low Levens. Pearson's article was extensively discussed by H.D. Rawnsley in *Lake Country Sketches* (1903).

A Crosthwaite respondent to a survey conducted by L.F. Newman and E.M. Wilson in 1951 for the journal *Folklore* recorded that a phantom black dog had been seen 'some years ago in the Lyth valley.'

CROOK

Footpaths lead to the slightly surreal sight of St Catherine's Church (SD450947), a tower and oval churchyard wall that is all that remains of a church built in 1620 and demolished in 1887. There are no gravestones. This is a strange, lonely and lovely place.

BURNESIDE

A malevolent headless dog goes for walkies around Eggholme. The Elba Monument at SD496951 just north of Plumgarths roundabout on the A591 was erected in 1814 by local Tories as a riposte to the 'liberty' monument on Castle Howe. It was meant to mark the imprisonment of Napoleon on Elba, but rather embarrassingly the wily old coyote escaped and went back on the warpath again, so the planned inscription was ditched. It took another century for it to actually be installed.

STAVELEY

A tale of (very) bad fairies is told in *Legends of Westmorland*. Simon Bell, a guard from Kendal Castle, was on the road just south-east of Staveley when he spied 'a band of dry-bellied, lantern-visaged Scots, all below the middle stature, all dressed in tartan, all carrying meagre rush lights in their hands.' The horde were running noiselessly, without bagpipe, drum, clank of weaponry or even footsteps. Terrified, Simon hid, until noticed by a 'little old gentleman, and as the latter raised his head, he perceived that he had two horns on his forehead, eyes set round with fiery eyelashes, a tail whisking nimbly under his kilt, and a couple of cloven feet for supporters.' Simon's panicked mare plunged into the throng, which unhorsed him and knocked him senseless. The next morning he walked to the castle and told his story. When, a year later, Kendal was ravaged by a Scots horde, all the remaining cattle went down with murrain, the crops were mildewed, and many people died of disease and hunger, Simon's fairy (or demonic) troop were viewed as supernatural harbingers of these various disasters. As with all the stories in this anonymous book, however, it's quite possible that the author simply made this episode up.

THE A6 NORTH OF KENDAL

A chapel once stood behind Skelsmergh Hall Farm (SD531959). Although many early churches were built near the site of wells and springs – here both the chapel and spring were dedicated to John the Baptist – this is the only case I know of where the stream actually ran through the chapel. A wooden floor prevented the congregation from getting their feet wet while at worship. There were still some parts standing when Thomas Machel visited in 1690 but nothing now remains of the chapel or the adjacent cemetery. In the sixteenth century a ghost at Selside Hall (SD535990) liked nothing better than to blow out candles and lamps. It appears to have been confounded by the advent of electricity.

LONGSLEDDALE

In the 1750s or so Dr Linkbarrow of Murthwaite (NY514007) had a reputation as a practitioner of magic (this probably just meant that he owned a few books and had a knowledge of healing). Sullivan's *Cumberland and Westmorland, Ancient and Modern* quoted an account of Linkbarrow from the *Kendal Mercury* of 1856. Whilst he was at church, an unnaturally strong storm blew up. Suspecting something was amiss, the doctor headed home, only to be waylaid by the Devil just below Beech Hill bridge. Curiously, His Satanic Majesty begged for work (the Devil is of course the master of dissimulation: if the one who has raised him cannot provide a task that justifies the journey from hell, Satan is entitled to claim his soul as compensation). Linkbarrow ordered Auld Horny to make a rope of sand (a common task for inconvenient fairies and demons). The Evil One asked for straw, which was refused him. This was clearly a common story: in *The Remains of John Briggs* (1825) an almost exact duplicate is told of Cockerham school near Lancaster. On his arrival at Murthwaite, the doctor found a servant in the study, surreptitiously reading a chained book. It was this imprudence that had caused the storm and Satan's arrival, so Longbarrow ejected the prying fool, and through his magic arts allayed the storm (and presumably returned the Devil to his lair).

The *Mercury* account included several more of Longbarrow's exploits, including his ability to recover stolen goods. As he lay on his deathbed, a white and a black pigeon engaged in combat on the roof of his house. When Longbarrow learned that the black bird had killed its opponent, he cried, 'It's all over with me, then!' and promptly expired. There is also a brief mention of another eighteenth-century 'wiseman', whose book, inscribed 'Dr. Fairer's book of Black Art', was apparently still in existence in the 1850s, 'Until very lately it was believed there was great danger in opening this book.' The work seems to have been a kind of jotter, mostly concerned with astrology. Where is it now?

Henry Cowper found an entry in the Hawkshead parish accounts for 1786: 'Journey horse hire and expenses to Eliner Preston to take her child to Mr. Kellet's of Long Sleddale to be cured of a scabbed head 2s.6d.' At the time a doctor was resident in Hawkshead, so the pilgrimage to Longsleddale must have been to visit an alternative practitioner, presumably a wiseman.

In *Robert Elsmere*, an 1888 novel by Mrs Humphry Ward (Mary Augusta Arnold), the servant girl Mary Backhouse, pregnant and betrayed, meets the bogle of Deep Crag, the ghost of a girl who had killed herself and her baby, and now walks on High Fell at Midsummer Eve. 'If you see her and she passes you in silence, why you only got a fright for your pains. But if she speaks to you, you die within the year.' Mary procures an abortion, and then declines physically and mentally, fixated on the idea that she will be dead by the following Midsummer Eve. Up among the lonely fells and tarns the main character, Robert Elsmere, muses on the way the landscape affects the imagination, 'How easily, with a mind attuned, one could people this whole path with ghosts!' The novel's setting, 'Long Whindale' is Longsleddale, and 'High Fell', the home of the bogle, is Harter Fell (NY460096).

GRAYRIGG

Thiselton Dyer's *Strange Pages from Family Papers* (1895) relishes in tales of posh families afflicted by curses, and he tells one of Justice Duckett of Grayrigg Hall. In the seventeenth century, when Quakers were widely persecuted, Duckett had jailed, among others, Francis Howgill. Howgill called on the judge at the Hall and uttered a prophecy:

> I am come with a message from the Lord. Thou hast persecuted the Lord's people, but His hand
> is now against thee, and He will send a blast upon all that thou hast, and thy name shall rot out of
> the earth, and this thy dwelling shall become desolate, and a habitation for owls and jackdaws.

All Duckett's children died without leaving any issue and several ended up in poverty, one even becoming a beggar. The imposing Grayrigg Hall passed to the Lowther family, who dismantled it, little more than its foundations being visible in 1777. After decades of the ruins being the 'habitation of owls and jackdaws,' they were removed altogether and a farmhouse erected upon the site. The Quaker's Curse had allegedly been fulfilled.

OLD HUTTON

In 1636 an apotropaic dobbie stone was brought to Bleaze Hall (SD 549891, private). Marjorie Rowling in *The Folklore of the Lake District* describes it as a prehistoric perforated stone hammerhead. Its purpose may have been to manage the route of a phantom funeral procession of a lady of the house who died of a broken heart when her lover did not return from the Crusades. The cortège has been seen passing around the Hall, but not since the early twentieth century at the latest, although a respondent to the *Folklore* survey claimed in 1952: 'When anyone is going to die at Bleaze Hall a coffin appears in the air in the farm-yard.' The dobbie stone is still hanging from the rafters, and ill luck will attend anyone who removes it from the house. In 2008 Bleaze Hall was on the market; the particulars noted that the stone was included in the sale.

More big black cats have been spotted around this area. All the following reports come from the *Westmoreland Gazette*: near junction 36 of the M6 (September 2000, and 26 November 2000, reported 1 December); near Holme (October 2000); Cracalt Farm, Natland (12 August 2002, reported 16 August); Burton Road near Oxenholme (January 2002); near Endmoor (January 2002); and in a field at the end of Popplemire Lane, Old Hutton (11 August 2006). In October 2000 plaster casts were taken of two massive paw prints in a garden at Gatebeck near Endmoor (reported 23 July 2004). A respondent to the 1951 survey for *Folklore* claimed: 'There is a black dog at Channel Hall, Endmoor. Several people have seen it run along the wall.'

CROOKLANDS

A corbel beneath an empty niche in St Patrick's Church (SD 537836) is carved with a demonic Green Man associated with a tongue-poking devil and an owl with a cloven hoof.

The heads of a king, queen, monk and nun decorate the exterior and there are gargoyles on the tower. The church was originally dedicated to St Gregory; St Gregory's Well, formerly used for baptisms, is on the path 150yds (137m) east.

SIZERGH CASTLE

This deservedly popular medieval-Elizabethan stately home (SD498878. National Trust. Open Easter-End of October 1 p.m.-5 p.m. – gardens from 11 a.m. – Monday-Thursday and Sunday. Admission free. Wheelchair access to some of the Gardens and ground floor of Castle only.) is peppered with grotesque carvings in dark wood. On the entrance porch is a lion's head on the central beam, and the carved doorway is flanked by two monsters with foliate back ends. In the hall there are two cherubs in mirror frame. The Dining Room has a wonderful overmantel with: two pairs of naked female and male torsos; a youth's head whose ears give rise to a duo of almost reptilian quasi-foliate lions; a Green Demon with goat's horns and ears spewing foliage; and a goat eating or spewing vegetation. In the Queen's Room the overmantel has: a shield supported by a lion and a dragon; two Green Men each with a flower sticking out of its mouth; a pair of human-looking lion heads spewing vegetation; and male and female figures. High up is a helmeted 'Pan' head hidden in foliage. Because the room was briefly occupied by Katharine Parr, a fatuous myth has grown up that her spirit is still active here.

In the Old Dining Room the overmantel features: female figures emerging from foliage; two bearded Green Men; and a pair of beasts spewing foliage. A goat-eared foliate head perches above the doorway to the Linen Fold Room, the corridor from which has panels of seventeenth-century stained glass that include heads, cherubs and lions along with a demonic bull. The bed in the Bindloss Room is made from a pre-Reformation pew reclaimed from Kendal church and has a quartet of heads on its bedboard. The Boynton Room contains several humans emerging from foliage on the overmantel, which also sports a grotesque bearded head and a pair of ape-headed birds. The Inlaid Chamber has horned goat-eared heads, which decorate the bedposts.

Sizergh is supposedly haunted by a woman screaming to be released from the room in which she was locked while her bloke went off to fight the foe. This story seems to have all the hallmarks of a legend of the 'it's a spooky castle so it must have a ghost' variety, and 'jealous husband imprisons wife' is a folktale motif with dozens of parallels in castles elsewhere. Peter Underwood, in *This Haunted Isle*, relates an undated, unprovenanced story of floorboards being repeatedly pulled up over an unspecified period, with the replaced boards always being disturbed again. No member of the managerial and volunteer staff I questioned had ever heard of this episode.

The BBC website http://news.bbc.co.uk on 7 March 2004 reported that a couple walking near the castle spotted a South American coati (for more coati sightings see GRASMERE).

LEVENS HALL (SD496851)

Open early April-early October Sunday-Thursday 12 p.m.-4.30 p.m. (Gardens open from 10 a.m.). Admission charge. Wheelchair access to gardens only.

Levens is a magnificent Elizabethan mansion with a medieval core. The gardens are justifiably famous, with more than ninety topiaries in the form of pyramids, columns, domes and other more abstract shapes, described in 1901 by A.G. Bradley in *Highways and Byways in the Lake District* as a 'quaint company of cardinals' hats and lions, peacocks and umbrellas, pheasants, forensic wigs and what not.' The ensemble gives the impression of a giant surreal chess set. Several rooms have gloriously extravagant seventeenth-century wooden carvings – apparently Levens and SIZERGH were always trying to out-do each other. The Smoking Room mantelpiece has five oak figures, three of which represent Wisdom, Justice and Beauty. The Great Drawing Room has a triple-decker chimney decorated with heraldic panels, with more heraldry in the stained glass. Best of all is the Small Drawing Room where the chimneypiece is ably supported by Hercules (with lionskin and club) and Samson (with the jawbone of an ass) and features two panels with representations of the Four Elements and the Four Seasons, while five other figures embody the Five Senses, with Touch, Smell and Taste in one group and Hearing and Seeing reclining at the top. Sensational.

The Hall is famous for its ghosts and legends, which typically come in four formats: the Grey Lady, the little black dog, the Pink Lady, and the white deer. Throughout the country, the birth of a white fawn has often been regarded as an uncanny event, and has often prompted either older traditions to be revived, or the creation of new superstitions. John Curwen's *Historical Description of Levens Hall* (1898) traced the local belief – that the arrival of a white deer would herald a significant event for the family at Levens – to the 1850s, when Lord Templetown was in residence:

> A white buck which had appeared in the herd was ordered to be shot, but the keeper was so horrified with the deed, which he thought to be 'waur ner robbin' a church,' that he actually went so far as to remonstrate with the Crimean veteran [Templetown]. Persuasion being of no use, he at last refused point blank to do the deed himself, and another man had to do it for him. In a few months great troubles came over the house. In quick succession it changed hands twice; the stewards, servants, and gardeners all lost their places; and the keeper firmly held to the belief that all was due to the shooting of this white deer.

Three further white deer were born, in 1883 (supposedly linked to the death of Gen. Upton), 1885 (on the day after the wedding of the new owners, Capt. and Mrs Bagot) and February 1896, when Mrs Bagot bore a son.

At some point the story of the white deer became entwined with the ghost of a gypsy, known as the Grey Lady, although most of the Lakes writers of the time – usually more than happy to pass on any ghostly gossip – are silent on the subject. Even books which include the white deer – such as Daniel Scott's *Bygone Cumberland and Westmorland* (1899) – make no mention of the ghost. The general story is that the woman, refused food at the Hall, placed a curse on the family, saying that no male heir would appear until a white fawn should be born in the park and the River Kent cease flowing. She then expired, to forever haunt the place where she was denied charity.

I, however, smell a rat. In spring 1897 Mrs Humphry Ward rented Levens while writing *Helbeck of Bannisdale*, wherein the fictional Bannisdale Hall is, from many descriptions, clearly Levens. In the novel there is a brief mention of the gypsy's curse, which is vaguely linked with the ghostly 'Lady of Bannisdale'. Ward has the curse as having been placed some forty years previously – which, if she was relaying local lore as she does elsewhere in the novel, puts the events in the 1850s. The decade when the white fawn was shot. Gypsy curses are a cliché, and were already so well before Victorian times, although they are still a staple of certain kinds of ghost stories. I suggest that three different elements have been melded together in folk memory: the actual events of the birth and death of the white deer, an episode inevitably surrounded by a foreboding aura of omens and auguries; real or imagined sightings of a female ghost; and the gypsy curse, either based on a genuine confrontation with itinerants, or derived from the rich stew of readily available stories about gypsy magic. Somehow the three have come together in a resonant mix.

Of course, I could be wrong. During the winter of 1895-96 the River Kent froze over, more-or-less coincidently with the birth of the male Bagot heir. In 1990 Levens' owner Hal Bagot spoke to J.A. Brooks, author of *Britain's Haunted Heritage*, and related the following. Hal Bagot, born February 1946: the Kent was frozen and a white fawn was born. His son, Richard Bagot, born 12 December 1981: the river was again frozen solid, and another white deer appeared. And when she was seven years old, in 1954, Hal's sister Lisa saw the Grey Lady so clearly she could describe the spectre's clothes – straw hat, heavy skirt and boots, all consistent with a gypsy of the period, although it could also apply to many other working-class women. In the 1954 encounter the phantom passed through the wooden walls of the stable. Hal's wife was driving to the house when she saw a woman rounding a corner in front of her. She expected to pass her as she came round the corner but there was no one there. In 1971 a female figure – possibly the Grey Lady, possibly not – was almost hit by a motorist negotiating a narrow bridge near the house. The woman moved unnervingly quickly from the side to the centre of the road. The encounter was recorded in Andrew Green's *Ghosts of Today*, where he noted this particular traffic hazard had last been seen in 1972.

Green's *Ghosts of Today* and *Our Haunted Kingdom* also record another female spirit, the Pink Lady, named after her mop hat, apron and long pink-print maid's dress. In August 1972 Hal Bagot's wife Annette told Green that some time previously a visiting party from the Women's Institute had seen her on the stairs, and he noted two other sightings by visitors in 1973. Her favoured locations included the hall and garden.

Andrew Green also recorded the visitations of the playful little black dog. According to Annette Bagot he was Levens' most frequent visitor, rushing down the staircase, confusing guests, and entering bedrooms and then disappearing. And there were named witnesses. He was seen by Don Stonor when he met Mrs Bagot in the village in the 1950s, when it appeared completely real to him. Visitors Raymond Leppard, Miss Rujickora and Harry Killard had also seen the dog, as had Annette Bagot. Hal told Brooks that in about 1980 a visitor was taking photographs of his family on the front steps when the entire group spotted the creature happily posing for the camera. Where are those photographs now?

Brooks' *Britain's Haunted Heritage* also describes a ghost which has not really made it to the Levens list of famous apparitions. Sometime before Hal Bagot was born, a priest on a sickbed visit heard a harpsichord being played in one of the rooms. After his visit, with the music still playing, he went into the library where Mrs Bagot was taking tea by candlelight because of a power cut. So how was it, the priest asked, that the harpsichord player he had just passed was wreathed in light? To which the answer was, of course, 'what harpsichord player?' Everyone promptly went upstairs, where there was no light, and no music.

In *The Folklore of the Lake District* Marjorie Rowling mentions two dobbie Stones at Nether Levens (SD488851); these particular apotropaic items were pieces of limestone with water-worn holes. The fragmentary ruins of the old Nether Levens Hall sit next

Sizergh Castle.

to the farm. In 1825 the *Gentleman's Magazine* noted that 'the side of the Kent is famous for petrifying springs that incrust vegetable bodies, one of them is called the "dropping [or dripping] well",' although I have been unable to locate this marvel.

WITHERSLACK

The craze for 'taking the waters' briefly led to the exploitation of the 'Holy Well' from 1656. The water was both laxative and purging; the well, which was about a mile (1.6km) has long since evacuated.

6

THE SOUTH-WEST
AND SOUTH

GRANGE-OVER-SANDS

The name tells it all: this entire coastal area is dominated by the vast stretches of sands that are revealed twice a day by the tide – which then rushes back in with such speed that it can overtake a galloping horse. The utterly flat, bleak estuaryscape is filled with quicksands and channels that can change their location between tides. Until the Turnpike Acts of the late eighteenth century produced slightly improved roads across the boggy mosses further north, and the railway arrived in 1857, the only effective route to the Furness area from the south was across the sands. Tacitus records Agricola and his invading Romans being taken across by native guides in AD 79. Other armies have taken the route, including those of Edward I (going north) to Robert the Bruce and Lambert Simnel (both heading south). The monks of FURNESS ABBEY often crossed to visit their properties elsewhere. In the fourteenth century drownings were so common the Abbot petitioned Edward II to appoint a coroner to enquire into the deaths. As Furness was part of Lancashire, officials, from tax-gatherers to lawyers, had to cross this way, and accused felons were transported to the courts in Lancaster. On 5 February 2004 twenty-three illegal Chinese workers collecting cockles near Hest Bank on the Morecambe coast were drowned by the incoming tide, a tragedy that led to several convictions for those who exploited the workers and changes in the law covering work gangs. Information on walks over the sands and the right-of-way across the bay is available from the Tourist Information Centre on Main Street. A guide is essential.

Crossing the sands was a fight against time and tide. Travellers took to the sands at Hest Bank and made landfall at Kents Bank, west of Grange-over-Sands. In 1909 A.M. Wakefield published a book of reminiscences, *Cartmel Priory and Sketches of North Lonsdale*, in which he described a perilous crossing:

> We were in great danger, even though we were pioneered by Carter, the guide. There had been much rain, and as the saying was, 'the fresh was out' and made many quick-sands and little streams, added to this a thick driving mist and drizzling rain came on, so that we could hardly see before us. When many miles out we found an unfortunate man who had utterly lost his way, wading aimlessly about, shoes and stockings in hand, and with not an idea of his whereabouts. With what joy he hailed our advent can be imagined … We had to skirt many miles out of our way to find a place where we could cross the channel; and to add to our

peril this loss of time brought the incoming tide so near that [John] Allen got more and more frightened, and at last, trusting more to the instinct of his horses than to himself or the guide, he plunged into the channel. The water washed into the chaise till we were obliged to lift our feet on to the opposite seat.

Wakefield also mentioned the experience of Revd Rigg, whose coach sank in quicksand, with some passengers having to be extracted through the windows. Several months later the coach washed up opposite Holme Island (SD422781), having been moved 4–5 miles (6–8km) by the waters and sands. Not surprisingly, the sands were deemed a good place in which to dispose of unwanted bodies; and corpses – of the drowned or murdered, no one could tell – would sometimes be disgorged many years down the line. In *This Haunted Isle* Peter Underwood, notes a belief that the sands are peopled with many ghosts, their dying cries heard when the wind comes off the sea.

Wakefield rented a cottage on Church Hill. The maid was convinced she had seen a ghost of an old woman, and gave a detailed description of the spirit's clothes. 'The girl at once wished to leave; but, happily, a lover turned up and so she then wished to stay!' Another of Wakefield's anecdotes concerned the notion that snakes swallow their young when danger threatens, a belief that goes as far back as ancient Egypt. 'Mr John Wakefield, of Sedgwick and Eggerslack, offered a reward of a guinea to any person who could verify this.' John Gregg, a woodsman from Lindale, saw a viper swallow its viperettes, so he killed it. 'Mr Wakefield on opening it found the tale quite true, and promptly sent the promised reward.' Snakes, however, do not swallow their young – anything that goes into a snake's stomach starts being digested, and anyway viperine parental care is almost entirely absent. The myth probably derives from the fact that many snakes give birth to live young: cutting open a pregnant snake would reveal young in the uterus, which could be mistaken for the stomach.

In a letter to the *News & Star* (30 May 2008) Mrs D.B. Ettrich wrote of seeing something strange by the railway bridge about 10.20 p.m. on 16 May. From behind the trees, came 'a bright, reddy-orange light,' swiftly followed by a second. Soon there were 'about 12 or 13 of these bright lights following each other up into the sky and disappearing into the clouds!' She thought it might have been a helicopter, but there was no noise. My suggestion is that they were Chinese lanterns floating away from a celebration.

The so-called Hampsfell Hospice on Hampsfield Fell (SD399793) was built in 1846 by the vicar of Cartmel as an eye-catching folly that doubles as an excellent fell-top shelter. Panels record, in verse, the builder's hopes that visitors will not damage the building, and a visitor's benign response. A Mr Williams contacted Tony Walker, author of *The Ghostly Guide to the Lake District*, with an experience from a misty summer's day in 1990. He was in a party of four looking for the hospice, but they had got lost. They all saw a tall woman in a long black robe pointing along what turned out to be the correct path. They checked the map and when they looked back she was no longer visible.

An anonymous correspondent in the *Big Cats in Britain Yearbook* 2006 recorded finding the carcass of a roebuck in Eggerslack Wood (SD410785) on 23 April 2005. It had not been dead for long, but had already been virtually stripped to the bone. The suggestion was that it was a big cat kill.

In 1965 new diesel engines were being introduced into Britain's railway fleet. One of the last steam locomotives, a 'Black Five,' clearly decided to have a final defiant fling. Somehow it started on its own and, driverless, ran from its depot at Carnforth right around Morecambe Bay, only stopping near Grange. The frantic driver had been giving desperate chase by car. The incident inspired a folk song. This wonderful episode is from the *Yorkshire Post* (21 October 1974).

LINDALE

Lindale's most famous son is John Wilkinson (1728-1808), notorious ironmaster, ruthless industrialist, original thinker and eccentric. He was a heavy-metal fanatic, obsessed with the production and potential of iron. The silted-up Newton Tarn (SD408826), near the summit of Newton Fell, is reputed to hide the wreck of one of his pioneering experiments, the first iron ship ever built. Lindale prepared his burial places and iron coffins well in advance of his death. Wakefield gives the best description of the legends that grew up around him and his home at Castle Head (SD421799):

> It was foretold to him that he should be buried three times before his body could find rest. Strange to say, this was literally fulfilled; for, dying away from home, his body was brought in the heavy coffin especially prepared, and on crossing the sands, perhaps owing to its great weight, the hearse sank in a quicksand and had to be dug out. The second burial took place in the cave at Castle Head as he had directed, but the next owner of the place, not caring for such gruesome relics, had the remains removed at dead of night, and he was buried for the third time in Lindale churchyard.

Lindale's remains were reburied yet again when the new church was built in 1828. The 20-ton (20,321kg) cast-iron obelisk he constructed as a memorial to himself can still be seen by the church (SD414803). Castle Head became known as a haunted house, 'The old caretaker always slept with a gun at his bed-head as a protection from spiritual visitations. Many were the tales told of awful sounds, rattling chains, groans and hurried flying footsteps, with all the necessary accompaniments of blood-stains to make a properly thrilling ghost-story.'

CARTMEL

Cartmel Priory is one of the great sights of the Lakes, a medieval treasure that survived the Dissolution of the Monasteries simply because, most unusually, the priory church was also the parish church. Today, with its equally unusual tower that sits at an angle of 45° to its base – a feature unique in England – it dominates the village.

Like all great institutions the priory has a founding legend. The Augustinian canons originally planned to build the church on nearby Mount Bernard but the next morning the foundation stones had been flung into a lower field. At the same time the architect had a dream in which St Cuthbert appeared, telling him to build the priory between two springs, one of which flowed south, the other north. The next morning two such directionally divergent streams were found flowing near the relocated stones. Cuthbert's role is significant, because sometime between AD 670 and 685 the Anglo-Saxon King

Egfrith granted Cuthbert 'that holy land which is called Cartmel and all the Britons therein' (the quote is from Camden's *Britannia*). It is not clear whether the grant was financial rather than spiritual, whether the area, or part of it, was already Christian, or even if 'Team Cuthbert' did any evangelizing in Cartmel. But clearly in spiritual terms Cuthbert 'owned' the area, and the Augustinians needed his blessing, something the vision story conveniently provides. When they arrived in 1188, the Augustinians monks possibly found a small parish church already in existence, and incorporated it into their grander enterprise. This may explain why part of the priory church was the parish church. In 1536-7 several of the monks were executed for taking part in the Pilgrimage of Grace (see FURNESS ABBEY) and most of the priory buildings were demolished, but the church remained.

The church has twenty-six fifteenth-century choirstalls with superbly carved misericords. The subjects include a range of Christian symbolism and Classical allusion, as well as some more earthy topics. Alexander the Great is carried into the sky by eagles (he encouraged them by dangling a spear baited with meat in front of their beaks); the Pelican feeds her young with her own blood (a cipher for Christ); a mermaid, symbol of vanity, combs her hair in a mirror; an ape holds a flask and an angel a shield; the unicorn is captured; three dogs chase a deer; there are angels and flowers; a crowned triple-faced Green Man spews leaves; there is the head of a man and one of a demon; and the menagerie includes hounds, a cock, an eagle, birds, a dragon and a griffin. Two oak chairs carved with scenes of the Ascension and Christ before Pilate sit in front of a wooden screen carved with symbols of the Passion, little animals and human figures.

The most striking monument is the huge – and hugely elaborate – fourteenth-century tomb of Sir John Harrington and his wife Joan. Large as it is, this is half its original size, and the damage to the adjacent arches of the sedilia shows where it has been brutally re-sited into a new niche. Angels pat the cheeks of the two effigies. On the base, monks read and chant and mourners – known as pleureurs (weepers) – mourn. The rest of the monument features grotesques, shields, the Virgin, Christ on a foliated cross, Mary Magdalene, a blindfold Christ being scourged by soldiers, Saints Philip, Catherine, Peter and Michael, John the Baptist, symbols of the Evangelists, angels carrying a soul to heaven, a broken crucifixion, and foliage. On top of the canopy Christ shows his wounds and the Virgin is crowned. The painted canopy ceiling has Christ in Glory with emblems of the Evangelists. When the tomb was opened it was found to contain bones of a man and a falcon.

For many years the eroded animal at the foot of the tomb of Sir Edgar Harrington, to the right of the altar, was claimed to be the Last Wolf (see HUMPHREY HEAD), but it is probably a lion.

Elsewhere in the church you can find many floor tablets for those drowned crossing the sands; a wooden door with bullet holes dating from the occupation of the church by Parliamentarian soldiers in the Civil War; and a memorial to William Myers (on the north wall) which states he died in 1762 – on 30 February. Arthur Mee in *The King's England: Lancashire* stated that the vestry had a 200-year-old umbrella which used to be held over the vicar at funerals, but I have no information if it still exists.

Apart from the church the only other building of the Priory to survive the Reformation was the Gatehouse, probably because it was the manor courthouse, so a structure of obvious utility. Tony Walker's informants told him of numerous sightings near the Gatehouse of a middle-aged chap with a tall hat and a double-breasted waistcoat. Footsteps had been heard on the stairs, and dogs often growled at or refused to climb the steps. An article in the *Whitehaven News* on 03 June 2008 reproduced some notes about life in old Cartmel published by the Women's Institute in 1928. One of the stories was of an underground passage from the church to one of the old buildings in Priory Close. The late owner of the house recalled that as a girl her mother had ventured into the passage and came up some steps into the church, near one of the columns in the nave. She startled the choir, who were at practice, and they fled, thinking she was a ghost.

HUMPHREY HEAD

The holy well at SD389739, long celebrated for healing and sometimes called St Agnes' Well, is easily reached from the beach car park at the end of the road. The spring still flows and, although a little litter-strewn, it's still worth a visit. A sign says 'Danger. Water not suitable for drinking.' Some editions of Mrs Jerome Mercier's *The Last Wolf* (see below) had a photograph of the building which once housed the well, a small shelter with a locked door. The key cost threepence to hire from a nearby farm. The shelter was demolished in the early twentieth century after a spa company in Morecambe abandoned its plans to sell the water. Those who are sure of foot and possess a head for heights can climb up to the natural arch called the Fairy Church (SD390738). When the arch is reached a cave can be seen beneath it but there is no access to this. Another precipitous climb starting from the same place on the shore footpath but angling slightly further to the left (north) brings you to a second small cave, the Fairy Chapel (SD390739). Another well, the Pin Well, used to be on the east side of the road down to the Head (SD388746) but is now a muddy patch. Here, bent pins were dropped into the water as offerings so that the *genius loci* of the spring would grant wishes. Cuming Walters, writing about another pin well further south in Lancashire in William Andrews' *Church Treasury of History, Custom, Folk-lore, etc* (1898) noted that it …

> … became customary for the Pin Wells to be much resorted to by sighing maidens and dejected lovers, as well as by people in search of 'good luck.' A new superstition also arose that whenever a new pin was dropped into the well all those which had been cast in previously rose to greet it. Eye-witnesses could be produced to attest to this fact. Why saints and fairies should be so easily propitiated by so small an offering, however, is more or less a mystery.

Humphrey Head is also where the last wolf in England was supposedly killed. There are many 'last wolves,' just as there are numerous 'the last time the fairies were ever seen' stories. Both are conventional, even stereotyped narratives deriving from both our collective obsession with 'last things' and our modern, urban fascination with the untamed and the unfettered — especially if they are comfortably just beyond our reach. 'Last wolf' narratives almost always have a threatened woman and a brave hero, and here we have both, in the shape of the beautiful Adela and the dashing John Harrington, her banished sweetheart who has secretly returned from the Crusades. In traditional style, with more than a nod to dragon/monster legends that stretch back to the Classical world, Adela's hand is promised to the knight who can slay the dread wolf ravaging the area. Guess who manages to kill the beast just before it attacks Adela? And then reveals his secret identity so he and Adela can be instantly married by a conveniently passing priest?

The story is derived from a booklet written by Mrs Jerome Mercier, *The Last Wolf: A Legend of Humphrey Head*, which was published some time in the late nineteenth century — there is no date on any of the several editions of what was a very popular book locally.

Anne Mercier, to give her real name, added endless romantic details and invented all the lovelorn subplots, but derived the main thrust of the story from Edwin Waugh, whose *Rambles in the Lake Country and its Borders* came out in 1861. He got it from John Briggs' posthumously published *The Remains of John Briggs* (1825). And there the trail goes cold, although Briggs was clearly relating a well-known traditional tale, in which the knight – just 'Harrington' – kills the wolf as it menaces a beautiful (unnamed) maiden, who instantly falls in love with the hero. The happy couple set up house in Wraysholme Tower (SD383754) which is visible from the road that passes its now-incorporated farm. The Harringtons were a prominent local knightly family so it is easy to see how the hero supposedly springs from their loins.

FLOOKBURGH

Near this place is a noted spaw, called Holy-well, found to be of great service in most cutaneous disorders, and much resorted to in the summer season from distant parts. It is an easy cathartic, restores lost appetite, and fully answers the ancient poetic description of a fountain: *Infirmo capiti fluit utilis, utilis alvo.*

Thomas West, *A Guide to the Lakes* (1778)

The Latin quote is from the first century BC Roman poet Horace. Philip Francis' *Poetical Translation of the Works of Horace* (1750) renders it as, 'Useful to ease an aching Head it flows, / Or when with burning Pain the Stomach glows.'

The *Sun* of 8 February 2003 reported that farmer Phil Lynott of Flookburgh was intrigued when a vet asked him why, when the average lifespan of a pony was twenty-five years, his retired ponies were living to thirty or more – one even reached forty-seven. Lynott discovered the animals were drinking from a spring containing minute traces of salicin, an anti-inflammatory agent used in a number of modern medicines. The spring was presumably the 'Holy-well' described by West. The water is now bottled in Flookburgh as Willow Water, named after the stratum of peat formed from compressed white willow bark that is the source of the salicin (see www.willowwater.com).

The *Westmorland Gazette* for 27 December 2002 reported sightings of big black cats, on the minor road between Cartmel and Flookburgh, and, during the previous summer, on the beach at HUMPHREY HEAD. But farmer Stuart Wilson claimed his sighting of a 'giant-sized' black cat with 'a fluffy coat' near Wyke Farm, Allithwaite, was simply a large domestic moggy that had taken to the wild and had been snacking on rabbits.

In older times the perilous crossing of the Leven Sands to CONISHEAD PRIORY started at Sandgate, just west of Flookburgh. These days signposts show the right of way from beside the railway across to Canal Foot near Ulverston. Follow this route at your peril unless you have a local guide.

HOLKER HALL (SD355775)

Open March-October, Sunday-Friday 11 a.m.-4:00 p.m. (gardens 10:30 a.m.-5:30 p.m.). Closed Saturdays. Admission charge. Wheelchair access to most parts (see www.holker.co.uk for full disabled access details).

The Cavendish family emblem is a snake, and crowned serpents can be seen in several places through this splendid stately home. Busty female sphinxes support a desk in the gallery, the light switches in the library are concealed behind imitation books with humorous titles, and in the grounds is modern piece of landscape art – a grass spiral punctuated by multiple standing stones.

In 1872 local historian James Stockdale published *Annales Caermoelenses: or Annals of Cartmel*, in which he related the legend of Dobbie Lane, the old road from Cark to Holker. In 1809 a young servant boy was sent from Cark Hall – which Stockdale owned – to deliver newspapers to Holker Hall. When he arrived back at Cark that night he promptly fainted. After being revived he described being chased all the way by a dobbie in the form of a ball of fire. The boy wasn't believed and became a laughing stock. Eight years later Stockdale's brother had a similar experience on the same road – a bobbing light or glowing ball of fire followed him, and he had to run to escape. Marsh gas? Earthlights?

The Cistercian Way long-distance footpath passes through the area, linking medieval religious sites. About 30yds (27m) east of the path at SD364780 is the Toad Stone, a standing stone that from one angle gives the impression of a squatting batrachian.

LEVEN RIVER

Stanley Clarke and his son Alan were swimming in the river somewhere near Ulverston when they saw a huge silver-blue fish with a spike repeatedly leap out of the water. It injured itself badly on some rocks so they killed it quickly. A photograph was sent to the Natural History Museum in London, which identified it as a white marlin, a fish common from Africa to Portugal, but never before seen around Britain. The marlin's thrashings were its death throes, caused by swimming into fresh water. This ocean-going fish – which was around 6ft (1.8m) long and may have weighed 58lb (26kg) – somehow ended up in an inland shallow river. The report was in the *Sunday Express* (18 September 1983).

CHAPEL ISLAND (SD321759)

The deadly nature of the shifting sands on the Leven crossing between Conishead and CARTMEL prompted the erection of a small chapel on this, the only piece of permanent solid land in the estuary. A monk prayed for the souls who had to cross before the morning tide rushed in, and travellers stopped (briefly) to give thanks for completing half of the crossing. Yet another mythical tunnel is supposed to link the island to the mainland. Braddyll (see CONISHEAD) transformed the chapel into a faux Romantic ruin, which is itself now storm-damaged. DO NOT attempt to reach the island, or venture anywhere on the sands, without a guide.

ULVERSTON

All the following reports of sightings big black cats are from the *North West Evening Mail*. The dates in brackets are when the story was printed.

In April 2004 Mike Hodgson took photographs of a 'spaniel-sized' black cat at Baycliff quarry. He released the (sadly inconclusive) images after another sighting at the same place on 15 July (reported 20 July 2004). There were sightings near Bouth (2 October 2004) and at Newland (24 September 2006, reported 27 September). Paul Caffrey saw a black cat run across the A590 dual carriageway south of Greenodd in late April 2007. As he passed it the lights of the bus he was driving 'lit up the cat's amber eyes.' (1 May 2007).

The main point of interest in St Mary's Church on Church Walk is the tomb of William Sandys, with an effigy of the man himself praying. Sandys was the owner of the Conishead Priory site before it was passed to the Braddylls. When the tomb was moved to its present position from the east end of the church it was found to be empty. From this discovery has sprung the local legend that he was murdered and his body disposed of in Morecambe Bay sands. The church also has a memorial to the Arctic explorer Sir John Barrow, in whose honour the Hoad Monument was built on Hoad Hill – a lighthouse without a light, and far from sea. A similar memorial can be found in the cemetery on Priory Road, where the monument to Thomas Watkins Wilson is a lighthouse on a rock carved with an anchor and chain, although sadly the gaslit lamp at the top no longer burns night and day. The light made a great impression on a certain young Ulverston lad. At the start of his career comic actor Stan Jefferson was superstitious about the thirteen letters in his name, and so changed it to Stan Laurel. The delightful Laurel and Hardy Museum contains everything you could ever want to know about the great comic duo. The museum is open 10 a.m.-4.30 p.m. daily February-December. Admission charge. Full wheelchair access (see www.laurel-and-hardy.co.uk).

The 1951 *Folklore* survey found the area still abounded in references to Jenny Greenteeth, a vicious water-monster. The green slime on the surface of stagnant pools was supposed to be her face. She was recorded in Ulverston, as well as Kirkby Lonsdale, Witherslack, Dalton-in-Furness and Askham-in-Furness. She provided a useful 'bogey' with which to warn children off playing in dangerous stretches of water.

PENNINGTON

St Michael's and All Angels' Church (SD262774) contains a reset Norman tympanum with the runic inscription 'Gamel founded this church; Hubert the mason wrought.' Gamel de Pennington was a twelfth-century magnate. An ancient carved head of a mitred bishop is in the porch, the graveyard contains a sundial dated 1680, and just outside the churchyard wall are the old village stocks. A footpath north of the church leads to the burial mound of Ellabarrow or Eller Barrow (SD264774). Arthur Mee's *The King's England: Lancashire* (1936) recorded the legend that it was the grave of Lord Ella and his golden sword – and that when a house was built on another barrow at Conynger Hurst nearby, bones were found, although the warrior's sword was simply made of iron.

For a Sheela-na-gig found in the church in 1926 see KENDAL MUSEUM.

CONISHEAD PRIORY (SD305758)

Open Easter-October 2-5 p.m. daily (from noon on weekends and bank holidays); November-Easter 2-4 p.m. daily (gardens every, day dawn to dusk). Admission charge and charge for guided tours of the house. Wheelchair access to the Temple and the ground floor of the house.

This Romantic Gothic revival mansion, built in 1836, is now the Manjushri Kadampa Meditation Centre and Buddhist College, the temple of which is freely accessible – and filled with mandalas, statues of revered figures and numerous Buddhas, including the largest bronze Buddha in the West. The Buddhist group who operate the centre have been in a fairly protracted theological dispute with the Dalai Lama.

A tour of the house (available at weekends and bank holidays during the season at 2.15 p.m. and 3.30 p.m.) is recommended if you want to catch an eyeful of the quasi-medieval tracery in the cloistered corridor, the badgers on the staircase, the stained glass, the seventeenth-century carved wooden panels with caryatids and male and female figures, and the other elements that go to make this fabulous fantasy building. The architect was Philip Wyatt, whose only other major work was the even more eccentric Fonthill Abbey near Bath, William Beckford's obsessive attempt to build the ultimate fantasy Gothic building. Things at Conishead are more modest. The arched doorway has heads of a queen, king and two monks, and is overseen by an angel, and there are more figures inside the exhibition area. The modern temple is a curious mix of Classical and Asian styles, with a golden stag and hind flanking a Wheel of Life on the roof, and another stag and hind, this time in bronze, in a nearby garden, the gateposts to which are topped with the bronze head of a horse. Col. Thomas Braddyll, who built Conishead, erected the octagonal folly on Hermitage Hill close to here, a castellated tower with cross arrowslits and a tiny bartizan turret. Another of his follies, this time triangular, surmounts the hill by the golf course (SD296751); in one of the three pointed niches is a sepulchral urn, although this is probably purely ornamental and not occupied.

Conishead is built on the site of a twelfth-century Augustianian priory that was reduced to its constituent stones and timber at the Reformation. Ian Morson's 1998 novel *A Psalm for Falconer* brings his Oxford scholar-detective Regent Master William Falconer to the priory for a medieval mystery involving missing manuscripts and monkish murder. Morson makes effective use of the atmospheric and sinister landscape as Falconer crosses the treacherous sands and tidal shallows of Morecambe Bay, which unexpectedly disgorge the skeleton of a monk killed fifteen years previously.

BARDSEA

The vestry within the nineteenth-century Holy Trinity Church has a seventeenth-century armchair carved with foliage and a long seat with four dragons.

BIRKRIGG

A Druidical Temple in which the sun and moon were worshipped … The twelve stones of the inner circle represented the twelve signs of the zodiac; and the nineteen stones of the outer, represented the years contained in the cycle of the moon.

Francis Evans, *Furness and Furness Abbey* (1842)

Birkrigg stone circle (SD292739) is also known as the Druid's Circle, although it was of course built millennia before any druids showed up. The circle is an easy walk from the road and has stunning views over the estuary. This is a double concentric circle – the inner ring of twelve stones is the most prominent, while the fifteen or so fallen stones of the outer ring are often covered by bracken in summer. On my visit one of the stones had sadly been vandalised with paint. Five cremation burials were found in the centre, along with a lump of red ochre, perhaps used for painting the corpse as part of the funerary rites. There are several intriguing ditches and banks nearby.

GREAT URSWICK

The delightful St Mary and St Michael's Church is full of interest, and has a very good guidebook available. The site is ancient and is probably the mother church of the Furness area. The west exterior face of the tower has a very worn fifteenth-century Pietà (the Virgin Mary cradling the dead body of Jesus) that may have come from FURNESS ABBEY. The door promises to 'ward against all winds and outer strife' and has panels carved with the Virgin and St Michael. A single rusted link is all that remains of the chain the vicar pulled across to prevent his cow from sleeping here in the porch. Scratch marks in the porch were either (a) where arrows were sharpened before archery practice or (b) made by the butcher when selling meat after morning services.

The twelfth-century hexagonal font now has a wooden cover carved with four sets of dolphins and cherubs, but originally was fitted with a locked heavy oak lid to prevent the holy water being stolen. Near the Sanctuary is the brass memorial plaque of Jacobus Barwick, with a dire warning and images of a skull and the Hand of Doom. Nearby are two carved graveslabs, one with a sword and shears. The most easterly oak beam is carved with the date 1598 and the initials of the then vicar 'WLV' and churchwarden 'JA'. There is a great deal of early twentieth century wood carving on the organ case (musicians playing the horn and the piano), vestry door (the Annunciation), chancel arch screen (angels, St James of Compostela, John the Baptist) and choir stalls (figures with instruments). The barrel-organ grinder and monkey were allegedly suggested by the vicar when the carver ran out of ideas.

The inner ring of Birkrigg Stone Circle.

Above left: The ancient rune-inscribed 'Tunwinni Cross'. St Mary and St Michael's Church, Great Urswick.

Above right: St Michael the Archangel dispatching the dragon. St Mary and St Michael's Church.

The church has two fragments of early crosses. The smaller one was not on display during my visit, but there is a life-size drawing of what it might have looked like in its glory days. W.G. Collingwood dated the larger piece, known as the Tunwinni Cross, to around AD 850 and translated the Anglo-Saxon runes inscribed on it as: 'This cross Tunwinni erected in memory of Torkbred [or Thorhtred] a monument to his son. Pray for his soul. Lyl wrought this.' Obviously the runes suggest there was a literate early Christian community at that time. There is also a panel showing two clerics, one holding a cross.

In 2002 archaeologist Steve Dickinson re-examined the stone and published a revisionist report entitled 'The Beacon on the Bay'. Dickinson's starting point is that the Tunwinni runes had been overcut on top of a much earlier inscription which commemorated a meeting between seventh-century representatives of the Roman and Celtic churches – the two men in the carving. Archaeological investigation turned up Roman masonry in the surrounding field walls and the church – including, intriguingly, a fragment of a possible pagan altar in the south nave. The main argument was that Urswick had been the site of a hitherto unidentified Roman fort; that following the departure of the Romans their masonry was re-used by the local people; and that by the late sixth century it was the site of a monastery based on the model of that on Iona – a community of Celtic Christian monks. This large monastic estate may have been the birthplace (one of many suggested around the country) of St Patrick. It's fair to say that Dickinson's bold ideas have not been fully accepted, but there is a very active ongoing archaeological and historical investigation – the Urswick Origins Discovery Programme – so this story may expand further.

Great Urswick Tarn, around which the village arcs, hides a legendary drowned town, Lile Ooston. Legend has it that either a priest was forced by the local people to conjure up fresh water during a time of drought and the resulting storm inundated the impious townsfolk, or the resident witches turned men into pigs or dogs and an earthquake buried the community as a divine punishment. On another slant, the tarn is supposed to be bottomless.

In 1958 *The Countryman* published 'A Furness Diary 1801-1807,' the journal of country gentleman William Fleming. In it is the following entry:

> Friday, May 24, 1801. About 100 yards [91m] to the West of Urswick Church in Furness in a Field called Kirkflat, adjoining to the Highway, stands a rough piece of unhewn Limestone, which the Inhabitants of Urswick were accustomed to dress as a Figure of Priapus on Midsummer Day, besmearing it with Sheep Salve, Tar or Butter and covering it with Rags of various Dyes, the Head ornamented with Flowers.

This is an extraordinary record of a rural pagan fertility ceremony. Priapus was the rampantly-erect Greek god of fertility, so this was clearly a name imposed on the ceremony by an educated gentleman, who perhaps did not want to use the cruder phrase 'fertility stone' or 'phallic stone.' There is no record of what the people who decorated and made offerings to the stone actually called it. The level of descriptive detail and Fleming's use of the word 'were' suggests the custom was still within living memory but had died out, although clearly the stone was still standing in his time. These days the stone is horizontal and built into the field wall on the north side of road opposite the playground south-west of the church (SD267741). There is a pattern of holes at one end which look modern, but their origin in unclear.

There are more fascinating stones in the area around. Closest is Great Urswick Burial Chamber (SD263745), where the overlying mound has vanished to reveal a cyclopean capstone balancing precariously on two equally titanic boulders. There is a footpath leading west from the village. Visible from one of the tangle of minor roads further west is Middle Barrow (SD255749), a standing stone so peculiarly shaped by weathering it resembles a piece of abstract modern art. Great Urswick hillfort (SD274751) to the north is prominent from a distance but barely discernable close up, although the views are good. The site is scattered with natural rock outcrops, within one of which were discovered four stone axes that appeared to have been deliberately hidden. At its foot is the more interesting Skelmore Heads long barrow (SD274754) with two standing stones.

GLEASTON

St Michael's holy well, also known as Micklewell, is on the north side of the street by the village hall (SD256708), but has been closed up and is no longer in use, or even accessible. The ivy-covered keep of Gleaston Castle (SD261714) is too dangerous to enter but there is a great view from the roadside. An ancient bronze 'celt' or axe was found during

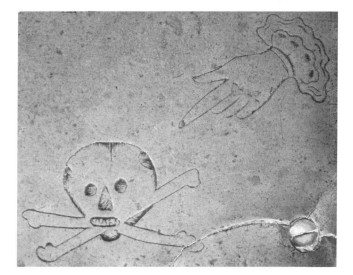

Right: Brass memorial of Jacobus Barwick, St Mary and St Michael's Church.

Below: The 'Priapus Stone', Great Urswick. A once-revered fertility stone now built into a wall.

digging in the ruins of the castle in 1776. In 1905 Henry Cowper, musing over the find with his folklorist's hat on, wondered if it had been built in as a sort of foundation deposit. Alternatively it could have been used as a charm against lightning strike, another common use of prehistoric tools in later times.

DENDRON

There were sightings of big black cats in the fields outside Dendron on 2 July 2002 (*Westmorland Gazette*, 5 July) and near Scales (25 July 2005 – *Hexham Courant* via Mark Fraser's *Big Cats in Britain Yearbook* 2006). A local person replying to the 1951 *Folklore* questionnaire noted that a place called Boggart Bridge was 'so-called because near it during hoar frost, a human figure is sometimes outlined on the grass.'

FURNESS ABBEY

English Heritage. Open 21 March–30 September 10 a.m.–5 p.m. daily, 1 October–31 March 10 a.m.–4 p.m. Saturday and Sunday. Admission charge. Wheelchair access to museum, ramp to monument, smooth grass in grounds.

Once one of the richest Cistercian monasteries in England and now an evocative, beautiful ruin, Furness Abbey is fabulous. The museum includes several superb effigies, including formidably armoured knights (one with an angel murmuring in his ear), an abbot, a cresset stone, and a fourteenth-century noblewoman, probably a benefactress. The church has several carved figures, including monarchs, angels, demons and dragons. A Nine Men's Morris frame is scratched on a doorway.

By 1535 it was clear to the Catholic Church in England that Henry VIII wanted to suppress the monasteries. This sacrilegious prospect aroused in the north an insurrection of sorts, the Pilgrimage of Grace, which fizzled out when several abbots, priors and monks were executed. In *Religion and the Decline of Magic* (1982), Keith Thomas describes how, during this period of political and religious turmoil, the embattled monks were invoking prophecies claimed to have been made by the Venerable Bede, Thomas the Rhymer, John of Bridlington, Geoffrey of Monmouth and Merlin, all of which were said to show that the Church would triumph. At Furness, the monks believed that the king would be slain by armed priests. In 1537 one of the brothers, John Broughton, spoke of a prophecy predicting the overturn of the new laws and the ultimate success of the Catholic Church, which if it survived for four years more would last forever. The prophecy, as prophecies tend to be, was suitably enigmatic: 'a.b.c. (Anne Boleyn? Thomas Cromwell?) and three t.t.t. (?) should sit all in one seat and should work great marvels' and the 'red rose' (Henry VIII) should die in his mother's womb (be killed by the Mother Church).

On 9 April 1537 Furness became the first of the larger monasteries to be dissolved. The abbot had negotiated a limited stipend for himself and the monks. Within a short time of the monks leaving, nobles who had previously worshipped at or donated to the abbey were ripping its fabric apart and carting away anything of value.

DALTON-IN-FURNESS

The solid pele tower of Dalton Castle in the Market Place (National Trust. Open 2–5 p.m. on Saturdays in summer, admission free) has four very damaged figures on its roof which appear to be jesters, although they could just as easily be judges.

The *Whitehaven News* for 29 August 2007 quoted the Trust's Morecambe Bay properties manager, Rowena Lord, as saying, 'The warden says he's seen a ghost here. He's seen a figure cut off at the knees going out through the wall.' This follows on from several apparitions reported over the years. On certain days you may see Morris Dancers in the Market Place. St Mary's Church nearby has a plaque which records the effect of plague in 1662: of a total population of 612, 320 were wiped out.

In 1874 limestone quarrying at Butts Beck (SD233747) unearthed a leaf-shaped bronze sword and bronze spearhead, while in the same year another discovery at Goldmire Quarry (SD218738) revealed a skeleton and a sword in a scabbard. Unfortunately, as the *Ulverston Mirror* for October 1874 noted, 'The whole of the bones were placed in a wheelbarrow … Difficulty was experienced in collecting the remains, as various portions were carried to Dalton, whilst the sword was broken into pieces, which were taken by the workpeople as mementoes or relics.' This source and much else on the archaeology and history of the area can be found on the excellent Dalton Online website.

Laura Houston saw a big cat near Thornton Park on 26 January 2007. This was her second sighting in less than a year. (*Westmorland Gazette* 2 February 2007.)

ASKHAM-IN-FURNESS

A respondent from here to the 1951 *Folklore* questionnaire said: 'If a black dog follows after you, comes near you and won't run away, it is a sure sign of a death.'

KIRKBY-IN-FURNESS

The Ship Inn's website states that strange footsteps and noises prompted the landlord of the time, along with some regulars, to hold a séance in the bar. They claim to have made contact with the spirit of a young girl who called herself Elizabeth and said she had died when she was nineteen. She was subsequently identified as Elizabeth S. Kendall, who was born in the pub in 1869 and appears in the ten-yearly censuses for 1871 and 1881 but not thereafter. Recent phenomena have included apparitions, footsteps in empty rooms, chills, a sense of being watched, and the forceful movement of small objects by unseen forces.

The Kirk is one of those stone circles whose past is more interesting than its present. The circle (shown as 'enclosure' on the OS map, SD251827) is on the fells above Beck Side and has lost all its stones. Up until what appears to be quite late in the nineteenth century, the ring was used for games of skill and strength on Easter Monday. The games were held under the benefice of the local lordly family, but when one of them was injured in the boisterousness, the sports ceased.

GRIZEBECK

A somewhat tortuous fell road north leads to the Giant's Grave ring cairn on the west side of the road (SD257879). Pevsner's *The Buildings of England: North Lancashire* claims that 100yds (91m) to the north-east are three pairs of stones which may be the remains of an avenue, although I can find nothing more about this. Across the fells to the north-west is the White Borran cairn (SD266891).

BROUGHTON IN FURNESS

The clock on the tower of the Victorian St Mary Magdalene Church on Church Street is cheerily inscribed 'Watch for ye know not the hour.' In the graveyard, a tombstone for one family gives their ages at death as 78, 80, 84, 92, 101 and 104.

As recorded by Tony Walker, the bedrooms at the Old King's Head nearby have a history of minor phenomena, including televisions switching on by themselves, small items disappearing, strange atmospheres and sensations of being touched.

The perfect circle at Swinside.

DUDDON BRIDGE

Of the two fallen standing stones east of Ash House (SD192873), one has eight curious polished grooves. Theories for their origin are: (1) used for polishing prehistoric stone axes; (2) work marks left by those attempting to demolish the monument; (3) the marks of wire cables used by timber felling gangs in the Second World War. All are plausible.

A sighting of a puma-like big cat in the garden of a house in the Duddon Valley was briefly reported in the *Westmorland Gazette* on 31 January 2006.

SWINSIDE STONE CIRCLE (SD172882)

> That mystic round of Druid fame,
> Tardily sinking by its proper weight
> Deep into patient earth, from whose smooth breast it came!
>
> William Wordsworth *The River Duddon* (1820)

In terms of location, size, preservation and ambience, this is easily the equal of the better-known CASTLERIGG. It can be reached by walking up the rough track of the public bridleway (signposted 'Swinside Farm: No unauthorised vehicles') from the road near Cragg Hall. The fifty-five large stones are set in a perfect circle, and the entrance is well-defined.

One of the Swinside stones showing 'terrain echoes' (the way the shapes of the stones mimic the landscape).

Another example of a stone at Swinside exactly following the line of the slope behind.

Several of the tops of the stones line up exactlly with the slope of the hills behind them, another example of the 'terrain echoes' phenomenon discussed at Castlerigg. Swinside is also known as 'Sunken Kirk' – the church was built by people by day and regularly pulled into the earth by the Devil at night. The stones are supposed to be the tips of the sunken church, the bulk of which lies, iceberg-like, beneath the sod.

MILLOM

Hob-Thross … the Goblin Fiend, that shunn'd their sight,
And wrought for the lords of Millom by night …
He scoured, and delved, and groom'd, and churned
But favour or hire he scorned and spurned.
Leave him alone to will and to do,
Never were hand and heart so true.
Tempt him with gift, or lay out his hire
Farewell Hob to farm and fire …
'Hob has got a new coat and new hood,
And Hob no more will do any good.'
Blight and change pass'd over the place.
Came to end that ancient race.

John Pagen White, *Lays and Legends of the English Lake Country* (1873)

The ruined shell of Millom Castle (SD172814, private) can be viewed from the adjacent Holy Trinity Church; an interpretation panel is next to the churchyard wall. E. Lynn Linton in *The Lake Country* (1864) wrote, 'in Millom grounds are the imperfect remains of a circle,' but I have found nothing more about this. White noted that the lords of Millom jealously guarded their unusual privileges, such as the right to execute without bothering with the courts – an active gallows still stood beside the castle in the seventeenth century – and the power to exclude the Sheriff of the County from their jurisdiction.

Hob-Thross, also known as Hob Thrust or Jack i' the Hob, a creature described as 'a body all over rough,' was the castle's brownie, or house-elf, 'a solitary being, meagre, flat-nosed, shaggy and wild in his appearance.' Those who did not eat a hearty meal on Shrove Tuesday would find their mouths crammed with barley chaff by Hob. Like brownies up and down the land, he speedily completed laborious household and agricultural tasks while everyone was asleep, asking in return only a quart of cream or a bowl of milk-porridge. Again like all brownies – the story is universal – he served notice to quit when, through mistaken kindness, a woman made him a coat and hood to keep him warm during the winter. With his departure the family's fortunes declined. There is an Elf Hall near Lady Hall, Hallthwaites (SD188859), but I can find no folklore for the name.

KIRKSANTON

The two stones of the Giant's Grave near Standing Stones Farm (SD13628109) are among the tallest in Cumbria, being 6ft 6in (2m) and 9ft 10in (3m) respectively. The north stone

The standing stones of Kirksanton, framing Black Combe.

has three cupmarks, the south four. This terrific site is an easy walk from the village. Hutchinson's *History of Cumberland & Westmorland* (1794) notes, 'near adjoining to this monument, several other large stones stood lately, placed in a rude manner.' In 1864 Linton recorded 'eight big blocks, which once formed part of a circle 25yds (23m) in diameter.' Tom Clare's *Prehistoric Monuments of the Lake District* traces other features in the immediate area, including a ring of pits around the stone pair, and henges or enclosures, although none of these can be seen by the casual visitor. There is a tradition of the burial mound of a giant killed in battle. Kirksanton itself is one of several places where the former church has supposedly sunk into the ground.

A footpath from Kirksanton crosses the railway and climbs the fell to a ruined farmhouse from where the four Lacra stone circles can be visited. All are damaged and relatively small but the overall cluster is impressive and the coastal views are magnificent. Lacra A (SD14988132) is the closest to the house, with eight low boulders. To the east is Lacra D (SD15118125), which is badly mangled but appears to be a circle with a large central stone – possibly a former capstone of a cairn – and a barely-discernable ring cairn on the other side of the track. Lacra B (SD14928098), the best circle, with six stones, is to the south-west. Lacra C (SD15018098) is now to the west. This was once thought to be the remains of a circle, but Aubrey Burl in *From Carnac to Callanish* identifies it as a three-stone row. An avenue of modest stones runs east-north-east and west-south-west from Lacra D, although tracking it can be challenging.

Millom Castle, former residence of Hob-Thross.

SILECROFT

A big cat was seen by a passenger on a train just south of Silecroft, while some years previously Netta Addison's husband had seen 'an ape-like animal with a long tail' in a wood between Silecroft and Waberthwaite. Both sightings are in the *Whitehaven News* 19 February 1998.

In *The English Lake District* Molly Lefebure calls Black Combe, 'fell of folklore and fairies,' based on Linton's descriptions, 'It is said there that the bees sing, and the labouring ox kneels in adoration at twelve o'clock at night on Christmas Eve.'

Traditionally a newlywed couple would never buy corn for their first sowing – to do so was to invite disaster. Instead they would take a sack around all their neighbours; when it was full the planting could begin.

BOOTLE

Not a trace remains of three stone circles that have been destroyed in this area: Annaside (SD099853), Hall Foss (SD112857) and Kirkstones (SD106843, with a large cairn 200yds/ 183m away, also gone). Almost equally eradicated is the Benedictine nunnery of Leakley, now just a fragment of gable on the site occupied by Seaton Hall farmhouse (SD107900).

7

ESKDALE
AND WASDALE

WABERTHWAITE

As well as a heavily worn tenth-century cross shaft outside St John's Church, located at a significant ford over the Esk (SD100951), the area abounds in prehistoric remains accessible to the fit and determined. The superb if enigmatic cluster on Barnscar (SD132958) comprises numerous low stone monuments – enclosures, cairns, round houses, walls, avenues and much more of the prehistoric settlement. Whelan's *History and Topography of Cumberland and Westmorland* (1860) describes it as 'the remains of a fort or encampment, called the ruins of the city of Barnscar.' There are more burial cairns (SD149968) on the path to Devoke Water, with further settlement fragments on Rough Crag above the lake (SD158973). A separate route onto Waberthwaite Fell leads to an extensive enclosure (SD134939) with cairns, hut circles and what may be a stone circle, with more cairns on the edges of the woods on Stainton Fell to the north (SD137942 and SD140945).

MUNCASTER CASTLE (SD104965)

Open February-October, Sunday-Friday (closed Saturdays) 12-4.30 p.m., (Gardens and Owl Centre open from 10.30 a.m.); open fewer but still regular days in winter (see www.muncaster.co.uk or telephone 01229 717614 for details).

The castle, a major attraction, is reported to be one of the most haunted buildings in Britain. In addition, there is tomfoolery, a Luck, legends of a king, a standalone boggle and a folly. So, something for everyone.

The castle's spectres are so famous there is a waiting list for people to attend all-night sessions in the Tapestry Room, where the ghostly events are concentrated. Numerous people have reported a range of phenomena – auditory (whispering, singing, children crying, bangs, footsteps, raps), visual (fleeting shadows, door handles turning), tactile (being touched, feeling a weight on the chest), olfactory (smells of burning), mental/emotional (feelings of a presence or being watched, a sense of foreboding), corporeal (severe headaches, dizziness, ringing in the ears) and physical (drops in temperature, interference with electrical equipment, vibrations).

Many of these experiences are concentrated on the bed in the room itself, and the room has been subjected to regular scientific investigation. In 2005 Dr Jason Braithwaite, a cognitive neuroscientist from the Behavioural Brain Sciences Centre at Birmingham University, and Maurice Townsend, from the Association for the Scientific Study of Anomalous Phenomena, published an article in the *European Journal of Parapsychology* (Vol. 20, No. 1) entitled 'Sleeping With the Entity – A Quantitative Magnetic Investigation of an English Castle's Reputedly 'Haunted' Bedroom.' The article described how the metal framework of the bed was associated with a very strong anomalous magnetic field, which extended for 6½ft (2m) beyond the bed and was particularly concentrated where your head would be while lying on the bed. Such powerful magnetic fields can have strange effects on the brain – laboratory experiments had shown that they could distort or even create sensations, especially if the person moved their head – as you would do when lying on a bed and trying to locate something you've just encountered in a 'haunted room.' The article cautiously notes that exposure to these complex and varying fields in the Tapestry Room could cause witnesses to 'bias their impressions of ambiguous stimuli towards a paranormal interpretation … or indeed such fields may induce more elaborate forms of direct sensory hallucination.' Of course this doesn't explain all the reported phenomena in other parts of the castle – such as the sound of footsteps on stone in a carpeted corridor, the apparition of a woman, doors being held shut by unseen hands – but it might give an indication that many of the invisible forces in operation might derive from the electromagnetic rather than the occult end of the spectrum.

Many of the supernatural phenomena have been attributed to the lingering presence of 'Tom Fool', the castle's last jester. A striking and slightly grotesque painting of him in a blue-and-yellow chequered cloak hangs in one of the corridors. Salaried fools, either in history or literature, have never struck me as particularly attractive individuals, they being more inclined to self-pity, smart-aleckery and sadism than genuine mirth, and what is told of Tom confirms this view. Dickinson's *Cumbriana* (1876) shows him as partial to cruel and distasteful practical jokes, as well as the odd spot of murder – such as decapitating the castle joiner. In some versions of the tale (for example, in Armistead's *Tales of the English Lakes*, 1891) Tom gets his axe out on behalf of Sir Ferdinand Hoddleston of Millom Castle, the carpenter's rival for the affections of Helwise, the daughter of Sir Alan Pennington of Muncaster. Elsewhere he is said to have deliberately misled travellers into crossing the potentially lethal quicksands of the Esk estuary. All of this unpleasantness is of course very much in the background these days, and the castle hosts an annual Festival of Fools – with much genuine mirth – at the end of which one Fool is voted as the official castle jester for the year.

But 'Tom Fool', or Tom Skelton to give him his real name, may not be all he has been made out to be. His portrait contains his will, written in doggerel verse, and within, there are many clues. In 1960 E. W. Ives embarked on a thoroughly scholarly literary excavation and published the results in *Shakespeare Survey* No. 13 ('Tom Skelton - A Seventeenth-Century Jester') and *Notes & Queries* ('Tom Skelton and Motley').

The will in the painting tells us that, 'I Thom Fool am Sheriff of ye Hall, I mean the Hall of Haigh.' Haigh is near Wigan, and, based on the dates of the other people mentioned in the document, it appears Skelton moved to Haigh from Muncaster in 1659, following the death of his employer Joseph Pennington of Muncaster. He posed for the lugubrious portrait in Haigh (where of course he was not 'sheriff' – that is one of his mock titles) sometime before 1665, and died in Wigan in 1668 in late middle age. He may have been born around 1618. Many of the tales around Tom place him in Elizabethan times, and credit him as the inspiration for both the Fool and/or mad Tom o'Bedlam in King Lear, and for the origin of the word 'tomfoolery.' Not so. The *Oxford English Dictionary* in its definition of 'tomfoolery' notes that mentally-ill or 'simple' people were often known as 'Tom foole,'

The much-haunted Muncaster Castle. (Courtesy of Muncaster Castle)

and gives supporting quotations dating to 1640, 1565 and even 1337. And Shakespeare wrote *King Lear* around 1608, a decade before Tom Skelton landed in the world. Skelton's use of the name 'Tom Fool' was based on a tradition dating back centuries.

The portrait was clearly painted when Tom lived at Wigan, although some of the place names in the will show he had previously been in Cumbria. Interestingly the only mention of Muncaster in the will is in the title, 'Thoms. Skelton late fool of Muncaster last will and Testament.' A cruder copy of the painting once hung in Haigh Hall. Ives suggests that once the new Pennington heir, William, came of age and left his guardian to live at Muncaster in 1676, he was offered the original, and the owners of Haigh Hall had the copy made for themselves. He also puts forward the notion that the story of Helwise and Ferdinand Hoddleston may have been confused with the real marriage of Bridget Pennington to Sir William Huddleston, whose father and son were both named Ferdinand.

To summarise: Tom Skelton did not spawn the word 'tomfoolery' or inspire Shakespeare; he lived a century later than the dates usually given for his exploits; few of the tales associated with him can be trusted; and although he certainly was the Fool at Muncaster he did not die there. So, does his motley-clad spirit still caper through the corridors?

Perhaps slightly more reliable is the story of the Luck of Muncaster. On 14 May 1464, in the climactic battle of the Wars of the Roses, Edward IV's Yorkists defeated the forces of Lancaster at the Battle of Hexham. The Lancastrian king, Henry VI, who had been deposed in 1461, had a reputation for being easily captured on battlefields, and so had been previously sequestered by his supporters at Bywell Castle in the upper Tyne Valley. When he fled Bywell he left behind his bycocket, a decorated cap. By this point the pious

The portrait of Tom Skelton, 'Tom Fool,' complete with his Will. (Courtesy of Muncaster Castle)

Henry was regarded by many as almost a saint, so the cap became a magical talisman that would ease headaches (a fine example of sympathetic magic; if he had left his shoe behind, it would no doubt have been claimed to cure athlete's foot). For the next twelve months Henry's loyal supporters became a small band of fugitives, moving the refugee king secretly from house to house in the north-west. At Furness Abbey he passed himself off as a monk and would probably have been quite happy to stay there.

This is the background to the now-famous visit by Henry to Muncaster (preceded by a less warm welcome at IRTON). Whether a shepherd did really encounter the travel-weary king in a hollow oak on Muncaster Fell or not, it does seem certain that Henry was sheltered in the castle by Sir John Pennington. A bedroom is still known as King Henry's Room. When Henry left, he expressed his gratitude by gifting one of his few remaining possessions, a glass drinking bowl, allegedly saying either 'The family shall prosper so long as they preserve it unbroken,' or, less likely but more poetically: 'So long as this cup shall stay unriven, Pennington from Muncaster shall ne'er be driven.' Or again, as gussied up in a poem in John Roby's *Traditions of Lancashire* (1872):

> But take this cup – 'tis a hallowed thing,
> Which holy men have blessed;
> In the church of the Holy Sepulchre
> This crystal once did rest;
>
> And many a martyr, and many a saint,
> Around its brim have sate;
> No water that e'er its lips have touched
> But is hallowed and consecrate …
>
> It shall bless thy bed, it shall bless thy board,
> They shall prosper by this token;
> In Muncaster Castle good luck shall be,
> Till the charmed cup is broken!

Of course, given Henry's holy reputation, the vessel was regarded as charmed, and became known as the Luck of Muncaster. It was placed in a box and promptly buried to await a more peaceful epoch, and when that epoch arrived it was dug up – and the box accidentally fell. So nervous were the Penningtons – after all, their fortunes as a family depended on the Luck being intact – that it was another forty years before a descendant summoned up the courage to peek inside the case. Both the intact bowl and the Penningtons are still in the castle. Roby went on to give more tales in his poem attached to his historical section, although it is not clear whether these are traditions recounted to him, or simply products of his poetic imagination. In one, an unscrupulous knight covertly obtained the cup and tipped it down a well. And at a later date a Pennington fancied a daughter of the house of Lowther, but she told him she would have nothing to do with a Luck-less man. Fortunately a passing fairy revealed the location of the lost Luck and the courtship was concluded successfully.

Henry VI was captured on 13 July 1465 while fording the River Ribble near Clitheroe, and was murdered in the Tower of London in 1471. Many people in the north of England worshipped him as a martyr, and although Henry VII had the body reburied in 1485 at the prestigious St George's Chapel in Windsor, he gave up an attempt to have Rome canonize the martyr-king because the process was simply too expensive.

The Luck is almost 6in (15cm) in diameter, with enamel and gold mouldings. According to Molly Lefebure's *Cumberland Heritage* the Victoria & Albert Museum had concluded it was Venetian and dated it to around 1500, so it could not have been owned by Henry VI. I have not been able to trace any confirmation of this report.

Close to the castle is Muncaster Church (SD104965), a Victorian building on a Norman site. In the churchyard stands a very worn tenth-century cross shaft at the base of which is a cross-head which may or may not belong to it. The stained glass includes two angels with wonderful polychromatic wings. A graveslab has the inscription:

Of your charitie preye for the sowle of Syr John de Penyngton ... Syr John resseved holie Kynge Harry whyche was Henry ye Sixtte at Molcastre 1461. Kynge Harry gave Sir John a brauve workyd Glasse Cuppe, with his Rod before at whyllys the familye shold keep hit unbrecken thei sholde gretelye thrif whyche Cuppe is kalled the lucke of Molcastre.

Jennifer Westwood, in *Albion: A Guide to Legendary Britain*, states that this inscription – which, if genuine, would confirm the story of the Luck – is actually faux antique writing inserted on the tomb of his ancestor by another Sir John Pennington. Who died, not in the fifteenth century, but in 1813.

In 1783 the same Sir John had erected a three-storey octagonal inspired Gothic folly at the spot where it was claimed shepherds found the fugitive King. It is in Chapel Wood about ⅔ mile (1km) north of the castle at SD111975. There is no access. When E.M. Hatt and Paul Sharp were researching their 1967 book *British Castles, Follies and Monuments* their artist irreverently nicknamed the structure a 'dolly folly' because it was home to a canoe, a rabbit hutch, and two dolls.

The Muncaster Boggle or White Lady, long reported as haunting the roads around Muncaster Castle, had always been linked in tradition to the death of a young housekeeper from Ravenglass named Mary Bragg. Local researcher David Bradbury has tracked down the boggle's origins (the complete documents can be found on his website www.pastpresented.co.uk, a treasure trove of local history). Bradbury started with the report of the coroner's inquest in the *Cumberland Pacquet* on 19 November 1805, a day after the actual inquest. Mary's body had been found at a place called Muncaster Steps in the Esk estuary on the 15 November. The *Pacquet* asserted that, 'a strong suspicion prevails that she had been strangled; but no discovery has yet been made of the perpetrator of this atrocious deed,' and after giving many paragraphs of witness testimony it concluded that Mary was 'found drowned and suffocated in the waters of the River Esk ... but how or by what means she became drowned and suffocated as aforesaid is wholly unknown to the jurors.'

A week later (26 November) the *Pacquet* had to print a retraction:

The paragraph in our last, concerning the body of a young woman, found at Muncaster-Steps, &c. was erroneous in several particulars – We have indisputable authority for saying, that after the most minute examination by Mr. Benson (the coroner) two surgeons, and a respectable jury, there did not appear a single circumstance to warrant an opinion of any violence or cruelty having been committed upon the body; but there were strong reasons for suspecting that the death of the unfortunate girl had been her own rash act. The jury returned a verdict – Found drowned.

Bradbury next located *The Muncaster Boggle*, a pamphlet published in Whitehaven in 1870. It purported to describe the experience of the anonymous author (actually J. Burroughs) on 1 May 1862. It was a wild and stormy night and after he had crossed over the Muncaster Bridge, Burroughs offered a lift to an old man heading to Ravenglass. In exchange his passenger told Burroughs a ghost story. It's hard to tell whether Burroughs really did meet the unnamed old man, or whether he was creating a convenient framing device for a well-known local tradition. Mary, apparently, had been in love with John Pike, the house steward at Muncaster. But Miss Littledel, a housekeeper at the castle, also had her eye on Pike. Littledel hired Scot, a hack chaise (carriage) driver, and Kit Gale, Muncaster's coachman, to do away with her rival. One night the two men called on Mary, claiming her sweetheart was seriously ill, and persuaded her to go with them to see Pike. At an old oak on the road through Muncaster wood (approximately NY096966) they murdered her, or, as Burrough's informant graphically put it, 'he ram'd his pistol intul her mouth and blew her brains oot.'

This was largely conjecture and was not reported at the inquest, although much circumstantial detail was. The old man was convinced something dodgy had happened at the inquest to avoid a further investigation for murder, and that Mary, having been denied justice, had returned to wreak supernatural vengeance. Certainly none of the principals in the story thrived thereafter. Kit Gales was hanged in London for highway robbery; within a year Scot lost his mind; Littledel moved to Whitehaven where she was snubbed as a murderess; and John Pike, who no one could say had a hand in the crime, nevertheless became an anxious, nervous wreck. The narrative concluded by noting that several local people, including Will Smith, had seen the Boggle, and the old man himself had been so scared by footsteps following him on a dark night that when crossing a beck he wasted no time looking for the stepping stones, but ran straight through the deep water, and never ventured along that road again.

Tony Walker's *Ghostly Guide to the Lake District* says that in the 1990s when 'Mary Bragg's Tree' – the cursed oak where she was killed – became old and dangerous, it took quite a search to find someone willing to cut the tree down. During the operation the worker's arm was sprayed with blood – courtesy of a hibernating bat that had been accidentally hit – and the tree's reputation appeared confirmed. No one would buy the timber so it was taken out of the area.

RAVENGLASS

Little now remains of the once-important Roman fort and naval base of Glanoventa, the only exception being the bath-house, also known as Walls Castle (SD087958). Here the structures are still over 12ft (3.7m) high. Ravenglass is one of several locations in England and Wales bruited as the fifth-century birthplace of St Patrick. About 1599 the antiquarian William Camden visited and recorded that the locals believed the ruins were the royal palace of 'King Eveling'. Later scholars followed a tortuous path through Welsh myths, Celtic literature – and a fair amount of guesswork – to relate Eveling to Evelac, also known as Avallach, the son of Urien and King of Rheged and the father of Modron, who became the legendary mother of Owain/Owen. As if this wasn't enough, Modron was said to have taken the grievously wounded King Arthur to her father's island Ynys Avallach – the Isle of Avallach – which later became corrupted to Avalon. Modron herself became translated into Morgan la Fée, the good healing fairy (or Morgan le Fay the wicked witch, depending on who you read). Another, separate, strand of myth was mined to show that Walls Castle was 'Lyons Garde,' the home of the fairy Lyones, the Lady of the Fountain. So Ravenglass is the ancestral home of the Kings of Cumbria, and the Isle of Avalon where Arthur lies, and the residence of two magical beings. Myth is such fun.

Ravenglass is the coastal terminus for the charming Ravenglass and Eskdale Railway, a former mining operation now converted to a major tourist attraction. Narrow gauge steam trains chug up to BOOT in Eskdale. In Richard Adams' anthropomorphic novel *The Plague Dogs* Snitter and Rowf, wrongly suspected of carrying bubonic plague developed in a secret bioweapons facility, escape the soldiers hunting them by jumping on one of the trains. The CryptoCumbria website reports that wallabies have been spotted living in the wild around Ravenglass.

BOOT

In 1976-77 Phil Hazlehurst, now General Manager of the Rum Story in Whitehaven but then working at Sellafield, was living at Gill Bank, the last house up the hill on the way to Burnmoor Tarn on the east bank of Whillan Beck (NY181018). One night, he told me, he had a persistent dream of driving along and seeing a policeman in front of him signalling him to stop, but the car's brakes weren't working and on each occasion he ran the policeman down – at which point Phil woke up. This happened several times. In the morning he decided to test his brakes just to make sure. He went forward, braked: fine. Reversed, braked: fine. He decided to do it one more time, went forward down a steeper slope, braked: nothing. No brakes. So he had the car taken for repairs. Later that day he got a telephone call from the garage: 'Did anyone have it in for him?'

'No, why?'

'Well …'

The outer lining brake pipe had been cut through – the pipe had not been severed all the way, so he had brakes on the flat, but if he needed to brake seriously they would fail. He had no enemies and could think of no one who would do it. Besides, you had to walk to the house, which was on a very steep untarmaced track – steeper than Hardknott Pass – and any car would have made a great noise. He reported it to the local police but heard no more. Around the same time he had another premonitory dream, and remembered it just as he and two workmates were driving to work at Sellafield and negotiating a nasty bend in Gosforth. He said, 'I dreamed about us doing this, and there was a sheep just there by the road …' and they saw the sheep. Then he said, 'You better slow down because a white van will come round the bend.' And one did.

At another time in the mid-1970s a friend of Phil's was living at Gill Bank. Having just come off a double shift at Sellafield he was relaxing, reading with some music and a glass of wine – when a book fell off a shelf. He put it back. A few minutes later the same book fell. He replaced it again, and now focused all his attention on the book, waiting for it to drop. It didn't – but instead the cutlery draw threw itself out and scattered its contents noisily on the floor. Phil's friend promptly climbed through the window and turned up at the pub in his dressing gown, and would not return alone.

St Catherine's Church (NY175003) may owe its location to an ancient set of stepping-stones across the Esk. The local website www.eskdale.info states that a sixth-century hermit lived on Armont Hill to the east. There is certainly an overgrown former holy well, St Catherine's, near the lane leading north to Beckfoot (NY175005). Writing in *Source – the Holy Wells Journal* (1986) Lesley Park noted that something called the Dogskin Fair was apparently held at the well on St Catherine's feast day, although this may have been an offshoot of the Catty (Catherine's) Fair held at the church the same day, when yarn was hung on the churchyard wall. The old practice of using well water for baptisms was briefly revived after 1925, following an excavation of the well; it may be back in vogue in the present day. In the churchyard is the elaborate gravestone of legendary huntsman Tommy Dobson, appropriately carved with a hunting horn, hound and fox.

ESKDALE

On a stone near Buck-Cragg, are the impressions of the foot of a man, a boy, and a dog, without any marks of tooling, or instrument.

William Hutchinson, *History of the County of Cumberland* (1794)

A huge Crag, called Buck Crag – & immediately under this is Four-foot stone – having on it the clear marks of four foot-steps. The stone is in its whole breadth just 36 inches [91cm], (I measured it exactly) but the part that contains the marks is raised above the other part, & is just 20½ Inches [52cm]. The length of the Stone is 32½ Inches [83cm]. The first foot-mark is an Ox's foot – nothing can be conceived more exact – this is 5¾ Inches [15cm] wide – the second is a Boy's shoe in the Snow, 9½ Inches [24cm] in length / this too is the very Thing itself, the Heel, the bend of the Foot, &c. – the third is the Foot-step to the very Life of a Mastiff Dog – and the fourth is Derwent's very own first little Shoe, 4 Inches [10cm] in length & O! It is the sweetest baby shoe that ever was seen … this really does work upon my imagination very powerfully & I will try to construct a Tale upon it / the place too is so very, very wild. I delighted the Shepherd by my admiration / & the four foot Stone is my own Christening, & Towers undertakes it shall hereafter go by that name for hitherto it has been nameless. – And so I returned & have found a Pedlar here of an interesting Physiognomy – & here I must leave off – for Dinner is ready –.

Samuel Taylor Coleridge, 6 August 1802, *Collected Letters*

Buck's Crag, where John Vicar Towers of Taw House Farm took Coleridge to show him the wonderful stone, does not appear on the modern map. It is probably part of High Scarth Crag (NY214037). I suspect very few modern people have seen Coleridge's Four-foot stone, which sounds like it may either be a simulacrum or some prehistoric rock art.

William Henderson's *Folk-Lore of the Northern Counties of England* (1879) has a very similar folktale to the witch story at OUTGATE. A mysteriously-regarded hare was shot with fragments of a silver coin. At that moment an old lady, carding wool for her spinning, cried out, 'They have shot my familiar spirit!' and fell dead.

The *Whitehaven News* for 26 February 1998 reported a sighting of a big cat at Stoney Tarn (NY200025). Nora Winter and her husband had seen it in September 1996.

HARDKNOTT PASS

> Aloft, the imperial Bird of Rome invokes …
> that lone Camp on Hardknot's height,
> Whose Guardians bent the knee to Jove and Mars

> William Wordsworth, 'The River Duddon' (1820)

Of all the Roman forts in the country, Hardknott Castle (NY219015) must be the most spectacularly-sited (and windswept – probably not a choice posting). Note that the road to here is very, very steep. Mediobogdum guarded the route from the forts at BROUGHAM and AMBLESIDE to the port at RAVENGLASS. The ruins are well-preserved and include walls, granaries, barracks and baths. The levelled area to the north-west, up the hillside was the laboriously-constructed parade ground. The website www.paranormaldatabase.com reports that on 8 May 2008 two people heard the sound of marching for about twenty seconds.

SEATHWAITE & DUNNERDALE

Seathwaite Footbridge (SD225963) has two inscribed stones, one marked 'AB,' the other with a star and the symbols for Alpha and Omega. In 'The River Duddon' Wordsworth described fairy footprints near Birks Bridge (SD239994): 'A sky-blue stone, within this sunless cleft / Is of the very footmarks unbereft / Which tiny Elves impressed / on that smooth stage.' Sadly the prints cannot now be identified.

ULPHA

A murder victim supposedly still hangs around the lonely ruins of Frith Hall (SD189916), which went from an aristocratic hunting lodge to a Gretna Green-like wayside marriage hall and smugglers' den.

MITERDALE

This relatively unvisited, road-free valley is home to another of the Lake District's established canon of ghosts, the Beckside Boggle – which probably never existed outside a local novelist's imagination. The story is that at a farmhouse at the top of the dale – exactly where, we'll come to in a moment – the farmer was away for the day when his wife saw a curious figure approach. It turned out to be an old woman, who begged shelter, which was granted. After asking some uncomfortably searching questions – such as when the farmer would be home, where they kept their money, and so on – the visitor fell asleep on a bench. At this point the farmwife realised that the old woman was in fact an armed man, clearly intent on robbing and perhaps murdering her. Lacking any other weapon, she poured boiling sheep fat down his throat until it covered his entire face. When her husband returned they buried the body in the ruined Nanny Horns pub and told no one about it. They also discovered the man's clothes, which he had changed out of just before arriving at the door, and a cache of stolen items from the thief's previous robberies. After the old couple died a few years later the brigand's ghost haunted the farmhouse, his head covered by a grotesque wax-like white mask of congealed sheep fat.

The only source for this episode is *The Beckside Boggle*, a short story published in 1886 by local author Alice Rea in *The Beckside Boggle and other Lake Country Stories* (it was reprinted in 1988 in Hugh Lamb's anthology of Victorian horror, *Gaslit Nightmares*). Miss Rea may have been drawing on local tales not recorded anywhere else, but I suspect she simply invented it, as you do when you're writing fiction. In short order, however, the Boggle made the leap from fiction to folklore, and today is frequently found listed in ghost books and paranormal websites as a 'real' haunting. Over the years, details have been added: the agonising screams of the monstrous spirit of the dead man are supposed to have been so ferocious that they caused the abandonment of the farmhouse; and the pub (which in the original story was already in ruins).

Rea called the cottage where the killing took place 'Beckside,' a name never used for any of the very few buildings at the valley head. She also appears to have invented not only the name Nanny Horns but also the pub itself. Local historian David Bradbury has been digging into this story for some time; in an email to me he noted that he had searched county licensing records – which go back to the mid-eighteenth century – and found no mention of any pub. There are also detailed surveys, maps and extensive local history documents going back to the sixteenth century on Alan Swindale's Family History website – again, no hint of an inn. In an area with only four buildings, it's hard to imagine that a pub might be omitted from the records. Bradbury's suggestion was one of the houses might have developed a tradition of informal hospitality for the weary traveller because the hamlet was the first sign of human life you encountered after miles of slogging over the fells from the north. Alternatively, Rea simply made it up.

And the notion that the ghost drove the farm tenants out? Miterdale Head was once two properties; inevitably they were consolidated and one, Sword House, slightly to the west (NY160024), became redundant and simply decayed away – it was empty before 1758, and has now almost entirely vanished, as has a neighbouring house, Browyeat, on the south side of the River Mite just east of its confluence with Robin Gill (NY160023). Miterdale Head (NY161025) itself can still be seen but is completely ruinous, having become empty by the later nineteenth century. These dwellings were abandoned for commonplace agricultural and economic reasons. The ghost story, however, gives a much more dramatic, and much more narratively pleasing, reason. Sometimes the hauntings are described as being in the Outdoor Pursuits Centre in the former barn of Bakerstead (NY159023): I suspect this is due to it being the only roofed building left in the immediate area – ghosts can move their billet if the demands of the narrative require them to do so. There have been no credible reports of the Beckside Boggle; it was born from fiction, and that is where it remains.

In *The English Lake Country* (1969) Dudley Hoys reported that twelve years previously a friend had discovered an old newspaper report of a crime in Whitehaven. Two sailors had quarrelled on the quay, one stabbing the other to death. The murderer had taken to the fells. A little while later a lonely farmhouse was broken into, and among the items stolen were some of the farmer's wife's clothes. David Bradbury thinks this may have occurred in the 1860s or slightly later. It is possible then, that Alice Rea read this report and used it as the inspiration for the boggle story, perhaps taking the 'death by boiling fat' motif from an almost identical tale that is told of Bewley Castle near King's Meaburn.

One of the other stories in *The Beckside Boggle* collection was 'How Our Fathers Went A-Burying.' This tells the tale of a funeral party taking the corpse of a young man for burial. The colt bolts on the fell and is lost. A few months later the mother dies and the old gray mare carrying her coffin bolts in exactly the same place. The search party looking for the mother come across the colt and give the son a proper burial, but the mother and mare are never found. As a result the ghostly grey horse can be seen galloping across the moors, still carrying its 'strange and uncanny burden.' This supernatural episode reads as if it has just been tacked on the end of the rest of the story, which tells of the old days of taking coffins along the Corpse Road.

Here, at least, we are on solid ground. Before the Wasdale Head churchyard was built at St Olaf's, England's smallest church (NY188087), funeral parties carried the dead on horse- or donkey-back across the moors to St Catherine's in BOOT. The path, via Burnmoor Tarn and Eskdale Moor, can still be walked. In 1980 the Ambleside Oral History Group interviewed 'AD', who was born in 1898. He remembered that many times he went up to the moors on a spring night to paint white crosses on the stones marking the Corpse Road. In *The Landnama Book of Iceland* the Revd T. Ellwood recorded a possibly-not-entirely-true anecdote told him by Will Ritson (see SANTON BRIDGE). A woman was being carried to her last rest when the coffin accidentally touched a rowan, a tree well known for its magical powers. The coffin was thrown off the horse and fell open, and the woman was found to be alive. After several more years of not being dead, she eventually took the same final journey. As the funeral party approached the rowan again, her alarmed husband shouted out, 'Tak' care o' that rowan tree!' This time there was no contact with the magical branches.

The general area through which the Corpse Road passes is littered with prehistoric monuments, although finding them on the moors can sometimes be a bit hit and miss. The centre of the cairn at Maiden Castle below Hard Rigg (NY184054) has been topped with a sheepfold and hollowed out for a shelter; sitting within its walls it feels like the cairn at the end of the world. The skeleton of an ancient settlement can be seen on Boat How (NY178034). The two small adjacent Low Longrigg stone circles (NY172028) are on the next summit to the south-west, while from them the largest circle, the low Brat's Hill circle, is about 440yds (400m) south (NY173023). Excavations of the circle's five internal cairns revealed funereal deposits of burnt bone and antlers. Best of all are the splendid twin circles of White Moss, a minute's walk away (NY172024). All the circles are marked as 'cairns' on the OS maps. Every one is worth visiting, not least for the scrumptiously desolate settings.

On the southern shore of Burnmoor Tarn is Burnmoor Lodge (NY184041), possibly the loneliest roofed two-storey dwelling you will ever encounter. You'd think it would be a welcome shelter on the moor, but several people have reported that something about it gives them the creeps.

WAST WATER

In 2005 the *News & Star* (12 February) reported on the gnome garden that had been created by divers at the bottom of this, the deepest lake in England. The forty-plus colony had included props such as a picket fence, a wooden aeroplane and a lawnmower. Rob Watkins, chairman of West Cumbria Sub Aqua Club, was quoted as saying 'When people see the gnomes they think they are hallucinating.' Unfortunately this unusual attraction had caused divers to spend too much time too deep searching for the gnomes and a few years previously there had been three deaths in quick succession. Police divers therefore removed all the items, which had been 157ft (48m) down. The 2005 reports claimed that more gnomes had now been planted deeper than 164ft (50m), the maximum limit for police divers. Needless to say, diving to this depth is extremely hazardous.

Wast Water is probably most notorious for its 'Lady in the Lake' case. In 1984 amateur divers searching for missing French hill-walker Veronique Marre discovered, at a depth of 110ft (34m), a carpetbag tied to a concrete slab. It turned out to contain the corpse of Margaret Hogg, who had gone missing in October 1976. The body was preserved like wax because of the lack of oxygen. Margaret's husband, Peter, was later found guilty of her manslaughter and served a four-year jail term. Had he rowed just 10yds (9m) further out, the weighted body would have sunk beyond normal diving depths. Veronique Marre's remains were eventually found at the foot of Broken Rib Crag; it was presumed she had fallen from a height.

Phil Hazlehurst (see BOOT) told me of a strange experience. In about 1976 he was at the south-west end of Wast Water with a girlfriend. They were waiting for the full moon to rise above the mountains over the lake, which they had heard was very beautiful. They had opened a bottle of champagne, it was about half past midnight and everything was lovely. But when the moon rose an unpleasant and cold atmosphere descended over the place. They started arguing over something trivial, and then panic gripped them so severely they had to flee. Only when the lake was out of sight did their mood improve and the panic subside.

WASDALE

In her *Guide to the English Lakes* (1855) Harriet Martineau recorded a curious local belief:

> … the children were dirtier than even in other vales … the state of children's skin and hair is owing to superstition … A young lady who kindly undertook to wash and dress the infant of a sick woman … exclaimed at the end 'O dear! I forgot its hands and arms. I must wash them.' The mother expressed great horror, and said that 'if the child's arms were washed before it was six months old, it would be a thief.'

The Times for 7 April 1860 reported that a snowstorm in Upper Wasdale on 16 March had deposited blocks of ice so large that at a distance they looked like a flock of sheep. A huge Bronze-Age cairn sits atop Seatallan (NY139084), but it has been damaged by walkers rearranging the stones for shelter. The Sphinx Rock, a simulacrum of a great head, can be seen from the path at Needle ridge on Great Gable, although the best view is only available to skilled climbers.

SCAFELL

A.H. Griffin's *In Mountain Lakeland* relates a classic 'crisis apparition' case from the First World War. A man ascending Scafell one summer afternoon was joined by his friend, a well-known climber. This was strange, as the climber was supposed to be fighting on the Western Front. After a convivial time together the soldier departed, promising to see the other later. Some days later the first man received a letter informing him that his friend had been killed in France on the very afternoon he walked with him on the fells.

On 9 September 2006 Scafell became the location for Britain's highest book launch, for the new edition of *Scratch & Co. The Great Cat Expedition* by Molly Lefebure, with illustrations by A. Wainwright, originally published in 1968. The book wittily chronicles the ascent of the mountain by a team of cat climbers, coping with terrier sherpas, rabbit porters, fox bandits, feline reporters and a crazed mongoose.

NETHER WASDALE

In *The Ghostly Guide to the Lake District* Tony Walker described how he arrived at the Screes Inn on 12 September 1998 just as an Australian couple were checking out because their room, No. 4, was haunted. The phenomena included footsteps, tappings, a strange atmosphere, the television suddenly going off and a force that held the door closed against the man coming in. Several other events had previously occurred in the kitchen, bar and gents toilet, an apparition of a man in a period white shirt with a large collar had been seen, and the previous owner had briefly witnessed an old fashioned pair of black shoes with shiny buckles in her room.

IRTON

Tradition, that unimpeachable source, states that following the Battle of Hexham Henry VI was refused shelter at Irton Hall and had to spend the night under (or, more usually in the story, within) a tree in front of the hall, which has henceforth borne the name the King's Oak. The lady of the house, Ann Lamplugh, took pity on the refugee king and brought him food, for which crime her husband John Irton imprisoned her in the pele tower. Presumably she ended her days there, for she is said to be the lady in black who now haunts the stairs and battlements of the tower. The next day Henry hoofed it over the fell to a more generous reception at MUNCASTER CASTLE. Irton Hall (NY105005) is private but has accommodation, and a footpath through the grounds gives sight of the oak as it leads to St Paul's Church (NY092005) and the 10ft (3m) high Irton Cross. Unusually for this area, this is a ninth-century cross with exclusively Celtic Irish-style interlace decoration, and dates from before the Norse occupation.

Within the Victorian church one of the stained-glass windows (designed by Edward Burne-Jones and William Morris & Co.) features the Tiburtine Sibyl, with her cat-headed fur cloak. The Sibyl was a pagan Roman oracle who featured in a fine piece of Christian propaganda: on being asked by the Emperor Augustus if he would be worshipped as a god, she pointed to a vision in the sky of the Virgin and Infant. There is a Virgin Mary Well above the banks of the River Irt south of Greengarth Hall (NY081003), but I have found no story pertaining to it.

Jason Braithwaite (see MUNCASTER) interviewed a father and son who separately and thirty years apart were each driving along Irton Levels near a 'tunnel' of trees when they passed right through the apparition of a woman walking along the lanes.

SANTON BRIDGE

Gerald Findler's *Ghosts of the Lake Counties*, which is often a bit short on confirmatory details, tells of an event a few years before 1969. Some young men from the Outward Bound School at Eskdale camped near Santon Bridge. It was a moonlit night, which brought strange sounds akin to dogs barking, geese gabbling and a woman's hysterical laughter. They searched the roads and found nothing, and thought that their remote location precluded pranksters.

Every year the Bridge Inn hosts the World's Biggest Liar Competition, in which candidates have just a few minutes to impress a panel of judges with their tall tales (Rule 7: 'Members of the legal profession and politicians are barred from entry.') The competition is held in honour of Will Ritson, a nineteenth-century pub landlord celebrated for his elaborately creative stories, which included such gems as a turnip so large its skin was used as a shed, and a hound which mated with an eagle and subsequently gave birth to a litter of winged puppies. Ritson gained the top liar crown in 1872, and the competition was held annually for a few years until dying out. It was revived in 1974 and I suspect that since then the culture surrounding the event – which must surely involve people practicing their whoppers and generally spreading the lies in as plausible manner as possible – has contributed to many of the weird tales in this chapter. I'm not saying everything is invented, but read on …

DRIGG

The *Daily Express* for 30 June 1978 reported that Michael King, a forestry worker, was working in a clearing in the woods at Drigg when he encountered … giant spiders. They were 'very brightly coloured – blue, red and yellow' and their webs were like steel, 'You could feel them pull tight against your body. You had to force your way through them. The spiders were over half an inch (1.3cm) across their bodies.' In addition, there were 'brambles the size of golf balls' and 'All the vegetation was very lush and quick growing. I felt the whole area and its insect life was being mutated by the presence of radioactive waste.' And there's the rub – the area was formerly used as a dump for low-level radioactive waste from Windscale (now Sellafield). I suspect that proximity to both Sellafield and Santon Bridge has fused radioactive mutation with tall-tale telling. Possibly related is the rumour that woodland near here is home to wild boar.

SEASCALE

Poor old Grey Croft Stone Circle (NY034023) has suffered more than most ancient monuments. In 1820 all but one of the stones were buried for agricultural convenience. In 1949 they were dug up again and restored, hopefully in their original positions. Ten of the twelve now remain, with several having been damaged in recent years, while an outlier which used to stand 37yds (34m) away has been uprooted and plonked in the circle. And to cap it all a short distance away is the titanic Sellafield nuclear facility. Despite all this it is still worth visiting (permissive footpath access over a stile from the road). The 1949 excavation discovered a LANGDALE axe buried close to the eastern stone, flints, a cairn containing cremated bone fragments, and a jet ring from the Whitby area.

Above left: The 14ft (4.3m) high Gosforth Cross, the 'apocalypse cross'. (NB all these photographs of the Cross are of the replica at Aspatria, as the carvings are clearer there.)

Above right: The hero Vidar, represented as a hart; the Fenris Wolf breaks its bonds and the forces of Evil gather. The Gosforth Cross.

Left: A dragon attacks Heimdal (identified by his watchman's horn). Below, Loki writhes in his bonds while his wife empties the bowl of poison dripping from the serpent (seen on the left).

Whitriggs, the southern part of Seascale, was once a large ironworks. In his 1774 *Tour in Scotland* Thomas Pennant described the weird sight of the 'Red Men': 'the ore ... is red, very greasy and defiling. The iron race that inhabits the mining villages exhibit a strange appearance: men, women and children are perfectly dyed with it, and even innocent babes do quickly assume the bloody complexion of the soil.'

According to legend, the Devil, as was his wont, was trying to build a bridge from Herding Neb to the Isle of Man when he dropped the foundation stone, which scuppered his plans. Unfortunately the stone, Carl Crag, is now covered by sand at SD044995, south of Seascale, so we cannot inspect its pair of white stripes, the marks left by the Satanic apron strings.

GOSFORTH

St Mary's Church (NY072036) has a fabulous collection of medieval monuments. The star attraction in the Gosforth Cross, a slim 14ft (4.3m) high Viking cross carved with both Christian and pagan symbolism. The carvings have provided much food for thought among learned commentators, and it is fair to say there is no one undisputed interpretation. There is general agreement, however, that the Viking elements are derived from the *Völuspá*, a poem telling of the creation and coming annihilation of the pagan Norse world. At its heart is the final conflict between the gods of Good and Evil; despite heavy losses, and apparent defeat, the forces of Good triumph in the end and a new world begins. The *Völuspá* was probably composed in the tenth century, and is known from its inclusion in the *Poetic Eddas*, a collection compiled in Iceland in the thirteenth century. If, as has been surmised, the Gosforth Cross was created before AD 1000, then it may be a response to the widely-expected end of the world that was anticipated with the approach of the first millennium. Its interwoven Christian and pagan myths, both of which promise a new world after the apocalypse, might have represented a message of hope for a half-pagan people who were still in transition from one belief system to another.

My interpretation of this 'apocalypse cross' is largely taken from that set out in M.D. Anderson's masterly *History and Imagery in British Churches* (1971), which itself references 'A reconsideration of the Gosforth Cross,' a paper providing a comparative table of the carvings on the cross and the subject matter of the *Völuspá*, written by C.A. Parker and W.G. Collingwood for the CWAAS in 1917.

The monument is topped by a ring-headed cross with a triquetra – symbol of the Christian Trinity – on each arm, but it is the symbols below that catch the attention. The lower part is round and carved with the foliage of Yggdrasil, the ash tree which supported the universe. Each of the four faces of the upper square section contributes part of a continuous narrative that runs up one side and down the other, moving in a clockwise (sunwise) direction. The south side starts with the hero Vidar, son of Odin, represented as a Hart (Good), opposed to the Fenris Wolf (Evil), which has just broken free from its bonds – the tangle at its feet. The escape of the imprisoned Fenris is the signal that the End Time has begun, with the final assault on the Gods of Order by the forces of Evil. Two plaited dragons on the west side continue the assault by attacking the horn-wielding Heimdal, the ever-alert Guardian of Heaven, who guards the rainbow bridge to Asgard (the realm of the Gods). The trickster god Loki lies, where he has been bound by the Gods, beneath a snake; his wife Sygin kneels above him, with the cup she uses to catch the poison dripping from the serpent. When the cup is full she has to empty it, during which time the poison falls on Loki's face: such is his punishment until the end of time, for he used guile to kill

Above left: The dragon of Hel, and possibly the fire-god Surt, originally a volcano demon, prepare for Ragnarök.

Above right: Vidar rends open the dragon's jaws, thus avenging the death of his father Odin.

Left: Baldur, symbol of the new world, is reborn. Here he is also Christ, standing above Longinus and Mary Magdalene and the dragon Nidhöggr.

the god Baldur. Loki must escape to help lead the assault. On the north face the evil forces gather before Ragnarök, the final conflict of the Gods. The many-winged dragon may represent the ship of Hel, the ruler of the underworld, and one of the horsemen may be the fire-god Surt. The great destruction of Ragnarök – which sees a great flood covering the earth and the death of, among others, the Gods Odin, Thor, Heimdall, Loki and Freyr – takes place off-screen as it were; and on the east and final side of the Cross, Vidar, the only survivor, rends open the jaws of Fenris – here shown as a dragon – thus avenging his slain father Odin and bringing the old world to an end. The image is common in later artworks, where Christ forces open the jaws of Hell. The promise of the new world to come is represented by the rebirth of Baldur, who will re-order creation, and who here is also Christ on the Cross, attended by Mary Magdalene and Longinus, who themselves stand above knotted serpents, possibly representing the dragon Nidhöggr, who gnaws at the roots of Yggdrasil. Which brings us back to where we started.

Winged souls flutter from gravestones nearby, while in the church are a pair of tenth-century hogback tombstones, one featuring a pair of crucifixions (the so-called 'saint's tomb), the other scenes from a battle ('the warrior's tomb'). There appear to have been three, if not four, great crosses at Gosforth, for on display are two cross-head fragments, one of which was – astonishingly – cut down in 1789 to make a sundial. No less than six wonderful Green Men leer from the capitals of columns, one spewing out foliage, which forms the hats of two of his companions.

Cemented into the wall – which means we can only see one side – is what is known as 'the fishing stone,' another carving mixing pagan Norse and Christian stories. It takes its name from the lower scene, in which two chaps in a boat are angling in waters filled with fish. The fishermen are the God Thor and the Giant Hymir using an ox-head as bait for Midgard, the World Serpent who encircles the earth. In the legend, Midgard is caught but escapes – clearly the biggest ever 'one that got away.' The great coils of Midgard are shown above the boat, and at the top is the much-used symbol of the Hart trampling the Snake, representing the Christian soul defeating Evil. Another dragon, but from a different culture, adorns the T'ang Dynasty bell kept in the church. It was captured in 1841 at Anunkry, a fort on the River Canton. The crack dates from the one time it was fitted with an iron clapper and used as a church bell, in 1896 – Chinese bells are beaten with padded hammers.

In *Best Pub Walks in the Lakeland Fringes* Neil Coates notes that the Lion and Lamb on The Square hosted several ghosts, including the victim of a stabbing in the small bar to the right, and a grey lady who apparently visits the main bar and upstairs on the same day each month.

Tony Walker reckons Room 11 in the Gosforth Hall Hotel is home to an apparition of a religious-looking figure sitting beside the priest's hole which leads downstairs to the fireplace in the bar. In the early 1990s, when the hotel was busy with contractors working at Sellafield, several men reported odd things in Room 11. Other phenomena included an unoccupied chair rocking gently by a fireplace in the lounge, footsteps from empty rooms, a face in the first floor window, and pewter tankards which would unhook themselves and fly across the bar. Several archaeological digs have taken place in the grounds and in 2005 a sunken-floored Norse Hall was discovered, dating to AD 920.

A footpath passes the hotel leading north to the holy well of Chapel Well (NY073041). Slightly neglected, with an enclosure of rusty railings and covered by a metal inspection cover, it once stood in a tiny medieval chapel. The booklet by Cumbria Holy Wells Trust mentions an 1884 account recording the tradition of pouring red wine into the well on feast days and drinking the mixture of water and wine as it came out of the spout, an act presumed to bring good luck and health. A strenuous walk to the north along the River Bleng brings you to several prehistoric upland sites on Stockdale Moor, including remains of settlements, numerous cairns, and the substantial stones of Sampson's Bratfull Long Cairn (NY098080), pockmarked with excavation holes.

CALDER BRIDGE

The attractive ruins of Calder Abbey (NY01064) cannot be visited but are easily viewed from the footpath which starts at Calder Bridge. When the abbey was dissolved in 1536 it possessed the Blessed Virgin Mary's miraculous girdle, which was used to ease pain at childbirth; presumably it was burnt as a 'superstitious relic'. St Bridget's Church (NY042056) has three medieval cross-slab grave covers and a seventeenth-century memorial with two strange-looking fellows wearing what appear to be bowler hats.

A hill walk taking in a fine range of ancient monuments begins near Cold Fell, from the junction of the fell roads to Haile, Wilton and Egremont at NY055101. First is a Bronze-Age tumulus at NY057100, very close to Friar Well. Then, north along Friar Gill is the lovely Monk's Bridge, the oldest packhorse bridge in Cumbria (NY064103). Further east on Tongue How, south of the path, are a series of prehistoric features including impressively sized stone hut circles, enclosures, field walls, funerary cairns and other signs of an ancient settlement (NY071096 and area).

BECKERMET

Probably one of the most extraordinary stories in this book appeared in the *Whitehaven News* on 5 March 1998. The anonymous writer of a letter claimed that on 25 January of that year, passing Nursery Wood, he had spotted 'a large creature covered in a sort of ginger brown hair.' It was drinking from a pond but then it stood up – to reveal itself as a human-like figure 6ft 6in (2m) tall weighing approximately 14st (89kg). It was naked except for its covering of hair. Nursery Wood (NY027064) is an irregular piece of woodland bounded on three sides by roads, including a busy access road between the A595 and Sellafield, which is 1¼ miles (2km) away. It covers around 600yds² (500m²). Even if such an 'ape-man' existed, there is no way the wood, or the environment around it, could support such a creature. The paranormal Chinese Whispers that takes place online has ensured that the original report, shorn of its detail, has turned up on UFO websites transmogrified into an encounter with a spacecraft and a humanoid alien. It has long been suspected that the letter is a hoax, perhaps a dry run for the lying competition at SANTON BRIDGE. However, the trail has gone cold. There were no follow-up reports, and my appeals in the local press in December 2008 solicited no responses.

Old St Bridget's Church outside the village at NY015061 has two fragments of pre-Norman Conquest cross shafts in its graveyard, one with interlace, the other bearing a runic inscription. The site may be on that of an Anglo-Saxon or even Irish-Celtic monastery. The Victorian church of St John, in the village, has several carved medieval graveslabs.

8

THE WESTERN LAKES

ENNERDALE BRIDGE

The eleven small stones of the moorland stone circle of Blakeley Raise (NY060140) sit next to the road in a lovely location. There appear to have once been thirteen stones, eight of which were removed to make a gateway, with most re-erected in 1925. To the east, by the corner of the wood, is the Great Stone of Blakeley (NY066141), a natural feature providing a superb platform from which to view the stone circle, and therefore may be connected to it in some way. There was once another circle at Standing Stones Farm to the south-west (NY061130), but this has been demolished.

Molly Lefebure, in *The English Lake District*, described how a friend found a mass of frogspawn on the highest and driest part of the track from Ennerdale to Buttermere via Floutern. Her friend could not conceive how it got there, but Molly suggested it was carried thence by a fox, frogspawn apparently being a vulpine favourite.

LAMPLUGH

A document held in the Cumbria Record Office and Local Studies Library in Whitehaven (document reference D/Di/4/53) purports to be a page taken from the Register of Deaths in Lamplugh parish. It claims to record the deaths in the parish from 'Janry ye 1 1658' to 'Janry ye 1 1663':

On a five bar gate, stag hunters	4
Two Duels, first fot [fought] with frying pan and pitchforks	1
Second between a 3 footed stool and a brown jug	1
Kild [killed] at Kelton fell raices [races]	3
Knocked on the head at Cockfight	2
Crost [crossed] in love	1
Broke his neck robbing a hen roost	1
Took cold sleeping at Church	11
Hanged for clipping and coyning [counterfeiting]	7
Of a sprain in his shouldr by saving his dog at bul bate [bull baiting]	1

Mrs Lamplugh's cordial water	2
Knocked on ye head with a quart bottle	1
Frighted to Death by faries	4
Of strong October [ale] at the hall	14
Bewitched	7
Broke a vein in bawling for a knight of ye shire	1
Old women drowned upon trial for witchcraft	3
Climbing a crows nest	1
Led into a horse pond by a will of the whisp	1
Over eat himself at a house warming	1
Died of a fright in an Excersise of ye traind bands	1
By the Parsons bull	2
Vagrant beggars worried by Esqr Lamplughs housedog	2
Choked with eating barley	4
Old age	57

The document, which is on aged paper, has been known for a number of years, having been discussed in the CWAAS in 1944 and in Marjorie Rowling's *The Folklore of the Lake District*. In 2006, however, a cleverly-worded press release from the Archives Service caught the attention of first local and then national press, culminating in a mention on the BBC's *Have I Got News For You*. In most cases the reports assumed that the original document was genuine, and the tone taken was 'weren't our ancestors superstitious/daft?' The more outlandish deaths – witchcraft, fairies and the like – are on a fake tombstone on display in The Beacon, Whitehaven.

The lonely moorland stone circle of Blakeley Raise.

Of course, the document is not what it seems. C.W.L. Bouch started the demolition in his 1948 book *Prelates and People of the Lake Counties*. 133 deaths are given for a five year period where the usual number would be between twenty-five and forty, and, most damningly, none of entries can be found in the actual Parish Register. Bouch concludes that the document's compiler was 'certainly some one with a nice sense of humour.' To underline his point, he indexes the entry as 'Lamplugh, a humourist at.'

Genealogist Chris Dickinson went further in an entry on a discussion thread on RootsWeb on 24 March 2007 (http://archiver.rootsweb.ancestry.com/th/read/ CUMBERLAND). The handwriting isn't mid-seventeenth century, being more likely to be early eighteenth century. The document claims to cover the years 1658-1663 but from 1658-1660 the Register records only sixteen burials, at which point it stops with the death of the parson, and the later Registers have no such record. Dickinson suggests the document was written for an after-dinner speech, possibly at an election meeting. It may well include jests directed at local people or events well-known to the audience, such as the armed combat between frying pan and pitchfork, or stool and jug. The Parson's bull or Mr Lamplugh's dogs may have been noted for their ferocity. Mrs Lamplugh, probably the wife of the landowner, was no doubt famous for making homemade cordials. So, no one was 'drowned upon trial for witchcraft' or 'Frighted to Death by faries.' Shame, really.

As compensation, St Michael's Church (NY089208) has three excellent demonic gargoyles which appear to be a monkey-demon, a dog-headed bird and a pig-headed bird, the last with a human face emerging from its belly. Two carved faces flank one of the small windows and the graveyard contains a worn medieval graveslab known locally as the Crusader's Grave. A pillar stands on a platform a short distance west, between Lamplugh Mill House and Mill Gill Head. This is a corpse cross, a resting place for coffins being taken from Loweswater to Burial at St Bees.

LOWESWATER

In 1964 Molly Lefebure published *The English Lake District* – a wonderful book – in which she described accidentally finding a small stone circle with traces of a ditch and embankment on Burnbank Fell. She wrote to A. Wainwright about it. His book *Fellwanderer* (1966) described in considerable detail how he tried and failed to find the circle. To her chagrin, he adopted a mocking tone, calling the fictional circle Molly's Shame and Molly's Folly. In *Memoirs of a Fellwanderer* Wainwright quotes letters from Lefebure, in which she describes being so stung by the comments that she and a group of friends twice searched the area, and found – nothing. She concluded that she had actually found a stone circle on Burnbank Fell – but that it was no longer there, and on that basis it should be named not her Shame or Folly but Molly's Magic Circle.

BUTTERMERE & CRUMMOCK WATER

There is a persistent tradition (and a complete lack of historical evidence) for a battle in the valley. Candidates include Romans *v* Britons, Normans *v* Cumbrians, and locals *v* Border reivers, a choice which spans fifteen centuries. In 1929 local publican Nicholas Size published *The Secret Valley*, a completely fictional account of the battle, set in 1092. In it, the people of Buttermere conceal the road around Hause Point on Crummock Water (NY162182) so that the invading Normans are tricked into the narrow blind valley of Rannerdale (NY168187) where they are ambushed and massacred. The spectacular annual bluebell display in the dale is said to grow from soil nourished by a pile of rotting Norman corpses – this, and other elements of Size's fiction, is now a staple of local folklore. In *Cumberland Heritage* Molly Lefebure notes that there used to be a large boulder near Gatesgarth at the foot of Honister Pass, marked with 'foreign' lettering. This was supposed to be a commemoration stone for the battle, but it was lost in the 1930s, probably broken up for roadbuilding.

In 1998 amateur divers found the body of Sheena Owlitt in Crummock Water, weighted down with an engine block. Her husband Kevin subsequently confessed to her murder and was jailed for life.

A. Wainwright's ashes were scattered at the side of Innominate Tarn (NY198129) on Hay Stacks on 22 March 1991.

LORTON VALE

In *Our Haunted Kingdom* (1975) Andrew Green reproduced a letter written to him in September 1972 by the Revd J.A. Woodhead-Keith-Dixon of Lorton Hall. There had earlier been reports (for example, in the *West Cumberland Times* 22 July 1967) of a phantom at the seventeenth-century manor house (NY153257, private). The reverend confirmed the reports, noting that the 'Grey Lady' appeared at the time of the full moon, and her usual activity was to open and close doors between 5 and 7.30 in the morning. Once, at the unexpected time of 9.20 a.m., he heard female footsteps. Thinking it was his wife, he went to the library door to speak to her, and saw a 'grey gauzy figure carrying a lighted candle.' She passed down the corridor and exited through the dining room window (where the front door used to be). This was in the early 1960s. Other sightings had been made by a 'down-to-earth tenant' of the home farm and by several Girl Guides camping in the grounds in the 1940s, who saw the ghost coming out of the front door and walking in the garden. An attempt to exorcise the spirit in 1923 was abandoned when, on the morning prior to the event, the designated priest dropped dead.

The ghost had been identified as Elizabeth Dixon, a member of the Dixon family living in the house in the late eighteenth century. She had been one of several children born with Down's Syndrome; unlike her siblings, who died young, she lived into her early sixties, although she was severely disturbed in her later years. There is no burial record for Elizabeth, and the family tradition was that she had been refused interment in the churchyard and so had been laid to rest in the hall's garden. The reverend also noted that in 850 the peripatetic monks carrying the coffin of St Cuthbert rested at Lorton, so when in 1089 Malcom III and Queen Margaret of Scotland made a pilgrimage around the holy places in the south of Strathclyde, they stayed at Lorton and attended Mass in the chapel built on the site of the coffin's resting place.

The Casshow Wood (NY151270) beside the road just north of Lorton was long held to be home to a boggle. F.J. Carruthers (*Lore of the Lake Country*) states it had its origins in memories of a suicide on the spot. A path leads from the layby opposite the wood to Stanger Well, aka Stanger Spa (NY141272), where a small stone building encloses a rusted grating over the well. It may have been a holy well, although there is little evidence other than a mention in an early deed of Fons Susannae (Susanna's Well, possibly corrupted from St Anna?). A sign reads 'St Anna. This is an ancient saline well, one of the few in this area. The building has existed since the eighteenth century, and until recently it had a roof. A doctor in the mid 1800s sold the water for its curative qualities for *6d* per bottle.' This plaque appears to date from the restoration of 1998.

MOCKERKIN

Mockerkin Tarn (NY084232), a small lake with a maximum depth of 11½ft (3.5m), is traditionally the site of the submerged palace of King Morken. Morken was the name of a pagan king based in Glasgow who in Jocelin of Furness' twelfth-century *Life of St Kentigern* opposes St Kentigern (and pays the price). After Morken's death his followers persecute Kentigern so badly he is forced to flee Scotland, thus accounting for the saint's time in Cumbria. Morken is always identified as having his palace in the Clyde valley and has no connection with Cumbria. The association with the tarn may have come from people working backwards from the name Mockerkin to find the only likely candidate in the literature, Morken (Morcant or Morcan in Old Welsh). Alternatively, the name could be related to the shadowy Morcant who may have betrayed King Urien of Rheged to his death – Morcant was a noted villain in ninth-century Welsh sagas.

In John Askew's *Guide to Cockermouth* (1872) someone known only as 'D' tells the highly coloured 'Tale of Mockerkin Tarn' over nine pages of energetic verse. Sir Mochar is a 4ft 3in (1.3m) tall dwarf with a taste for plunder and battle. His huge black charger Rook never grows old, as if it is a magical familiar. When Mochar goes hunting alone and kills a stag or boar he – despite being a dwarf – mysteriously manages to place the heavy body onto Rook's back. The king has three maidens stolen from their homes to serve as his concubines. The girls escape, only to be killed by Mochar, his dogs, or by jumping into a lake. Appalled by what he has done, Mochar blasphemes and curses himself, causing the castle to be destroyed by a storm and flood. Black Rook haunts the tarn to this day, with the dwarf on its back.

> The stones of the tower may still be discerned
> When the tarn is tranquil and clear,
> About twenty feet deep, by those who are learned
> And have eyes of the wizard or seer.

Robert Charles Hope's *The Legendary Lore of the Holy Wells of England* (1893) states, 'It is affirmed that at times the roofs and chimneys of the houses may be seen.'

DEAN

St Oswald's Church (NY071254) is a real gem, with three medieval gargoyles. One appears to be indicating it has toothache, another is a bear (?) in a harness strapped to a two-armed cross, and the third is an acrobat pointing his posterior at us (guess where the rainwater exits). The carved gravestones include a cheery pair of winged souls buddying up, and there is the base and stem of a preaching cross and a fragment of a graveslab carved with a sword. Inside the church, more medieval graveslabs are re-used in the south-west window of the chancel (with an elaborate cross and chalice, indicating the grave of a priest); above the window behind the altar (long sword and cross-headed shorter sword); in the south-east window of the nave (foliated cross and shears); within the north wall of the nave (Celtic cross and sword pommel); and in the floor (cross head with three circles incorporating floral insets, and a sword and shield). The nave contains a cup-and-ring-marked stone, a mason's mark and a stain on a paving slab that forms the simulacrum of an elephant. The pew ends, lectern base, choir stalls and pulpit all have tiny mice carved on them – twenty in total. The mouse, symbolising industry in quiet places, is the trademark of the early twentieth-century master craftsman Robert Thompson, as described in Patricia Lennon's 2001 book *The Tale of the Mouse, the Life and Work of Robert Thompson, the Mouseman of Kilburn*. More Thompson mice can be found in THORNTHWAITE and PATTERDALE.

COCKERMOUTH

The spire of the Victorian All Saints' Church on Kirkgate is alive with zooform gargoyles. Dogs predominate (Cocker Spaniels?), one carrying a bone, but there are also sheep, what may be bears, and other beasts, as well as grotesque humans, all with eyes daubed with a black substance that makes them even more creepy than they were originally. There is also a collection of heads on the corbels of the window arches. In the graveyard is the large monument to George Biddall, who died in Cockermouth in 1909. Biddal ran a famous travelling ghost illusion show, the showfront emblazoned with signs such as 'Phantospectra Biddall's Ghostodramas.' An article that appeared in *The World's Fair* following his death described how the ghost show seemed to have convinced some people that the family had the evil eye. In subsequent years a local rumour developed of a ghost in the graveyard, which too must have stemmed from Biddall's association with spectral illusions. Biddall's story is in the locally-published booklet *The Past People of Allerdale*.

Above left: Rainbow, clouds and sun …

Above right: … and the full moon. Gargoyle on St Oswald's Church, Dean.

Elephant head simulacrum in the floor of St Oswald's Church.

Above left: One of the twenty Thompson mice in St Oswald's Church.

Above right: Cocker spaniels and other creepy black-eyed critters adorning All Saints' Church, Cockermouth.

The still-substantial Cockermouth Castle (private) wedges itself on a boat-shaped strategic eminence above the meeting of the Rivers Cocker and Derwent. In 1724 the antiquarian Stukeley noted, 'they report that the earth of the vallum on the outside the walls was fetched from Ireland, whence no venomous creature can pass over it.' Ireland was famously free of snakes because St Patrick had banished them; hence Irish soil would have made an effective serpentine prophylactic. It will come as no surprise to learn that there is a secret underground tunnel between the castle and the former Roman fort of Papcastle to the north, although the deep, wide River Derwent in between might have been thought to provide an impediment to this.

A terrific source for stories about Cockermouth is John Askew's *Guide to Cockermouth* (second edition 1872, revised by Thomas Thompson after Askew's death). He tells us of the skull at Threlkeld Place, which used to be on the road to Loweswater, possibly near Threlkeld Leys (NY117272). The new tenants of the farm found the skull in a dark room. It was given a Christian burial, but returned to its spot. The family took it to the sea and threw it into the sea off St Bees Head some 30 miles (48km) away, but by the time they returned it was back in its niche. Askew says that several more attempts failed, 'but as to how it disappeared at last, tradition does not inform us.' There is no solid source of a reliable witness who saw the skull, and the details seem to suggest it is simply the replanted tale of the skulls at CALGARTH or BROUGHAM growing in local soil.

Askew describes several standing stones in the area – one in a field opposite Fitz Tollgate, somewhere on the south side of the Derwent; three stones in a line 'in the sixth field from

Papcastle, right of the road to Great Broughton,' and one close by in the second field above Broughton Beck. All these appear to have disappeared. Somewhere south of Cockermouth was the farm of Cleety Bank, home of the elderly Charley Dickinson and his wife. Two robbers, Redhead and Wadlad, invaded the farm. Charley barred them inside and ran for help to the neighbours, who arrived just in time to prevent the duo placing the old woman on the heated griddle to torture the location of the money out of her. The thieves were hanged, as was the custom, within sight of where the crime was committed, 'and the bodies remained a terror to evil-doers till they dropped piecemeal to the ground' as Askew puts it. The site was renamed Gallowbarrow, but this place name too seems to have vanished.

BRIGHAM

St Bridget's Church (NY086309) has five medieval graveslabs inside while the graveyard has a fine selection of carved gravestones, an early cross base, and the table tomb of Fletcher Christian, the mutineer on *The Bounty*. A Nuns' Well formerly flowed near here, suggesting that the former parsonage may have been a nunnery in times past. A much-repeated story is that the Carlisle hangman Joseph Wilson was buried in the churchyard after drowning himself from Cocker Bridge in 1757. A stone rope was carved on his headstone – as a grisly tribute to his choice of career – but it was stolen as a souvenir and so his spirit started to hang around the area. Supposedly the manifestations only stopped when his grave was opened and his skull relocated to his former cottage. Desecrating a sepulchre was a serious business, and as this is meant to have happened as late as 1860, and the author of the act was supposed to be

'Richard he me wrought, and to this beauty me brought.' Richard the mason at work. Norman font, St Bridget's Church, Bridekirk.

Two of the several dragons carved by Richard on the font.

the sexton or vicar, I wonder how much credence we can place on this story. It is also curious that Askew, normally a keen collector of this kind of tale, does not mention it. However, this is one boggle the original report of which I have failed to track down, although I wonder if the following vague account from the *English Lakes Visitor and Keswick Guardian* of January 1882 is somehow connected to the persistence of the place's uncanny reputation:

> For the last few weeks all the girls and timid people of Brigham have been terribly 'flayte' of a boggle … it touched a man on the shoulder and, not despising material things, asked him for a 'pipe o' bacca.' The story goes that when the man turned to speak with his mysterious visitant it had departed and he was unable to catch it, but this was just after 'closing time.' Others also are said to have seen 'something,' but could not say what, except that it was 'like a woman' – certainly not human.

BRIDEKIRK

The amazing Norman font in St Bridget's Church (NY116336) is not only carved with dragons, double-headed monsters, griffins, Adam and Eve and the baptism of Christ, it is signed by the man who did it. A runic inscription reads 'Richard he me wrought, and to this beauty me brought,' and on one side we see Richard of Durham himself, at work with his mallet and chisel, carving a flower and leaf.

Elsewhere in this treasure trove of a church is a very worn figure of Christ on the tympanum of the west porch, a cross-shaft fragment, and, high up on the capitals of the crossing, two owls, a dragon, and a crocodilian monster. Arranged around the exterior of the apse are a number of medieval graveslabs, some with simple crosses, others with swords, and one with sword, shears and an elaborate cross. The walls of the ruined twelfth-century church moulder are in the graveyard.

The Angel of the Last Judgement, with trumpet and book. Gravestone, St Michael and All Angels' Church, Isel.

ISEL

The lovely St Michael and All Angels' Church (NY163334) has two large fragments of an Anglo-Saxon cross shaft, a sundial etched into a stone on the porch, and two more faint sundials on the left side of the exterior south chancel window. A now-empty niche once held the 'Triskele Stone,' a Norse work carved with the triskele (a three-legged spiral, sign of the god Woden) a sun-snake, and a swastika (this being the fylfot, the sign of Thor's hammer). Unfortunately the stone was stolen. There is a photograph inside the church.

The gardens and walls of Isel Hall nearby (NY158338) are decorated with amazing sculptures of pairs of arms holding the sun, this pagan-looking device in fact represents the sun supported by the arms of the law, this being the crest of the Lawson family. In an interview in the *Whitehaven News* (25 October 2007) the Hall's owner, Mary Burkett, described the ghostly lady in a blue dress who had been seen sitting at the end of their bed by four young men on separate occasions over twenty-five years. Isel Hall is open on Mondays, 2-4 p.m., from the last Monday in March to the first Monday in October. Admission charge.

BIBLIOGRAPHY

Those works marked with an asterisk* are highly recommended.

TCWAAS = Transactions of the Cumberland and Westmorland Antiquarian and Archaeological Society

ARCHAEOLOGY, HISTORY, LITERATURE & GENERAL

Anon. 'Druidical Temple, near Keswick, in Cumberland' in the *Saturday Magazine* No. 161 (3 January 1835)

Anon. *Keswick and its Neighbourhood* (Garnett; Windermere, and Whittaker; London, 1852)

Allan, Sue 'Beautiful Borrowdale' in *Cumbria Life* April/May 2007 No. 111

Allerdale Borough Council *The Past People of Allerdale: Tales and Stories of the Interesting and Famous People of West Cumbria* (Allerdale Borough Council; Workington, n.d.)

Anderson, M.D. *History and Imagery in British Churches* (John Murray; London, 1971)

Andrews, William (ed.) *The Church Treasury of History, Custom, Folk-Lore, etc.* (William Andrews & Co.; London, 1898)

Armitt, Mary L. (ed. Willingham F. Rawnsley) *Rydal* (Titus Wilson; Kendal, 1916)

Askew, John *Guide to Cockermouth* (Isaac Evening; Cockermouth, 1872 – facsimile reprint by The Printing House; Cockermouth, 2000)*

Automobile Association *The Lake District and Lancashire* (Reader's Digest Association; London, 1988)

Barnett, John 'Monuments in the Landscape: Thoughts from the Peak' in Gibson, Alex and Derek Simpson (eds) *Prehistoric Ritual and Religion* (Sutton Publishing; Stroud, 1998)

Beckensall, Stan *British Prehistoric Rock Art* (Tempus; Stroud, 1999)

————— *Prehistoric Rock Art in Cumbria* (The History Press; Stroud, 2002)

Blair, John *The Church in Anglo-Saxon Society* (Oxford University Press; Oxford, 2005)

Blamires, Gabriel M. *Guidestones to the Great Langdale Axe Factories: Ancient Ways to Stone Axe Working Sites in the English Lake District* (Gabriel M. Blamires; Cumbria, 2005)

Bogg, Edmund *A Thousand Miles of Wandering Along the Roman Wall, the Old Border Region, Lakeland, and Ribblesdale* (E. Bogg & James Miles; Leeds, 1898)

Bouch, C.M.L. *Prelates and People of the Lake Counties* (T. Wilson; Kendal, 1948)

Bradley, A.G. *Highways and Byways in the Lake District* (MacMillan & Co.; London, 1901)

Briggs, John *The Remains of John Briggs* (Arthur Foster; Kirkby Londsdale, 1825)

Buckley, Norman *Lake District* (Landmark Publishing; Ashbourne, 1998)

Burl, Aubrey *The Stone Circles of the British Isles* (Yale University Press; New Haven & London, 1977)

————— *Rites of the Gods* (J.M. Dent & Sons; London, 1981)

————— *The Prehistoric Stone Rows and Avenues of Britain, Ireland and Brittany* (Yale University Press; New Haven & London, 1993)

————— *A Guide to the Stone Circles of Britain, Ireland and Brittany* (Yale University Press; New Haven & London, 1995)

──────── *Prehistoric Henges* (Shire Publications; Princes Risborough, 1997)

──────── *Great Stone Circles* (Yale University Press; New Haven & London, 1999)

Calverley, Revd William Slater *Notes on the Early Sculptured Crosses, Shrines, and Monuments in the Present Diocese of Carlisle* TCWAAS Extra Series: Vol. XI (T. Wilson; Kendal, 1899)

Camden, William (Trans. Philemon Holland) *Britannia* (Online at www.philological.bham.ac.uk; originally published 1586 & 1610)

Clare, Tom *Prehistoric Monuments of the Lake District* (Tempus; Stroud, 2007)*

Clarke, James *A Survey of the Lakes of Westmoreland, Cumberland and Lancashire* (the Author; London, 1789)*

Coates, Neil *Best Pub Walks in the Lakeland Fringes* (Sigma Leisure; Wilmslow, 1999)

Coleridge, Edith (ed.) *Memoir and Letters of Sara Coleridge* (Henry S. King & Co.; London, 1873)

Coleridge, Samuel Taylor (ed. Earl Leslie Griggs) *Collected Letters of Samuel Taylor Coleridge* (Oxford University Press; Oxford, 2000)

Collingwood, W.G. 'The Home of the Derwentwater Family' *TCWAAS* New Series Vol. 4 (1903-4)

Cook, Tim 'Rock Carvings in Patterdale: A Neolithic Puzzle' in *Year Book 1999 and Transactions of the Matterdale Historical and Archaeological Society*

Cooper, A.H. Eaton & W.M.T. Palmer *The English Lakes* (Adam and Charles Black; London, 1908)

Cowper, Henry Swainson *Hawkshead: (The Northernmost Parish of Lancashire) Its History, Archaeology, Industries, Folklore, Dialect, etc* (Bemrose & Sons; London and Derby, 1899)*

──────── 'Some Miscellaneous Finds' *TCWAAS* New Series Vol. 5 (1905)

Cox, J. Charles *Churches of Cumberland & Westmorland* (George Allen & Co.; London, 1913)

Cumbria Federations of Women's Institutes *Cumbria Within Living Memory* (Countryside Books; Newbury, 2005)

Curwen, John F. *Historical Description of Levens Hall* (Titus Wilson; Kendal, 1898)

──────── *Kirkbie-Kendall: Fragments Collected Relating to its Ancient Streets and Yards; Church and Castle; Houses and Inns* (Titus Wilson; Kendal, 1900)

Darvill, Timothy *Prehistoric Britain from the Air* (Cambridge University Press; Cambridge, 1996)

Defoe, Daniel *A Tour through the Whole Island of Great Britain* (Yale University Press; New Haven & London, 1991) (first published 1727)

De Quincey, Thomas *Recollections of the Lakes and the Lake Poets* (Adam Black; Edinburgh, 1862)*

──────── *Literary Reminiscences* (Ticknor & Fields; Boston, 1865)

Dickinson, Alexander Craig *Cumbriana or, Fragments of Cumbrian Life* (Whittaker & Co,; London, Callanader & Dixon; Whitehaven, 1876)

Dickinson, Steve *The Beacon on the Bay: The Discovery of an Early Christian Church and Monastic Site at Great Urswick, Low Furness, Cumbria and the Case for its Connections with St Ninian, St Patrick, St Hild and St Columba* (Steve Dickinson; Ulverston, 2002)

Dixon, John *Hawkshead Revisited: A Walk in Time through Hawkshead* (Helm Press; Kendal, 2000)

Dymond, C.W. *Mayburgh and King Arthur's Round Table* reprinted from the *TWAAS* (T. Wilson; Kendal, 1890)

Edwards, B.J.N. *Vikings in North West England: The Artifacts* (Centre for North-West Regional Studies, University of Lancaster; Lancaster, 1998)

Ellwood, Revd T. *The Landnama Book of Iceland as it Illustrates the Dialect, Place Names, Folk Lore, & Antiquities of Cumberland, Westmorland, and North Lancashire* (T. Wilson; Kendal, 1894)

Ewbank, J.M. (ed.) *Antiquary on Horseback: The First Publication of the collections of the Rev. Thos. Machell, Chaplain to Charles II, Towards a History of the Barony of Kendal* (Cumberland and Westmorland Antiquarian and Archaeological Society, extra series, 19; Kendal, 1963)

Evans, Francis *Furness and Furness Abbey, or, a Companion through the Lancashire part of the Lake District* (D. Atkinson; Ulverston, 1842)

Farrah, Robert W.E. *A Guide to the Stone Circles of Cumbria* (Hayloft; Kirkby Stephen, 2008)*

Ferguson, The Worshipful Chancellor 'The Bears at Dacre' *TCWAAS* Vol. 11 (1890-91)

Fiennes, Celia *Through England on a Side Saddle in the Time of William and Mary (including travel book, manuscript record of Journeys through England including parts of the Lake District 1698)* (Field and Tuer; London, 1888)

Fleming, Simon D.I. *A History and Guide to St Andrew's Church, Penrith* (Skiddaw Grove Productions; Penrith, 1997)

Fleming, William 'A Furness Diary 1801-1807' in *The Countryman* Vol. LV No. 1 (1958)

Gaythorpe, Harper 'Pre-Historic Implements in Furness' *TCWAAS* Part 1 Vol. XV (1898)

Gerrard, Mike & John Morrison *AA Leisure Guides: Lake District* (AA Publishing; Basingstoke, 2007)

Gibson, Alexander Craig *The Old Man; or, Ravings and Ramblings Round Conistone* (Whittaker & Co.; London, J Hudson; Kendal, 1849)

——————— 'The Lakeland of Lancashire. No. II. – Hawkshead Parish' in *Transactions of the Historic Society of Lancashire and Cheshire* New Series – Vol. VI (1865-66)

——————— *The Folk-Speech of Cumberland and Some Districts Adjacent* (Russell Smith; London, 1869)

Gilpin, William *Observations, Relative Chiefly to Picturesque Beauty, Made in the Year 1772, On Several Parts of England; particularly the Mountains, and Lakes of Cumberland, and Westmoreland* (R. Blamire; London, 1792)

Green, William *The Tourist's New Guide Containing a Description of the Lakes, Mountains, and Scenery, in Cumberland, Westmorland, and Lancashire* (R. Lough & Co.; Kendal, 1819)

Griffin, A.H. *In Mountain Lakeland* (The Guardian Press; Preston, 1963)

——————— *Inside the Real Lakeland* (The Guardian Press; Preston, 1965)

——————— *The Roof of England* (Robert Hale; London, 1970)

Harris, Robert *Walks in Ancient Lakeland* (Sigma Leisure; Wilmslow, 2001)

Hatt, E.M. & Paul Sharp *British Castles Follies and Monuments* (The Reprint Society; London, 1967)

Headley, Gwyn & Wim Meulenkamp *Follies* (Jonathan Cape; London, 1986)

Hutchinson W. *The History of the County of Cumberland* 2 Vols. (F. Jollie; Carlisle, 1794)

Ives, E.W. 'Tom Skelton – A Seventeenth-Century Jester' in *Shakespeare Survey* No. 13 (1966)

——————— 'Tom Skelton and Motley' in *Notes & Queries* New Series Vol. 7, No. 12 (December 1960)

Jackson, Robert *Dark Age Britain: What to See and Where* (Patrick Stephens; Cambridge, 1984)

Lefebure, Molly *The English Lake District* (B.T. Batsford; London, 1964)*

——————— *Cumberland Heritage* (Victor Gollancz; London, 1970)*

Lindop, Grevel *A Literary Guide to the Lake District* (Chatto & Windus; London, 1993)*

Linton, E. Lynn *The Lake Country* (Smith, Elder & Co.; London, 1864)

Livingston, Helen *In the Footsteps of Caesar: Walking Roman Roads in Britain* (Dial House; Shepperton, 1995)

Long, Peter (ed.) *The Hidden Places of the Lake District and Cumbria* (Travel Publishing; Aldermaston, 2003)

McCracken, David *Wordsworth & The Lake District: A Guide to the Poems and their Places* (Oxford University Press; Oxford, 1985)

MacRitchie, William *Diary of a Tour through Great Britain in 1795* (Elliot Stock; London, 1897)

Mannix & Whellan *History, Gazetteer and Directory of Cumberland* (M. Moon; Beckermet, 1974 – Facsimile reprint of 1847 original)

Marsh, Terry *The Lakeland Dales* (Halsgrove; Tiverton, 2004)

Martineau, Harriet *A Complete Guide to the English Lakes* (John Garnett; Windermere, 1855)*

——————— 'Lights of the English Lake District' in *Atlantic Monthly* Vol. 7 No. 43 (May 1861)

Mee, Arthur *The King's England: Lancashire* (Hodder & Stoughton; London, 1936)*

——————— *The Lake Counties* (Bracken Books; London, 1994 (first published 1937)*

Monson-Fitzjohn, G.J. *Drinking Vessels of Bygone Days* (Herbert Jenkins; London, 1927)

Moore, Margaret F. *The Lands of the Scottish Kings in England* (Augustus Kelly; Clifton, 1973) (first published 1915)

Morris, Francis Orpen *A History of British Birds* (Groombridge & Sons; London, 1852)

Newby, George *Henllywarc, or Druids Temple Near Keswick: A Poem* (Longman, Brown, Green, and Longmans; London, and James Ivison; Keswick, 1854)

Nicholls, Arthur R *Kendal Town Trail* (*Westmorland Gazette*; Kendal, 1986)*

Otley, Jonathan *Guidebook, Concise Description of the English Lakes, later A Description of the English Lakes* (the author; Keswick, and J. Richardson; London, and Arthur Foster; Kirkby Lonsdale, 1823 onwards)

Palmer, William T. *The Verge of Lakeland* (Robert Hale; London, 1938)

Pearsall, W.H. & Winifred Pennington *The Lake District: A Landscape History* (Collins; London, 1973)

Pevsner, Nikolaus *The Buildings of England: North Lancashire* (Penguin; Harmondsworth, 1969)

———————— *The Buildings of England: Cumberland and Westmorland* (Yale University Press; New Haven and London, 1967)

Radcliffe, Ann *A Journey Made in the Summer of 1794 through Holland and the Western Frontiers of Germany, with a Return Down the Rhine, to which are Added Observations During a Tour to the Lakes of Lancashire, Westmoreland and Cumberland* (G.G. & J. Robinson; London, 1795)

Raine, Michael *The Wars of the Roses* (Wheaton; Exeter, 1969)

Rawnsley, H.D. *Lake Country Sketches* (James MacLehose & Sons; Glasgow, 1903)

Rice, H.A.L. *Lake Country Portraits* (Harvill Press; London 1967)

———————— *Lake Country Towns* (Robert Hale; London 1974)

Richards, Mark & Christopher Wright *The Westmorland Heritage Walk* (Cicerone Press; Milnthorpe, 1987)

Salter, Mike *The Castles and Tower Houses of Cumbria* (Folly Publications; Malvern, 1998)

———————— *The Old Parish Churches of Cumbria* (Folly Publications; Malvern, 1998)

Scott, Daniel *Bygone Cumberland and Westmorland* (William Andrews & Co.; London, 1899)

Shaw, W.T. *Mining in the Lake Counties* (Dalesman Books; Clapham, 1975)

Smith, Gavin D. *Gavin D. Smith's Lake District: An Alternative View of the Lakes* (The Serpent Press; Oldham, 1997)

Stockdale, James *Annales Caermoelenses: or Annals of Cartmel* (William Kitchin; Ulverston, 1872)

Thorley, John 'The Ambleside Roman Gravestone' *TCWAAS* 2 (2002)

Trench, Richard *Travellers in Britain: Three Centuries of Discovery* (Aurum Press; London, 1990)

Trollope, Thomas Adolphus *What I Remember* (Richard Bentley & Son; London, 1887)

Wainright, Martin *Wainwright: The Man Who Loved The Lakes* (BBC Books; London, 2007)

Wakefield, A.M. *Cartmel Priory and Sketches of North Lonsdale* (H.T. Mason; Grange-over-Sands, 1909)

Walker, J. *The History of Penrith* (B.T. Sweeten; Penrith, 1858)

Watson, George 'Notabilia of Old Penrith' in *Transactions of the Cumberland and Westmorland Association for the Advancement of Literature and Science* Vol. 14 (1888-89)

Watson, John (ed.) & 'A Country Parson' *The Annals of a Quiet Valley* (J.M. Dent & Co.; London, 1894)

Waugh, Edwin *Rambles in the Lake Country and its Borders* (Whittaker & Co.; London, 1861)

West, Thomas *A Guide to the Lakes* (W. Pennington; Kendal, and J. Richardson; London, 11th edition, 1821)

Whiteside, Joseph *Shappe in Bygone Days* (Titus Wilson; Kendal, 1904)

Williamson, George C. *Lady Anne Clifford Countess of Dorset, Pembroke & Montgomery 1590-1676. Her Life, Letters and Work* (Titus Wilson & Son; Kendal, 1922)

Wordsworth, William *Guide to the Lakes* (Frances Lincoln; London, 2004) (first published 1810)

———————— *Selected Poems* (Penguin Classics; Harmondsworth, 1994)

Wyatt, John *The Lake District National Park* (Webb & Bower; Exeter, 1987)

'Y.A.C.' 'Ballad of Dick and the Devil' in *Notes & Queries (A Medium of Inter-Communication for Literary Men, Artists, Antiquaries, Genealogists, etc.)* No. 29 (18 May 1850)

FICTION

Adams, Richard *The Plague Dogs* (Allan Lane; London, 1977)

Mercier, Mrs Jerome (Anne) *The Last Wolf: A Story of England in the Fourteenth Century* (H.T. Mason; Grange-over-Sands, n.d.)

Morson, Ian *A Psalm for Falconer* (Orion; London, 1998)

Rea, Alice 'The Beckside Boggle' (1886) in Lamb, Hugh (ed.) *Gaslit Nightmares* (Futura; London, 1988)

Size, Nicholas *The Secret Valley* (Frederick Warne & Co.; London, 1930)

Stagg, John *The Minstrel of the North: or, Cumbrian Legends; Being a Poetical Miscellany of Legendary, Gothic, and Romantic Tales* (the author; Manchester, 1816)

Twemlow, Cliff *The Pike* (Hamlyn; London, 1982)

Walpole, Hugh *Rogue Herries* (Sutton Publishing; Stroud, 1994) (first published 1930)

——————— *The Bright Pavilions* (Macmillan; London, 1940)

Ward, Mrs Humphry *Robert Elsmere* (Smith, Elder; London, 1888)

——————— *Helbeck of Bannisdale* (Smith, Elder; London, 1898)

Williamson, Shaun *Mauler* (Hayloft Publishing; Kirkby Stephen, 2005)

MYSTERIOUSNESS

Anon *Legends of Westmorland and the Lake District* (Hamilton B. Adams; London, and Rawson B. Lee; Kendal, 1874)

Amos, William *Tales of Old Cumbria* (Countryside Books; Newbury, 1998)

Armistead, Wilson *Tales & Legends of the English Lake District* (Simpkin, Marshall & Co.; London, 1891) [first published in c.1850 as *Tales and Legends of the English Lakes, Collected from the Best and Most Authentic Sources* (Longmans; London) by 'Lorenzo Tuvar']

Ashton, John *The Devil in Britain and America* (Ward and Downey; London, 1896)

Automobile Association *Secret Britain* (Automobile Association; Basingstoke, 1996)

Bailey, Richard N. 'Apotropaic Figures in Milan and North-West England' in *Folklore*, Vol. 94, No. 1 (1983)

Bell, Harry 'Drawing Down the Hills: Terrain Echoes at Castlerigg,' in *Northern Earth* magazine No. 79 (1999)

Bird, Christopher *The Divining Hand* (Schiffer Publishing; Atglen, Pennsylvania, 1993)

Bord, Janet *The Traveller's Guide to Fairy Sites* (Gothic Image; Glastonbury, 2004)

——————— *Holy Wells in Britain* (Heart of Albion; Loughborough, 2008)

Bord, Janet & Colin Bord *Mysterious Britain* (Paladin; St Albans, 1974)

——————— *The Secret Country* (Book Club Associates; London, 1977)

——————— *Earth Rites: Fertility Practices in Pre-Industrial Britain* (Granada; St Albans, 1982)

——————— *Modern Mysteries of Britain: One Hundred Years of Strange Events* (Grafton Books; London, 1987)

——————— *The Enchanted Land: Myths & Legends of Britain's Landscape* (Thorsons; London, 1995)

Bowker, James *Goblin Tales of Lancashire* (W. Swan Sonnenschein & Co.; London, 1883)

Bradford, Anne and Taylor, David *Haunted Holidays* (Hunt End Books; Redditch, 2002)

Braithwaite, Jason J. and Maurice Townsend 'Sleeping With the Entity – A Quantitative Magnetic Investigation of an English Castle's Reputedly Haunted Bedroom' in *European Journal of Parapsychology* Vol. 20, No. 1 (2005)

Brand, John *Observations on Popular Antiquities in Britain, Chiefly Illustrating the Origin of Our Vulgar and Provincial Customs, Ceremonies, and Superstitions* 3 Vols (Henry G. Bohn; London, 1855)

Brewster, David *Letters on Natural Magic* (Chatto & Windus; London, 1883)

Brooks, J.A. *Ghosts and Legends of the Lake District* (Jarrold; Norwich, 1988)

——————— *Britain's Haunted Heritage* (Jarrold; Norwich, 1990)

Carrick, T.W. 'Scraps of English Folklore, XVIII. Cumberland' in *Folklore* Vol. 40, No. 3 (30 September 1929)

Carruthers, F.J. *Lore of the Lake Country* (Robert Hale; London, 1975)

Carter, R.O.M. and H.M. 'The Foliate Head in England' in *Folklore*, Vol. 78, No. 4 (Winter, 1967)

Cumbria Holy Wells Trust *Holy Wells of Cumbria – A Seeker's Guide* (Cumbria Holy Wells Trust; Ambleside, 2008)

Davidson, H.R. Ellis (1990). *Gods and Myths of Northern Europe* (Penguin Books; Harmondsworth, 1964)

Davies, Owen 'Healing Charms in Use in England and Wales 1700-1950' in *Folklore*, Vol. 107 (1996)

——————— 'Charmers and Charming in England and Wales from the Eighteenth to the Twentieth Century' in *Folklore*, Vol. 109 (1998)

——————— *The Haunted: A Social History of Ghosts* (Palgrave MacMillan; Basingstoke, 2007)

Devereux, Paul *Earth Lights Revelation* (Blandford Press; London, 1989)

——————— *Places of Power* (Blandford Press; London, 1990)

——————— *The Sacred Place* (Cassell; London, 2000)

Dugdale, Graham *Walks in Mysterious North Lakeland* (Sigma Press; Wilmslow, 1998)

Dyer, T. F. Thiselton *Strange Pages from Family Papers* (Sampson Low, Marston & Co.; London, 1895)

Farrah, Robert W.E. 'A Sacred Space Odyssey' in *Northern Earth* magazine No. 85

Findler, Gerald *Legends of the Lake Counties* (Dalesman; Clapham, 1967)

————— *Ghosts of the Lake Counties* (Dalesman; Kendal, 1969)

Fortean Times 'All New Improved British Roswell' *Fortean Times* No. 197 (June 2005)

Forbes, John Foster and Iris Campbell *Giants of Britain … with Additional Psychometric Interpretations by Miss Iris Campbell* (Thomas's Publications; 1945)

Fort, Charles *The Book of the Damned* (John Brown Publishing; London, New Ed. 1995)

————— *New Lands* (John Brown Publishing; London, New Ed. 1996)

————— *Lo!* (John Brown Publishing; London, New Ed. 1997)

Fraser, Mark (ed.) *Big Cats in Britain Yearbook* 2006 (CFZ Press; Woolfardisworthy, 2006)

————— *Big Cats in Britain Yearbook* 2007 (CFZ Press; Woolfardisworthy, 2007)

Freeman, Richard 'The Case of the British Thylacine' in *Animals & Men* No. 19 (1999)

Freitag, Barbara *Sheela-na-gigs: Unravelling an Enigma* (Routledge; London, 2004)

Gates, Barbara T. 'Wordsworth's Use of Oral History' in *Folklore*, Vol. 85, No. 4 (Winter, 1974)

Gomme, George Laurence (ed.) *English Traditional Lore: To Which is Added Customs of Foreign Countries and Peoples; The Gentleman's Magazine Library: Being a Classified Collection of the Chief Contents of the Gentleman's Magazine from 1731 to 1868* (Elliot Stock; London, 1885)

Green, Andrew *Our Haunted Kingdom* (Fontana/Collins; London, 1975)

————— *Ghosts of Today* (Kaye & Ward; London, 1980)

Grinsell, L.V. 'Notes on the Folklore of Prehistoric Sites in Britain' in *Folklore*, Vol. 90, No. 1 (1979)

Grundy, Thirlie *Going in Search of the Green Man in Cumbria* (Thumbprint; Carlisle, 2000)

Halton, J.W. 'Beliefs regarding Death in Cumberland' in *Folklore*, Vol. 31, No. 2 (30 June 1920)

Hannigan, Des *Eccentric Britain* (New Holland; London, 2006)

Hayman, Richard *Riddles in Stone: Myths, Archaeology and the Ancient Britons* (The Hambledon Press; London and Rio Grande (Ohio), 1997)

Henderson, William *Folk-Lore of the Northern Counties of England and the Borders* (The Folk-Lore Society / W. Satchell, Peyton & Co.; London, 1879)

Hicks, Clive *The Green Man: A Field Guide* (Compass Books; Fakenham, 2000)

Hitching, Francis *Earth Magic* (Picador; London, 1978)

Hope, Robert Charles *The Legendary Lore of the Holy Wells of England* (Elliot Stock; London, 1893)

Hutton, Ronald *The Triumph of the Moon* (Oxford University Press; Oxford, 2001)

Ingram, John H. *Haunted Homes and Family Traditions of Great Britain* (Gibbings & Co.; London, 1897)

L'Estrange Ewen, C. *Witchcraft and Demonism* (Heath Cranton; London, 1933)

Linahan, Liz *The North of England Ghost Trail* (Constable; London, 1997)

Lofthouse, Jessica *North-Country Folklore* (Robert Hale, London, 1976)

McMahon, Joanne & Jack Roberts *The Sheela-na-Gigs of Ireland and Britain* (The Mercier Press; Cork, 2000)

Maple, Eric *Old Wives' Tales* (Robert Hale; London, 1981)

Merrifield, Ralph *The Archaeology of Ritual and Magic* (B.T. Batsford; London, 1987)

Michell, John *A Little History of Astro-Archaeology* New edition (Thames & Hudson; London, 1989)

————— *The Traveller's Key to Sacred England* (Harrap Columbus; London, 1989)

Newman, L.F. and E.M. Wilson 'Folk-Lore Survivals in the Southern "Lake Counties" and in Essex: A Comparison and Contrast' in *Folklore*, Vol. 62, No. 1 (March 1951), Vol. 63, No. 2 (June, 1952) and Vol. 64, No. 1 (March, 1953)

Nickel, Kenneth 'Five Specters on a Roman Road' in *Fate* April 1998 Vol. 51, No. 4, Issue 577

O'Donnell, Elliott *Ghosts Helpful and Harmful* (W. Rider; London, 1924)

Palmer, Martin and Nigel Palmer *Sacred Britain: A Guide to the Sacred Sites and Pilgrim Routes of England, Scotland & Wales* (Piatkus; London, 1997)

Park, Lesley 'Cumbrian Well Walking' in *Source – the Holy Wells Journal*, Issue 6 (Winter 1986)

Partridge, T.B. 'Lancashire Folklore' in *Folklore*, Vol. 26, No. 2 (30 June 1915)

Richardson, Alan *Spirits of the Stones: Visions of Sacred Britain* (Virgin; London, 2001)

Richardson, Jack *Jack in the Spirit* (Bridge Studios; Berwick upon Tweed, 1989)

Roberts, Andy and Clarke, David 'Heads & Tales: The Screaming Skull Legends of Britain' in
  Fortean Studies Vol. 3 (John Brown Publishing; London, 1996)

Roby, John *Traditions of Lancashire* 2 Vols (George Routledge & Sons; London, and L.C. Gent;
  Manchester, 1872)

Rollins, Hyder E. 'Notes on Some English Accounts of Miraculous Fasts' in *The Journal of
  American Folklore*, Vol. 34, No. 134 (October-December, 1921)

Rowling, Marjorie *The Folklore of the Lake District* (B.T. Batsford; London, 1976)*

Satchell, John 'The Green Man in Cumbria' in *Folklore*, Vol. 110, (1999)

Sharpe, James *Instruments of Darkness: Witchcraft in England* 1550-1750 (Hamish Hamilton; London, 1996)

Spencer, John and Anne Spencer *The Ghost Handbook* (Macmillan; London, 1998)

Straffon, Cheryl *The Earth Goddess: Celtic and Pagan Legacy of the Landscape* (Blandford; London,
  1997)

Sullivan, Jeremiah *Cumberland and Westmorland, Ancient and Modern: The People, Dialect, Superstitions
  and Customs* (London; Whittaker, 1857)*

Thomas, Keith *Religion and the Decline of Magic: Studies in Popular Beliefs in Sixteenth- and
  Seventeenth-Century England* (Penguin; Harmondsworth, 1982)

Timpson, John *Timpson's England: A Look Beyond the Obvious* (Jarrold; Norwich, 1987)

——————— *Timpson's Leylines: A Layman Tracking the Leys* (Cassel & Co.; London, 2000)

Underwood, Peter *This Haunted Isle* (Harrap; London, 1984)

——————— *Guide to Ghosts & Haunted Places* (Piatkus; London, 1996)

Walker, Tony *The Ghostly Guide to the Lake District* (The White Rabbit Press; Penrith 1999)*

Waugh, Edwin *Rambles in the Lake Country and its Borders* (Whitaker & Co.; London, 1861)

Westwood, Jennifer *Albion: A Guide to Legendary Britain* (Book Club Associates; London, 1986)

White, John Pagen *Lays and Legends of the English Lake Country* (G. and T. Coward; Carlisle, and
  John Russell Smith; London, 1873)

Williamson, Tom and Liz Bellamy *Ley Lines in Question* (The Windmill Press; Tadworth, 1983)

Wilson, Edward M. 'Folk Traditions in Westmorland' in *Journal of the Folklore Institute*, Vol. 2, No. 3
  (December 1965)

NEWSPAPERS AND MAGAZINES

Carlisle Journal – 5 October 1869

Cumberland & Westmorland Herald – 10 March 2001; 17 August 2002; 9 May 2006; 23 February 2007

Cumberland Chronicle or Whitehaven Intelligencer – 27 August 1778.

Cumberland Pacquet – 19 & 26 November 1805

Daily Express – 30 June 1978

English Lakes Visitor and Keswick Guardian – 1878: March; July; December 1881: July 1882: January;
  September

Fortean Times – July 2004; June 2005

Lake District Life – January/February 2006

Lakeland Echo – 14 September 1989

Land and Water – 4 September 1869

News & Star – 19 February 1997; 12 February 2005; 30 May 2008; 2 October 2008

News of the World – 1 June 1986

North West Evening Mail – 2004: 20 July; 2 October; 9 October; 2006: 27 September; 2007: 1 May

Practical Photography – April 2007

Sun – 8 February 2003

Sunday Express – 18 September 1983

Sunday People – 14 July 1974

The Times – 7 April 1860

Yorkshire Post – 21 October 1974

West Cumberland Times – 22 July 1967

Westmorland Gazette – 1992: 28 August. 1998: 5 March. 2000: 13 October; 1 December. 2001: 10 August. 2002: 19 April; 5 July; 16 August; 8 November; 20 December; 27 December. 2003: 13 March. 2004: 13 March; 23 July; 8 October; 15 October. 2005: 9 March. 2006: 31 January; 28 July; 4 August; 11 August. 2007: 2 February. 2008: 16 January; 8 April; 27 September

Whitehaven News – 1998: 19 February; 26 February. 2007: 2 March; 29 August; 9 September; 25 October; 2008: 03 June; 9 July

WEBSITES

Addenda to Floating Islands – A Global Bibliography: http://www.cantorpress.com/floatingislandsaddenda/FI%20Addenda.pdf

The Aetherius Society: www.aetherius.org

Alan Swindale's Family History: www.fivenine.co.uk/family_history_notebook/background/miterdale/miterdale.htm

Ambleside Oral History Group: www.aohg.org.uk

Big Cats in Britain: www.scottishbigcats.co.uk

Centre for Fortean Zoology: www.cfz.org.uk

CryptoCumbria: http://members.lycos.co.uk/crypto/cumb.html

Dalton Online: www.daltononline.co.uk

Edgar Rice Burroughs Tribute Site: www.erbzine.com

The Far Away Centre: www.farawaycentre.com

Freedom of Information: www.whatdotheyknow.com

Glasgow Network of Aligned Sites: www.geocities.com/leylinequest

Gosforth Hall Hotel: www.gosforthhallhotel.co.uk

Guides to the Lakes: www.geog.port.ac.uk/webmap/thelakes/html/lakemenu.htm*

Heritage Action: www.heritageaction.org

Horse and Ferrier pub: www.horseandfarrierdacre.co.uk

Images of Cumbria: www.stevebulman.f9.co.uk/cumbria

Langdale Estates: www.langdale.co.uk

Low Graythwaite Hall B&B: www.lowgraythwaitehall.co.uk

The Modern Antiquarian: www.themodernantiquarian.com*

Overwater Hall: www.overwaterhall.co.uk

Paranormal Database: www.paranormaldatabase.com

The Past Presented (David Bradbury): www.pastpresented.co.uk*

Rick Gemini's Blog: http://caldbeck-ufo-crash.blogspot.com/search/label/Caldbeck%20UFO

ScubaSpooks: http://myweb.tiscali.co.uk/freshwaterdiver/Web%20Pages/ScubaSpooks-Index.htm

Shap Community: www.shapcumbria.co.uk/Shap-Standing-Stones-and-Stone-Circles.htm

The Ship Inn: www.theship1691.co.uk

The Twa Dogs Inn: www.twadogs.co.uk

Visit Cumbria: www.visitcumbria.com*

INDEX